This book is impressive; it fills a gaping void in international relations theory. The past several decades have pushed religion to the forefront of issues facing decision makers and IR scholars. This book is a must read for anyone interested in these salient issues.

Manus Midlarsky, Moses and Annuta Back Professor of International Peace and Conflict Resolution, Rutgers University, USA

The book probes tenaciously many of the key concepts, assumptions, and possible connections to religion in each of the main theories, paradigms, or traditions of thought in international relations. It does so in ways that will help all of us - regardless of our theoretical or methodological commitments, to think more systematically about the ways religion has an impact on international relations. It is going to be essential reading for the next generation of scholars of religion and international relations

Scott Thomas, Senior Lecturer in International Relations and the Politics of Developing Countries, University of Bath, UK

For over a decade now, a vibrant community of scholars working on religion and politics has emerged and has been growing rapidly. Few, though, have sought to ask systematically whether and how religion can be studied fruitfully through the reigning theories of international relations. The wait is over. Sandal and Fox have done a great service to everyone working on the subject.

Daniel Philpott, Associate Professor of Political Science and Peace Studies, Notre Dame University, USA

Religion in International Relations Theory

There is a growing realization among international relations scholars and practitioners that religion is a critical factor in global politics. The Iranian Revolution, the September 11 attacks, and the ethno-religious conflicts such as the ones in the former Yugoslavia and Sri Lanka are among the many reasons for this increased focus on religion in international affairs. The rise of religious political parties across the world ranging from the Christian Democrats in Europe to the Bharatiya Janata Party in India similarly illustrated religion's heightened international profile.

Despite all this attention, it is challenging to situate religion within a discipline which has been dominantly secular from its inception. Only a few existant works have ventured to integrate religion into core international relations theories such as Classical Realism, Neorealism, Neoliberalism, Constructivism, and the English School. This work is the first systematic attempt to comparatively assess the place of religion in the aforementioned theoretical strands of international relations with contemporary examples from around the world.

Written in an accessible and systematic fashion, this book will be an important addition to the fields of both religion and international relations.

Nukhet A. Sandal is Assistant Professor in the Political Science Department at Ohio University, USA.

Jonathan Fox is Professor in the Department of Political Studies at Bar Ilan University, Israel.

Routledge Studies in Religion and Politics
Edited by Jeffrey Haynes
London Metropolitan University, UK

This series aims to publish high-quality works on the topic of the resurgence of political forms of religion in both national and international contexts. This trend has been especially noticeable in the post-cold war era (that is, since the late 1980s). It has affected all the 'world religions' (including Buddhism, Christianity, Hinduism, Islam, and Judaism) in various parts of the world (such as the Americas, Europe, the Middle East and North Africa, South and Southeast Asia, and sub-Saharan Africa).

The series welcomes books that use a variety of approaches to the subject, drawing on scholarship from political science, international relations, security studies, and contemporary history.

Books in the series explore these religions, regions, and topics both within and beyond the conventional domain of 'church–state' relations to include the impact of religion on politics, conflict, and development, including the late Samuel Huntington's controversial – yet influential – thesis about 'clashing civilisations'.

In sum, the overall purpose of the book series is to provide a comprehensive survey of what is currently happening in relation to the interaction of religion and politics, both domestically and internationally, in relation to a variety of issues.

Religion in International Relations Theory

Interactions and possibilities

Nukhet A. Sandal and Jonathan Fox

Routledge
Taylor & Francis Group

LONDON AND NEW YORK

First published 2013
by Routledge
2 Park Square, Milton Park, Abingdon, Oxon OX14 4RN

Simultaneously published in the USA and Canada
by Routledge
711 Third Avenue, New York, NY 10017

Routledge is an imprint of the Taylor & Francis Group, an informa business

British Library Cataloguing in Publication Data
A catalogue record for this book is available from the British Library

Library of Congress Cataloging in Publication Data
Sandal, Nukhet A.
  Religion in international relations theory : interactions and possibilities /
  Nukhet A. Sandal and Jonathan Fox.
    pages ; cm
  1. Religion and international relations. I. Fox, Jonathan, 1968– II. Title.
  BL65.I55S36 2013
  201'.727–dc23

                                                    2012047751

ISBN: 978-0-415-66262-8 (hbk)
ISBN: 978-0-203-69443-5 (ebk)

Typeset in Times New Roman
by Wearset Ltd, Boldon, Tyne and Wear

Printed and bound in the United States of America by Publishers Graphics,
LLC on sustainably sourced paper.

Contents

Acknowledgments

We would like to thank Patrick James, Jeffrey Haynes, and Shmuel Sandler for their support in this project.

1 Religions, paradigms, and international relations

There is a growing realization among scholars of international relations that religion is an important factor in global politics. The numerous events that led to this realization include the Iranian Revolution, the September 11 attacks, widespread employment of religious discourse in politics worldwide, the rise of Al-Qaeda on the international scene, and the ethno-religious conflicts such as those in the former Yugoslavia, Northern Ireland, Sri Lanka and Iraq. The successes of religious political parties and groups across the world ranging from the Christian Democrats in Europe to the Bharatiya Janata Party in India similarly illustrate religion's expanding international profile. There is also a growing recognition of the impact of religion on individual policy-makers and the influence of international religious figures such as the Pope and the Dalai Lama. While the Iranian Revolution was likely the earliest widely recognized event which showed religion's influence on contemporary international relations, Toft et al. (2011) argue convincingly that religion's international influence had been increasing since the 1960s.

Recently, there have been increasing efforts to grapple with understanding religion within a discipline which has been dominantly secular from its inception. Yet, only a few of the extant works have attempted to integrate religion into core international relations theories such as Classical Realism, Structural (Neo) Realism, (Neo)Liberalism, the English School, and Constructivism. The purpose of this book is to assess whether an understanding of religion can be systematically integrated into these theories without losing the core insights these theories already bring to international relations. Accordingly, in this chapter we discuss the current state of religion in international relations, why we believe there is a need to accommodate religion in the existing international relations paradigms, and our basic methodology for accomplishing this task including why we selected these five theories as our focus.

A brief overview of the current state of religion in international relations thought

The existing literature on religion and international relations theory may be divided into four categories. While individual treatments of religion in international relations may fall into more than one category, the categories themselves are distinct. The first is the simple realization that religion has been neglected in international relations theory. For example, Daniel Philpott (2002: 67) argues that "with few exceptions, international relations scholars have long assumed the absence of religion among the factors that influence states." Katzenstein and Byrnes (2006: 680–681) similarly assert that:

> In the analysis of Europe and its international relations, the rediscovery of religion is overdue. Specifically, scholars of Europe's emerging polity have so far neglected this topic in their voluminous writings. This oversight is true, specifically, for analyses grounded self-consciously in secular liberal and cultural realist perspectives. Instead of multiplicity, these perspectives stress uniformity of outcomes: the absence of religion in either a progressive and cooperative secular politics for liberals or a divided and conflictual one for realists.

Scott Thomas (2005: 3) more broadly attributes this gap to academics, the media and the policy community:

> Since the Iranian revolution religion has been marginalized in our understanding of international affairs. There is still the attempt by the media or by policy-makers to portray the reformist pressures in Iran only in a secular, liberal, democratic way – a Western way – rather than to recognize that they aim to form a political order that is representative, democratic, and still responsive to traditional values.

Interestingly, the writings in this category and nearly every other study which seriously addresses religion in international relations were published after September 11, 2001. Philpott (2002: 69), in an examination of major international relations journals between 1980 and 1999, found only six articles which considered religion to be a serious impact on international relations. Similarly, using a search in the Library of Congress online catalog, Hassner (2011: 38) reports that the average yearly output of books on religion and international affairs has sextupled, from about one book a year in the 1970s, 1980s, and 1990s, to approximately six books a year since 2002.

The second type of treatment of religion has been through discussions of why religion has been neglected. There is little disagreement over the reasons for this lacuna in international relations theory. Most scholars who discuss the topic place much of the blame on secularization theory – the argument that religion will come to a demise in modern times[1] (Bellin, 2008; Fox and Sandler, 2004; Fox, 2013; Goldewijk, 2007; Hurd, 2004a; Philpott, 2009). Thomas (2005) calls this tendency a political myth based on normative aspirations rather than on reality. Another common argument is that political leaders exiled religion from international relations with the Treaty of Westphalia which declared religion a domestic matter in the seventeenth century (Farr, 2008; Hanson, 2006; Hurd,

2004a; Laustsen and Waever, 2000; Philpott, 2002). Finally, positivist inter-national relations studies are accused of ignoring religion as religion has been difficult to operationalize (Fox and Sandler, 2004; Thomas, 2005; Philpott and Shah, 2012).

The third type of discussion includes the studies which identify influential religious factors in global politics but which make no attempts to integrate these factors into existing international relations theories. The next chapter is devoted to creating a comprehensive list of such factors and draws extensively on this literature.

The final, and perhaps the least common, type of discussion has been attempts to grapple with how religion can be addressed by international relations theory. While most such discussions of which we are aware are noted in more detail in the following chapters, a typology of such attempts is useful to illustrate the current state of affairs in the theoretical discussion.

One branch of the literature argues that contemporary theories and paradigms of international relations are incapable of dealing with religion and, therefore, it is necessary to build new theories. Some of these theorists identify and often describe in detail religious factors that are important in specific areas. Although their work undoubtedly contributes to our understanding of religion, these scholars do not actu-ally construct comprehensive theories of international relations. Some of the factors identified in this literature include religious identity (Kubalkova, 2000; Katzenstein and Byrnes, 2006), religious motivations for behavior (Kubalkova, 2000), religious human rights (Richardson, 2007), religious non-governmental organizations (NGOs) and other non-state actors (Katzenstein and Byrnes, 2006; Thomas, 2005), religion in global justice (Wilson, 2010), and religious violence (Thomas, 2005).

A few other scholars have developed models that integrate limited aspects of theory and religion. That is, they do not develop overarching paradigms but they have devised workable theories for understanding the role of religion. For example, Hassner (2009) uses the concepts of divisible and indivisible conflicts to understand conflicts over holy spaces such as the Temple Mount in Jerusalem. Hurd (2004a) develops a theory that describes two trends in Western secularism and how these two perspectives result in different foreign policies. Halliward (2008: 12) introduces a model stating that secular–religious boundaries can influ-ence how "individuals and organizations negotiate the relationship between these rival sites of authority and the contexts in which they attribute (or withhold) legitimacy." Lynch (2011: 405) adopts a Neo-Weberian approach to religion in international politics that provides "conceptual tools to link ethical motivations and interpretations to both context and action" and notes that "this approach does not provide simple, parsimonious explanations of behavior derived from the reli-gious beliefs of actors." Jack Snyder (2011) brings insightful snapshots of inter-national relations theory and religion in an edited book; the authors discuss how aspects of international relations–religion research agenda can benefit discussion of international relations theory. These are certainly illuminating exercises, and in this book we aim to systematize and considerably widen these debates on reli-gion and international relations theory.

Other efforts to integrate religion into international relations theory, while falling short of building models, similarly focus on limited aspects of international relations and rarely directly address the major international relations paradigms. For example, several studies look at the role of religion in legitimizing specific foreign policies (Froese and Mencken, 2009: 103–104), civil wars (Rummel, 1997; Toft, 2007), or transnational issues such as human rights (Akbaba, 2009).

This brief discussion certainly does not do justice to a diverse literature, and in the following chapters we discuss much of this literature in more detail. However, this review is sufficient to demonstrate that the efforts to integrate religion into international relations theory are in their earlier stages. There is a realization that this gap needs to be addressed. Sandal and James (2011), in their survey of how the mutual links between religion and international relations theory can be established, point to the possibilities and the need for in-depth studies that explore these links. As they argue, systematic attempts at a comprehensive integration of an understanding of religion into existing international relations paradigms such as Classical Realism, Neoliberalism and Neorealism are noticeably lacking. Although there are some ad hoc efforts to account for certain aspects of religion in some aspects of the theory, many scholars specifically note that such integration is not the appropriate avenue for understanding religion within the context of international relations (Kubalkova, 2000; Thomas, 2005).

Approaches to integrating religion into international relations theory

There are three possible approaches to integrating religion into international relations theory. The first is to construct new theories. As noted above, a number of theorists advocate this option and have begun the process of using alternative approaches to accomplish this task. This approach has already provided important insights and it has the potential to provide new theories which may, eventually, evolve into a new paradigm of international relations. However, this approach has a major drawback. It effectively tosses out the decades, and in some cases centuries of research and insights into international relations accumulated within the context of existing paradigms.

Put differently, the approach of discarding existing theories to explain religion throws out the baby with the bath water. As discussed in Chapter 2, religion influences international relations in multiple significant ways. However, we make no claim that religion is the only influence. Military and economic power as well as the structure of the international system – the foci of the different branches of the Realist paradigm – remain important. Similarly, the dynamics of the international economy and non-state actors described in the Neoliberal paradigm have also the potential to interact with religion. Given these links, we posit that the option of scrapping existing theories is an option that should be considered only after efforts to find a way to understand religion within the context of existing international relations theories have utterly failed. We argue that we are not yet at that point. Barnett (2011), in his discussion of religion and world orders, makes a similar argument, expressing his belief that existing theoretical approaches provide a useful starting point for discussion on religion and politics.

The second approach is to examine an existing international relations theory to fit religion into it in as many ways as possible. This approach has the advantage of keeping the insights from existing international relations theories. However, we argue that it is also an inefficient methodology to accomplish the task at hand. This becomes most apparent when examining the final approach.

The final approach is to first develop a comprehensive list of ways in which religion can potentially influence international relations, then to take this list and examine whether and how each item can be integrated into an existing international relations paradigm. This approach has several advantages in comparison to the first two. Like the second approach, it maintains the insights contained in the existing paradigm. However, beginning with an examination of religion's role in international relations and then examining how religion fits into the theory at hand results in a more comprehensive and comparable approach without preconceptions regarding the ability of each theory to accommodate religion.

Comprehensiveness: The second approach essentially looks for convenient places to integrate religion into a theory. One examines the theory and seeks places where religion will fit. In contrast, our approach (the third approach) begins with a comprehensive list of ways in which religion can potentially influence international relations and seeks to fit each item on this list into a theory. This approach significantly increases the likelihood that one will consider and hopefully find ways to integrate more aspects of religion into the theory. Put differently, using a checklist ensures that every item on the list will be examined, which is not necessarily the case with a less organized approach. Thus, this approach is more comprehensive.

Comparability: Similarly, the approach of beginning with a theory or paradigm and then integrating religion where it seems to fit is basically an ad-hoc approach. It can function well in the context of a single theory or paradigm. However, it will prove to be difficult to compare results between the theories. In contrast, the methodology of beginning with a list of potential influences and examining the compatibility of each one with each theory allows for a clear comparison across theories. That is, this approach allows us to compare the ability of each theory to accommodate each item on the list. It is well known that each international relations paradigm has its strengths and weaknesses – things which it explains better than others. As is demonstrated in this book, this is also true of how well these paradigms can accommodate religious factors. A standardized list of religious influences on international relations that is applied to multiple paradigms allows for a clear comparison of which aspects of religion can be better addressed by which paradigm as well as which paradigm can, overall, best deal with religious factors.

An open inquiry without preconceptions: This approach allows for an examination of several theories without any preconceptions. Taking advantage of the increased comparability among theories, it allows for a more objective evaluation of which theory, if any, is most suited to account for religion's influence in international relations. Such an approach also brings different literatures and different cultures together to explore the role of religion in the existent frameworks, even filling an existent gap in political theory (Dallmayr, 2004). Furthermore, it allows for future efforts to use similar methods on theories not included in the initial analysis and to compare them to those previously analyzed. Thus, rather than providing a contained analysis of the five theories we examine here, this approach permits our analysis to be the starting point for an open discussion which can potentially include additional approaches to understanding international relations.

Goals, structure, and methodology

Our goal in this volume is to create a list of ways in which religion can influence, intersect or interact with international relations and to integrate an understanding of these issues into existing theories of international relations. This list of potentially significant religious phenomena, developed and explained in Chapter 2, is as follows:

- religious legitimacy
- religious worldviews
- religious states
- non-state religious actors
- transnational religious movements (including religious fundamentalist movements)
- transnational issues which intersect with religion including human rights, proselytizing, holy places, family planning and stem cell research
- religious identity.

In Chapters 3 through 7 we integrate all of these items into five major theories of international relations: Classical Realism, Neorealism, Neoliberalism, the English School, and Constructivism. Each of these chapters is organized around the influences of religion we identify above, with each influence being evaluated in the context of each theory.

In order to accomplish our task of integrating religion into these theories, we rely on several literatures. First, we rely on the core literatures of the theories themselves. In many cases a close examination of these literatures reveals that the issue of religion is not as distant from these theories as many assume. For example, core Classical Realists such as Morgenthau, Machiavelli, and Hobbes directly addressed religion in their writings. Second, we rely on multiple methodological approaches to international relations. In addition to the aspects of this literature which directly addresses religion, we also examine the literature which focuses on integrating a wide variety of factors including culture and ethnicity into international relations theories. We then apply these methodological approaches to the investigation of religion and international relations. Third, we draw from the general political science literature on religion. Finally, we draw from the religious studies literature. We believe that building this bridge between religious studies scholarship and international relations is necessary.

In Chapter 8, we evaluate each of the ways in which religion influences international relations, this time comparing and contrasting how well each theory is able to account for each potential influence. All of the theories are found to be able to account for all of the potential religious influences on international relations. However, as one would expect, each theory has its strengths and weaknesses in that each handles some issues better than others.

Why Classical Realism, Neorealism, Neoliberalism, the English School, and Constructivism?

An obvious question is: Why do we select these five theories of international relations to the exclusion of all other theories and approaches? We select them because they are among the most mainstream theories in international relations. As one of our aims is to find ways to theorize and understand religion in international relations without losing the insights provided by extant works and paradigms, using those theories which are among the most widely used has obvious advantages.

Our selection of these theories should not be taken as a statement that other theories and approaches such as Marxism, critical international relations, feminist and postmodernist theories, among others, are of no use and cannot contribute to a sophisticated understanding of religion in international relations. In fact, we believe that those theories that we do not address are most likely able to accommodate an understanding of religion and in doing so provide useful insights. The purpose of this book is not to examine all theories and approaches that exist in the international relations literature. Such a task is too large for a single book and, of necessity, we must select from the available international relations theories. We select these five theories because we believe that anyone making the argument that religion can be accommodated within existing theories would need to address these theories precisely because they are among the most influential theories in international relations.

We posit that this proof of concept is especially potent for at least two reasons. First, we are successful in integrating religion into five mainstream theories. Second, these theories include Neorealism which, at first glance, one would assume is among the international relations theories least compatible with religion. We further hope that this will inspire others to follow a similar model in integrating religion into other theories and approaches to understanding international relations. Thus, the use of these five theories is not intended to be limiting; rather it is intended to be an illustrative example that will begin a conversation which we hope will include theories and approaches other than the ones we address in this book.

We should also note that we take the constructivist approach as a methodology as much as a theoretical approach. Klotz and Lynch (2007) acknowledge that the term "constructivism" means different things to different scholars, but there is an agreement that the focus is on "capturing processes of mutual constitution." Barkin (2003: 338) also argues that, unlike Realism and Liberalism, constructivism is about how to study politics and it is, indeed, "compatible (as are other sets of assumptions about how to study politics, such as rationalism) with a variety of paradigms, including realism." Throughout the book there are examples of the constructivist epistemology, since it is almost impossible to divorce it from the Realist, Neoliberal, and the English School perspectives. In short, although we treat the Constructivist literature separately in Chapter 7, it is also a methodology or a social science approach that has its place in other theoretical strands we study in this book.

It is important to reiterate and emphasize that we do not investigate all avenues to understanding religion's influence on international relations in this volume. Nor is it our intention to imply that anyone wishing to understand religion's influence must use all of the theories and all of the avenues within those theories detailed in this volume. Rather, we intend to accomplish the following. First, we demonstrate that there is room in existing theories of international relations to understand and theorize about religion. Second, we provide potential avenues for this understanding and theorizing in the hope that others will make use of these avenues and develop new ones for understanding religion's role in international relations. We see this book as a template and a starting point for others rather than as a compendium of all possible knowledge on the topic. Every scholar of international relations has her own approach which inevitably favors some theories of international relations over others. In this vein, we expect that scholars seeking to understand religion's multiple roles in international relations will have preferences as to general theoretical frameworks and approaches within those frameworks.

The remainder of this section addresses two significant issues that are critical to understanding the methodology and goals of this volume.

Paradigms lost?

A potentially important issue when integrating a new factor into an existing paradigm is whether the paradigm remains the same after such a treatment. For instance, can Neorealism remain Neorealism after religion is integrated into its framework or does it become a new theory? Unfortunately the answer to this question is subjective. Some theorists would not welcome any alterations to or deviations from international relations theories, since this process might result in a new theory or paradigm. Others would likely be more flexible.

Yet, in the end, such issues have more to do with labels than with understanding. However, more broadly considered, our goal is to find a way to understand religion's multiple influences on international relations without sacrificing the insights contained in these paradigms to the extent possible. The question of whether the result can be considered to be within the formal boundaries of the existing paradigms or whether it has evolved into a new set of paradigms has no objective answer.

A social science view of religion

Religion is a multifaceted phenomenon that can be perceived and examined from diverging viewpoints. As the discipline of International Relations is usually regarded as a branch of social science, it is critical to view religion from the point of view of a social scientist for the purposes of this exercise. Social scientists are primarily interested in human behavior, both as individuals and in groups of varying sizes. This focus on behavior is something common in international relations, political science, sociology, anthropology, and psychology. Accordingly, our primary concern here is how religion influences the behavior of the various actors which are the subjects of study in international relations theory.

Given this focus, theological definitions and the many issues that arise from these definitions, while important in other contexts, are not critical to the topic at hand. This is because we are asking how religion, in its many manifestations, influences international politics. The contexts in which we study religion do not require us to understand religion's nature, but its translation into the kinds of activities we associate with politics (Nexon, 2011: 156; Sandal, 2012). In this vein, we deem it more efficient to set aside specific definitions of religion and accept that religion is, among other things, a powerful social and political force which influences human behavior and that our task is to uncover its influences in the international arena. This acknowledgment allows us to set aside difficult theological issues which often have a minimal and indirect impact on the topic at hand. Instead, we focus on those aspects of religion which have a clearer and more significant impact on international relations. These aspects are described in more detail in Chapter 2.[2]

Although we would like to avoid any theological discussions regarding the nature of the belief, the operational definition of religion comes on the scene even in social science investigations. For example, the definition of religion can influence which groups are considered religious communities. As an illustration, in 1996 an Italian court maintained that the Church of Scientology is not a religion. The court noted that Italian law does not include an absolute definition of religion, and chose to use the following definition: "a system of doctrines centered on presupposition of the existence of a supreme being, who has a relation with humans, the latter having towards him a duty of obedience and reverence." The court interpreted the term "supreme being" narrowly to mean that a religion includes the belief in a specific God. Consequently, the non-theistic worldview of Scientology is not considered a religion. In 1997, the ruling was overturned on appeal because it was based on a narrow "biblical" paradigm religion, and as such it would exclude Buddhism, a religion that was already recognized in Italy as a religious denomination since 1991 (Massimo, 2001). In order to avoid these complicated legal and theological debates, this study uses a similarly broad non-theistic approach to religion in order not to exclude potentially important religious actors.

Yet this illustration highlights another challenge we encounter when we focus on how religion impacts international politics rather than on the specific content of religious theology. Specifically, it is often the content of specific theologies that motivate religious actors – which is one of the several potential religious influences on international relations we address in this volume. How can one understand this aspect of the impact of religion on international politics without understanding the content of these ideologies? While in principle this concern is important, it is impractical to address in studies of international relations. There are numerous religious traditions which can potentially influence international politics, and most of them have numerous and contradicting religious doctrines which are open to multiple interpretations. Whether it is possible to even catalog all such traditions and interpretations is questionable. Building or adopting general theories based on this ground-up approach is certainly an impossible task. Given this reality, we simplify this vast and complex universe of theology into the simpler proposition that theological motivations can influence behavior.

Finally, when discussing religion, it is important to also discuss secularism. While there is considerable debate about the nature and definition of secularism, it is clear that it is at least in part the negation of religion in the public sphere. While secularization theory is in crisis in that it is becoming increasingly clear that religion is not disappearing, new reformulations of the theory remain firmly linked to the negation of religion. For instance, Charles Taylor (2007: 3) argues that secularization is "a move from a society where belief in God is unchallenged … to one in which it is understood to be one option among others." Thus the presence of secular ideologies which challenge, or negate, religion in the public sphere is what constitutes secularization for Taylor.

Like religion, secularism is not monolithic and includes multiple trends. The difference among these trends is primarily the extent and nature to which each form of secularism seeks to remove religion's influence on the public sphere in general and the purview of government specifically. Hurd (2004a) divides Western secularism into two dominant trends. The first, Judeo-Christian secularism, is a secularism which is informed by religious values. More specifically, "members of a political community agree upon an ethic of peaceful coexistence and political order common to all Christian sects, or even all theists. Historically, this represented a successful compromise between warring sects" (Hurd, 2004a: 246–247). Put differently, this form of secularism was a compromise that developed in order to avoid religious wars between sects which wished to impose their religion on the state. Thus, Judeo-Christian secularism is not necessarily opposed to a role for religion in society. Rather it involves the avoidance of a dominant religion. However, since it is based on the Judeo-Christian tradition, it is less tolerant of other religious frameworks. Madeley (2003) further divides this form of secularism into two categories. The first, "neutral political concern," requires that the state neither helps nor hinders any particular ideal more than others. This conception of secularism allows government involvement in religion as long as this involvement is similar and equal for all religions. Second, the concept of "exclusion of ideals" requires that the state should not base its actions on a preference for any particular way of life. This understanding of secularism focuses on the intent to remain secular rather than on a secular outcome. It allows greater government involvement in religion than does the neutral political concern conception.

The second form of Western secularism discussed by Hurd (2004a: 242) is laicism. This version of secularism consigns all religion to the private sphere and tolerates no expression of religion in the public sphere. One example of this is the continuing controversy over the wearing of headscarves in French public schools which culminated in a 2004 law that bans the wearing of headscarves and other conspicuous religious symbols and ornamentation in schools. The headscarf issue has also manifested in Germany, Spain, Switzerland, and even in a Muslim majority country, Turkey.

Kuru (2006: 571) discusses a similar dichotomy in secularism using more general terms:

> Passive secularism, which requires that the secular state play a "passive" role in avoiding the establishment of any religions, allows for the public visibility of religion. Assertive secularism, by contrast, means that the state excludes religion from the public sphere and plays an "assertive" role as the agent of a social engineering project that confines religion to the private domain.

When examining the role of religion in international relations, these conceptions of secularism are undoubtedly important. This is because one aspect of religion's potential influence is the tension between religious and secular ideals. There exists a fundamental debate over what should be the proper role of religion in government. While the discussion is considerably more complex than a simple secular vs. religious dichotomy, the tension between secularism and religion is a central element of the debate.[3]

In the following chapter, we examine religion's multiple potential influences on international relations. We follow this review with an examination of how each of these influences can be integrated into each of five major international relations theories. In the conclusion, we compare these theories' overall ability to address religion in the international arena. Before we begin our investigation, we would like to acknowledge that despite our efforts to include debates in multiple religions, some readers might say that there is a bias towards Abrahamic traditions. There are two main reasons for that. First, although it is gradually changing, this bias is embedded in the international relations theory and politics of religion literature. There are not as many pieces that cover Eastern, Native American, or other spiritual traditions in the international relations literature as those that study the political manifestations of the Abrahamic traditions. Second, neither of this volume's authors is sufficiently familiar with the East or South Asian cultures and languages (or the culture of any other religious tradition we may not be treating in enough detail) to be able to probe into the native literature and news sources to follow the contemporary debates that are not widely discussed in the international media. This makes it difficult for us to offset the existing bias in the literature. Like many other international relations scholars, we look forward to the increase in the number of such works of international affairs and religion that go beyond the Abrahamic traditions.

2 Religion and its influence in the international arena

The overall goal of this book is to find a way to understand the influence of religious phenomena in the public sphere without losing the insights provided by mainstream international relations theories. Before we address these interactions, we must identify the multiple ways in which religion can influence international politics. In order to accomplish this task in a systematic manner, we catalog the ways in which religion can influence international relations in this chapter. In subsequent chapters, we use this catalog as a basis for the discussion of whether these elements can be incorporated into each of these bodies of theory. This approach also allows us to compare the ability of these five theoretical strands to include an understanding of religious influences on international relations.

It is worth repeating that while we consider this list comprehensive, we do not claim that no other potential religious influences on international relations can be identified. Rather, we consider this catalog to be a list of major influences which any attempt at understanding religions' influence on international relations should address. We recognize that our insights cannot possibly be exhaustive and myriad other avenues of integration exist. Our goal is to prove that existing international relations theories can accommodate religion without making any claim that we address all possible avenues for doing so. Thus, while to our knowledge the listing of religion's influences on international relations that we build in this chapter is one of the most comprehensive to date, it certainly does not exclude the possibility of other influences.

The multiple influences of religion

Following the social scientific definition of religion we outline in Chapter 1, we argue that the influence of religion in international relations is neither singular nor monolithic. Religion is a multifaceted phenomenon that has cross-cutting influences on all levels of politics and society including international relations. Thus, rather than identifying a single and overarching manner in which religion influences international relations, we seek to catalog the many potential avenues through which religion can somehow shape international politics.

The various forms of religious influence described below are interrelated and in some cases overlap. For example, worldviews are connected to identity and non-state religious actors are linked to transnational religious actors. This is unavoidable when dealing with a phenomenon as complex as religion. Nevertheless, a theory is intended to be a simplification which helps us to understand the complex reality. Thus, for the purposes of building a catalog of the various influences of religion, treating them as distinct has value.

Religious worldviews

The argument that religious beliefs influence people's worldviews is well grounded in the social sciences literature. For instance, Seul (1999: 558) argues that "no other repositories of cultural meaning have historically offered so much in response to the human need to develop a secure identity. Consequently, religion often is at the core of individual and group identity." Mark Juergensmeyer (1997: 17) similarly avers that religion "provides the vision and commitment that propels an activist into scenes of violence, and it supplies the ideological glue that makes that activist's community of support cohere." These basic insights from the sociology and to a lesser extent the political science literature are clearly applicable to the study of various actors in international relations.[1]

Religion can influence international relations through worldviews in two ways. First, religion can influence the belief system or the worldview of a policy-maker. To the extent that this is true, religion has the potential to influence that policy-maker's decisions. Guner (2012: 19) argues that "state leaders and decision makers can ascribe meanings to reality by assessing foreign policy through their religious lenses." Thus religion can influence how they "identify causes of global problems, allies, enemies" as well as how they assess national interests (Guner, 2012: 219).

Sometimes this influence can lead to extreme and intractable policies because "religion deals with the constitution of being as such. Hence, one cannot be pragmatic on concerns challenging this being" (Laustsen and Waever, 2000: 719). On the one hand, these intractable policies can result in international incidents including war. On the other hand, religion can also encourage peace and reconciliation (Appleby, 2000a; Gopin, 2000; Philpott, 2012).

The literature on conflict is beginning to acknowledge the influence of religious worldviews. For example, one aspect of the conflict literature focuses on the difference between divisible and indivisible conflicts:

> A good or issue is perceived as indivisible if it is perfectly cohesive, has unambiguous boundaries and cannot be substituted or exchanged for another good or issue. All sacred places fulfill these three conditions....The international relations literature defines indivisible conflicts as situations in which the utility functions of risk averters are such that no compromise settlement is mutually preferable to conflict.
>
> (Hassner, 2003: 8–9)

This focus on preferences is applicable to situations where the utility functions of one or both sides are influenced by religion to the extent that the conflict becomes indivisible (Svensson, 2007: 931). In addition, in cases of holy sites or other important religious objects or goals, the object of the conflict cannot be divided in people's minds, and therefore there is no room for compromise (Hassner, 2003).[2]

Examples of the influence of religious beliefs and motivations on policy are numerous. Joseph Kony, the leader of the Lord's Resistance Army in Uganda, called himself God's spokesperson and created a political theology that is a combination of Acholi nationalism and Christianity. The motivation behind the 9/11 attacks was based at least in part on an extreme version of Wahhabi Islamic worldview. Sinhalese Buddhist nationalists in Sri Lanka, Hindu nationalists in India, and ultra-orthodox Jews in Israel believe that it is their duty to behave in line with their traditions and they have a special political mandate. In addition, several studies have found that countries which intervene in ethnic conflicts tend to intervene primarily on behalf of minorities which belong to their religion (Fox, 2004; Khosla, 1999). This implies that having similar religious worldviews can be a strong motivation for international intervention.

Even if a policy-maker's worldview is not completely religious, religion can still influence their decision-making process. Most individuals' worldviews are based on a number of factors including, but not limited to, their religion, upbringing, education, friends, family, cultural heritage, political ideologies, and personal experiences. That being said, even if religion is only one influence among many, its power cannot be underestimated. Even secular worldviews are influenced by religion in that they consciously take a stance against religion's public reach. Only those who are entirely apathetic to the issue of religion may be said to have worldviews that are religion-free. Such apathy is almost non-existent in global politics.

The second influence of religious beliefs and worldviews on international relations is through constraints placed on policy-makers by widely held religious beliefs among their constituents. This is true even under autocratic regimes. It may be unwise for policy-makers to take an action that runs counter to some belief, moral, or value that is cherished by their constituents. To do so could easily undermine the legitimacy of a regime and its rulers. For example, in the Arab–Israeli conflict, leaders from both sides need to weigh how their populations will react to any agreement between the two sides. This is particularly true of agreements dealing with the disposition of holy sites like the city of Jerusalem, which are widely considered indivisible issues.

In a more general context, while there are few empirical studies which focus specifically on the religious constraints that can be placed on policy-making, studies show that religion itself can influence the political and cultural mediums through which policy-makers act. For example, several investigations show that religious tradition influences the extent to which governments are authoritarian or democratic (Fisch, 2002; Midlarsky, 1998). Toft et al. (2011: 9) also demonstrate that political theologies – defined as "the set of ideas that a religious community holds about political authority and justice" – significantly influence whether a specific strand of religion will support war or peace at a given time.

There is also no shortage of studies showing that religious affiliation is associated with political attitudes (Beyerlein and Chaves, 2003).

Religious legitimacy

Legitimacy may be defined as "the normative belief by an actor that a rule or institution ought to be obeyed" (Hurd, 1999: 381). Legitimacy has proved to be a powerful tool in international relations. The key in this process is to make the other actor feel morally obligated to support one's policies. While it would be naive to argue that all actors in international politics behave morally, it would be equally naive to argue that engaging in an action which is seen as immoral and illegitimate does not have consequences. Thus, legitimacy and morality clearly have an impact on behavior.

Few would dispute that religion is a potential source of legitimacy. Religion is actually one of the oldest sources of legitimacy in the context of domestic politics. Religious actors can lend legitimacy to governments as well as to specific policies followed by governments. However, religion is clearly not the only source and there are some set boundaries on what is and what is not considered legitimate in the international arena. For instance, self-defense is near-universally considered legitimate and genocide is not. However, there exists a substantial gray area where the legitimacy or illegitimacy of an action or policy can be debated. This area is one in which policy-makers seek to convince others – including their constituents, other policy-makers, both from their own state and from other states, and the populations of other states – of the legitimacy of their actions and policies. Religion is a potential source of persuasion in this sense. For example, many US presidents have used religious imagery to legitimize their foreign policies (Kelley, 2005). Carter's conciliatory religious discourse enabled him to bring different worldviews to the table, especially within the context of the Middle East peace process. Ronald Reagan called the USSR an "evil empire." George W. Bush has repeatedly used religious imagery in his justification for the war in Iraq and the "war on terrorism." Bush's worldview and the legitimacy of his policies have been challenged numerous times. Many Muslim leaders have characterized Bush's policies constituting a war against all Muslims, invoking religious imagery in order to oppose these policies. In addition, there exist Christian-based challenges to Bush's policies (Kimball, 2002; Laaman, 2006).

Legitimacy's domestic–international nexus

While the concept of religious legitimacy as a factor in international politics is underdeveloped, this is not the case for domestic politics. Until a few centuries ago, it was taken for granted in the West that religion was the basis for the legitimacy of the state itself with the Church, as God's agent, granting rulers the right to govern (Turner, 1991: 178–198).

Today, the role of religion in legitimizing state policies in the West is not nearly as central in the modern era as it was in the past but religion is still a significant factor. In modern times, the state's legitimacy rests on multiple sources but "a strong residual element of religion" continues to perform basic legitimizing functions (Geertz, 1977: 267–268). Many argue that this legitimizing function of religion is becoming increasingly important as governments guided by secular ideologies are seen as failing to provide basic needs like security, economic well-being, and social justice (Juergensmeyer, 1993). Empirical results tend to support this argument. A study of 175 states shows that nearly all of them continue to legislate religion and otherwise engage in religious issues. Furthermore, the extent of this legislation and other forms of engagement with religion increased between 1990 and 2002. While the study notes that it is not always clear whether this is in order to support religion or control it, these results show that nearly all states either seek to use religion to legitimize state policies or fear its power to undermine the status quo (Fox, 2008).

The prevalence of religious legitimacy in domestic politics is significant for international relations because to a great extent all politics, even international politics, are local. That is, much of the persuasion relevant to international politics takes place in the context of domestic political arenas. Depending on the nature of the state's regime, policy-makers need to satisfy domestic constituencies, opinion leaders, and other actors in their own states that their course of action is legitimate. Policy-makers have two types of international audience. The first is their counterparts in other states. The second audience is the citizens of the other state(s). That is, if one can convince the citizens of another state of the legitimacy of one's cause, the policy-maker who is representing those citizens will feel considerable pressure to support one's policy preference. Thus, the mechanisms which link religious legitimacy to domestic politics are not far removed from those that link it to international politics.

The limits of religious legitimacy and persuasion

Religion is a versatile tool of persuasion. Most religions include multiple traditions which policy-makers can draw upon to justify different and often contrasting policies. Religious traditions have been evoked at various times to justify both policies of war and violence as well as policies of peace and reconciliation. Religion is in many ways a double-edged sword; just as a policy-maker can use it to support a policy, so can other political actors use it to oppose that policy.

Despite its potency and versatility, there are at least three significant limitations on the use of religious legitimacy as a means for persuasion. First, this persuasion is often limited by cultural and religious boundaries. For example, invoking Jesus is more likely to sway Christians than Muslims or Jews, much less Hindus or Buddhists. Religious arguments have a theological context and their ability to persuade is limited to those who share this theological context. Obviously it is possible to find religious themes which cross the boundaries of specific religions, but their prevalence and potency are in most cases significantly limited.

Second, religious persuasion is limited by the extent to which someone believes in that religion. Simply put, some people are more religious than others and, thereby, more likely to be swayed by religious arguments. The extent to which religious persuasion will be effective may be described as a function of the strength of one's religious beliefs, and the centrality of these beliefs and others to one's decision-making process. In fact, this function predicts a situation where religious persuasion will have the opposite intended effect. Some people are disposed to resent and oppose anything associated with religion. Accordingly, religious persuasion may make them more likely to oppose a policy.

Finally, religious persuasion is to a great extent dependent on the credentials of the one using it. Religious persuasion works best when the one using it is seen as actually believing in the religious theological framework that is used for the persuasion and living by its tenets. Someone who is known to be not particularly religious will have more difficulty using religious persuasion than someone with good religious credentials. For example, the Pope or the Dalai Lama will have little difficulty invoking religious legitimacy to support a cause. In contrast, a secular leader invoking religious legitimacy would be viewed with suspicion. Even a leader known to believe in religion, but who is also widely known to have engaged in "immoral" behavior, may have a compromised ability to invoke religious legitimacy as a tool for persuasion.

Religious states

The international system is usually regarded as not having any religious qualities. However, in this largely non-religious context there are numerous religious factors which can influence international relations. A number of states clearly embrace religion as their national ideology or at least as an element of their national ideology. Fox (2013) in a study of 177 states' religion policies between 1990 and 2008 demonstrates that in practice official support for a single religion is common. Forty-one states (23.1 percent) have official religions and an additional 44 (24.8 percent), while not declaring an official religion, support one religion more than others. Thus, nearly half of the world's states consider a single religion sufficiently important to single it out in official policy, at least on the domestic level.

As would be expected, "official religion" means different things to different states. While the United Kingdom and Saudi Arabia both have official religions, few would claim that the impact of religion on domestic policy in these two states is the same. For this reason Fox (2013) also tracks several other aspects of government religious policy including the extent of support for religion. Fox tracks 51 types of support and finds that all of these states, other than South Africa, had at least one religion in 2008. States which do not single out a specific religion support religion less than those which support a single religion with an average of 5.6 types of support as compared to 13.6 in states which single out an official religion. However, some states which do not single out a specific religion still engage in as many as 19 types of support. While even with information this specific, it is difficult to define an exact cut-off between religious states and other states, it is accurate to say that many states' domestic policies are to varying degrees influenced by a religious ideology.

This ideology–state relationship has significant implications for international relations. For one, it means that many of the religious phenomena described in this chapter which can influence international relations are likely to be more significant for states influenced by or based on a religious ideology. Religious legitimacy would certainly be a more defining factor in political discourse, including those with regard to foreign policy. Religious identity, and the tendency to support others across the world who share that identity, would be stronger. Policy-makers from such states would be more likely to have religious worldviews, as would their constituents. Some of these states try to actively export their religious ideology. This does not have to be through only violent means. Saudi Arabia, for example, follows an overt policy of spreading its particular state-supported version of Islam, Wahhabism. The relevant initiatives include:

> building and funding new mosques, Islamic cultural centers, schools and universities, as well as providing generous scholarship and assistance to perform the hajj (pilgrimage to Mecca). Another important activity is the diffusion of the Qur'an and religious textbooks as well as the publication and distribution of works by Islamist intellectuals ... Saudi-financed schools abroad recruit their students from all over the globe and train a new generation of mosque leaders and clerics who, once returned to their own countries, open schools and religious centers spreading the Wahhabi-inspired worldview from Morocco to Indonesia, thereby creating an international network. The kingdom also sponsors several pan-Islamic organizations, such as the Organization of the Islamic Conference and the World Association of Muslim Youth, to promote the Saudi version of Islam.
>
> (Prokop, 2003: 83–84)

These actions indicate that religious ideology can be more than just an influence on the foreign policy goals of a state. Rather, exporting the religious ideology of a state, at least for some states, is in and of itself an important foreign policy goal. Thus, international relations theories need to take into account religion as a policy-defining state ideology.

Non-state religious actors

Thus far, we have focused mostly on how religion can influence the state – though the concepts of religious worldviews and legitimacy can clearly also apply to non-state actors. However, when assessing the influences of religion on international relations, it is important to also account for the specific roles played by non-state actors. Few would dispute the proposition that religious institutions can play a significant role in domestic politics. For one, they can be potent agents of political mobilization. Classic mobilization theory (McCarthy and Zald, 1976; Tarrow, 1989) states that an existing set of institutions, including religious institutions, are capable of being the basis for mobilizing groups for political action.

Thus, all religious institutions are potential bases and facilitators of political mobilization. For instance, organizing a pro-Israel demonstration in the US is far easier if it is accomplished by contacting as many synagogues as possible and asking them to help mobilize their congregants than building the organizational structure to mobilize demonstrators from scratch. This is exactly what happened to mobilize over 100,000 people for a pro-Israel demonstration in Washington DC in April 2002.

This mobilization strategy is effective because religious institutions generally have most of the organizational resources necessary for political mobilization. These resources include meeting places in which people regularly congregate. While these meetings are usually religious and social meetings, using those meetings to announce the details of a political mobilization campaign requires very little additional effort. Religious institutions also have communication networks. Active members of religious organizations tend to develop organizational and leadership skills that may also be applied to political activities. Religious institutions also often have considerable economic assets and good access to the media. In some cases they are part of international networks (Fox, 2013; Hadden, 1987a; Harris, 1994; Johnston and Figa, 1988; Verba et al., 1993).

Religious institutions are also related to religious worldviews. One of the purposes of religious institutions is to safeguard and propagate the religious worldview and belief system upon which the institution was founded. Political activities intended to accomplish this goal are not uncommon. Comparative research shows that in cases where religious institutions benefit from the status quo, they have a tendency to support that status quo. When some aspect of the status quo is a threat to these institutions or the religion they represent, religious institutions tend to support the opposition. For example, Anthony Gill (1998) asks why the Catholic Church supports the governments of some Latin American states but supports the opposition in others. He finds that historically in most Latin American states the Church had benefited from a religious monopoly supported by the government, undermining any interest in opposing the government in favor of social economic and political change. In many Latin American states citizens were disillusioned with the church support for unpopular governments. This alienation from pro-establishment churches has contributed to conversions away from Catholicism to North American-style Evangelical denominations. In such competitive settings, the Catholic Church started to support the opposition in order not to lose any congregants. Put differently, religious institutions tend to support opposition movements when they feel their institution or religion itself is threatened and the loss of a significant number of congregants constitutes such a risk.

This combination of the mobilization potential of religious institutions, their aim to foster the interests of the institution as well as its religious philosophy, and the desire to remain relevant to congregants all have the potential to influence international politics. Religious organizations often pursue political objectives in the international arena. For example, the World Council of Churches played a key role in leading and supporting various initiatives which led to the fall of the Apartheid regime in South Africa. Religious NGOs are active through-out the world, engaging in humanitarian and missionary work as well as support-ing political causes.

On a more general level, the understanding that religious individuals, institu-tions, and transnational groups may be considered actors in international rela-tions is inherent in the discussion throughout this chapter. Any theory of international relations is profoundly influenced by the actors it recognizes and "various religious actors have taken the view that involvement in politics is essential as part of their ethics" (Haynes, 2008: 294). These actors are not limited to fundamentalists of different religions with radical agendas. They include individuals and organizations representing more moderate religious denominations who pursue goals influenced by their religious worldviews. In fact, "any individual, group, or organization that espouses religious beliefs and that articulates a reasonably consistent and coherent message about the relation-ship of religion to politics" can be a religious actor (Toft et al., 2011: 23). Accordingly, any international relations theory which accounts for the impact of religion must in some way recognize the existence and influence of religious actors.

Local religious issues and phenomena cross borders

Religion is rarely confined to a single state. Local religious issues and phenom-ena often have an impact which reaches beyond state borders. While this cat-egory is not analyzed systematically in this volume, it is one that is both worthy of note and important to other aspects of the discussion in this chapter.

The concepts of interdependence and "global" politics are applicable to reli-gion. What happens locally will have global consequences in an interdependent world. Perhaps this is most obvious with regard to religious conflicts. While there are few international wars that are overtly religious, local conflicts with religious overtones are common. These conflicts can influence international pol-itics in a number of ways. First, since the end of the Cold War, humanitarian intervention in these conflicts has become increasingly accepted. This interven-tion may range from mediation and humanitarian aid to outright military inter-vention on behalf of an oppressed minority. The NATO intervention on behalf of the Albanians in Kosovo is one example of the latter. However, this case is actually atypical in that when looking purely at the religious identities of those involved, it is an intervention by Christians on behalf of a Muslim minority. Most interventions tend to be along religious lines. That is, when states intervene on behalf of ethnic minorities, over 80 percent of the time they intervene on behalf of minorities with which they share a religion (Fox, 2004).

Second, local conflicts may and often do cross international borders in several ways. Intense local conflicts result in war-affected populations seeking refuge in neighboring states. When the combatants share ethnic or religious affinities with a group in a bordering state, this bond may cause the group in the bordering state to become involved in the conflict. It may also inspire a similar conflict in the bordering state. All of these ethno-religious bonds–conflict interactions were observed in the Former Yugoslavia in the 1990s.

Shared borders are not necessary for a conflict to spread to other settings. A conflict in one part of the world can cause conflicts elsewhere both passively and actively. Passively, the success of one group may inspire similar groups elsewhere. Many argue that the Iranian revolution had exactly this influence on Muslim opposition movements around the world. On the active side, if a religious revolution is successful, as happened in Iran and Afghanistan, those states often seek to spread the revolution and support violent opposition movements elsewhere.

Third, the conflicting parties can seek to internationalize a conflict through the use of international forums. The Israeli–Palestinian conflict provides a good example of a more recent form of internationalization of conflict. There is an increasing belief that certain crimes transcend borders, and international courts such as the International Criminal Court must punish war criminals and offenders of human rights norms. A number of European countries have passed laws which allow their courts to hear such cases, claiming a form of universal jurisdiction over these types of crimes. These courts also provide potential forums for the sides of religious conflicts. Palestinian organizations have been active in pursuing prosecutions of Israeli soldiers and officials in these forums, claiming that they are responsible for crimes which fall under this universal jurisdiction.

Fourth, religious conflicts have an impact on economic interdependence. Local economic disruptions caused by local religious conflicts ripple across the international economy. Local events are often known and even viewed in real time across the world, placing greater pressure on policy-makers to react to these events when, in the past, these leaders might have been able to ignore them. The attacks of 9/11 demonstrate both of these trends. It is likely that the second plane hitting the World Trade Center was viewed by a significant percentage of the world's population in real time and many more saw the video within hours. The uncertainty caused by the attacks strongly influenced the world economy in the short term and the reactions to the attacks likely had a more profound long-term economic influence.

These avenues through which conflicts spread across borders are not unique to religious conflicts. Nevertheless, this does not detract from the potential for local religious conflicts to spread across borders and, thereby, influence international relations. Since the late 1970s, religious conflicts have comprised an increasingly greater proportion of all conflicts. Based on an analysis of the State Failure dataset which provides a list of the most violent domestic conflicts between 1948 and 2009,[3] religious conflicts rose from 25 percent of all local conflicts in 1974 to 62 percent in 2009.

Manifestations of religion other than religious conflict can also cross borders. The question of the proper role of religion in government is a significant one with which all states must deal. Most do so at a constitutional level. Of 172 states with active constitutions in 2008, 75 (43.6 percent) declared some form of separation of religion and state, and another 32 (18.6 percent) declared official religions. Some 158 (91.9 percent) of these states' constitutions have clauses protecting religious freedom.[4] The debate over the proper role of religion in government is on its surface a local issue in that it deals with how sovereign states will organize their governments. However, the preference for communism or capitalism was also a "local" issue during the Cold War. When it comes to modes of governance based on any ideology, it is difficult to argue that what happens in a state will stay in that state. Various states and non-state actors have been seeking to further their preference on the international stage. Perhaps most obviously, Al-Qaeda, among other radical Muslim organizations, has been seeking to propagate its concept of a strict theocracy across borders.

Another cross-border issue is diaspora politics. Religious diasporas have always been vocal in international relations. However, as the world's population becomes increasingly mobile, countries are becoming more religiously diverse through immigration. This diversity impacts state policies toward government involvement in religion. It also creates a constituency in many states which lobbies for the interests of their co-religionists abroad. The Jewish lobby in the US in support of Israel is a classic example of this. More recently, Muslims in Europe and the United States have become increasingly active over foreign policy issues including the Arab–Israeli conflict and the wars in Afghanistan and Iraq.

Transnational religious movements

In practice, the dividing line between local religious issues and transnational religious phenomena is blurred. In theory the distinction is more straightforward. Local religious issues focus on issues and phenomena that stem primarily from a single state but have an impact outside that state. Transnational issues stretch across multiple states and are not limited by state borders. Despite the difficulty of applying this theoretical distinction in practice, it is important because issues, actors, events, and phenomena that are limited to a single state must be treated differently in international relations theory than those which are truly transnational. The fact that there is an overlap does not prevent the analytical separation of these categories.

It is important to note that in this context the term *transnational* does not refer in particular to the transnationalism school of thought that emerged in international relations theory during the 1970s (Keohane and Nye, 1977). Rather, it is used to refer to religious phenomena which transcend state borders. While this concept is similar to this earlier school of thought, we do not rely on nor are we bound by its specific definitions and propositions.

Transnational religious movements include any religious ideology or phenomenon that operates in multiple states and pursues an agenda on a transnational level. This pursuit is the key to understanding the impact of these movements on international relations. Despite the significantly different ideologies, agendas, tactics, and organizational structure of these movements, they are similar in this respect. From this perspective violent movements seeking to impose their religious ideology on others such as Al-Qaeda and the Christian Identity Movement are similar to international religious hierarchies such as the Catholic Church or pacifist religious groups such as the Quakers. Whether organized around a specific religious ideology, organization, or issue, all of these movements seek to significantly shape political agendas and do not confine themselves to a geographical location. Of course, on a practical level, the ideologies, agendas, and tactics of these movements are critically important but on a theoretical level their pursuit of a transnational agenda is a common denominator that makes all of them similar for theoretical purposes. The discussion of specific movements below is designed to identify prominent examples of such movements.

Religious fundamentalisms and religious political ideologies

Religious fundamentalism is arguably the most widely discussed transnational religious phenomenon. Both the agenda and origins of religious fundamentalism may be considered transnational. Scholars of fundamentalism argue that it is a reaction against modernity (Almond et al., 2003). In the past, many predicted that processes inherent in modernity would lead to religion's demise. These predictions were correct in that these modern processes would pose a challenge to religion, and even profoundly influence how it manifests in society, but were incorrect in their prediction of the end of religion as a significant social factor. In fact, religion reacted and evolved to survive and even flourish in its modern environment (Fox, 2008, 2013). Fundamentalism and its rejection of many of the values of modernity and the Enlightenment is one of the results of this process. One of the primary goals of fundamentalists of all religions is to protect their religious identities and traditions from modernity and secularism. They seek to accomplish this, in part, by creating a society which strictly follows their religious ideals. Some, though not all, fundamentalists seek to also impose their ideology and preferred sociopolitical structure on others (Appleby, 2000a: 87–94). Ultimately, many fundamentalist movements hope to create a worldwide religious society that knows no borders. Thus, their goal is clearly a transnational one.

Most religions present their beliefs as universal truths and, accordingly, these beliefs, at least in theory, do not recognize international borders. This is also true of fundamentalist movements. The feeling of threat caused by modernity makes such movements particularly likely to pursue their goals politically in both the domestic and international arenas. The international aspect of this agenda is accomplished through a number of strategies. First, many movements seek to influence or take control of state and local governments. This desire has international implications because when fundamentalists manage to gain control of a state their agenda does not stop at enforcing their religious ideals locally. They often also use the state to spread their ideologies worldwide.

Second, fundamentalists try to take over religious institutions and become the sole arbiters of religious legitimacy and authority. When successful, they can use this monopoly of religious legitimacy and authority to portray their goals as moral and to paint any who oppose them as evil and subversive. Third, these movements form transnational linkages with other like-minded movements worldwide. These linkages may be formal or informal, but clearly represent an effort to build and execute a transnational agenda. Fourth, they make use of the media and other tools of international communications to both coordinate activities and spread their message worldwide.

While fundamentalist successes at taking over states are sensational and have an important impact in international relations, these events are relatively uncommon. It is likely the successes of fundamentalists in framing public debate, persuasion, and influencing governments (rather than taking them over) that have the greatest influence. Such influence is most likely more significant than their material impact on international relations. Thus, the grass-roots efforts of fundamentalists to gain converts to their ideologies will likely have the longest lasting impact on politics.

Fundamentalist or not, religious ideologies have also transnational influence as they are not confined to one state. Arguably, the two most visible transnational religious ideologies in terms of their activism have been political Islam and evangelical Christianity. Political Islam, as a transnational religious ideology, has been the subject of heated debate. Political Islam may be defined as "a form of instrumentalization of Islam by individuals, groups and organizations that pursue political objectives" (Denoeux, 2002: 61), and it is not necessarily equal to Islamic fundamentalism (Fuller and Lesser, 1995: 6). Political Islam, as we understand it today, is defined as an ideology that is the product of political, social, and military interactions of the Muslims with the West in the past centuries – usually in the form of an asymmetric relationship (Ayoob, 2004: 2). Although it is sometimes argued that there is no concept of separation of religion and state in Islam (Dalacoura, 2000: 879; Gellner, 1992) or Islam makes no room for opposing viewpoints (Jaggers and Gurr, 1995: 478; Juergensmeyer, 1993: 19–23; Lewis, 1993: 96–98), many scholars contest the notion that Islam is any different from other Abrahamic traditions when it comes to separation of the political and the religious, or tolerance toward the religious "other" (Ayoob, 2004; Brown, 2000a). Comparative studies show that about half of all Muslims live in democratic and semi-democratic states (Stepan, 2000: 48–49). Scholars also argue that the link between Islam and autocracy (established by Fisch, 2002; Midlarsky, 1998) is contextual. It is restricted mostly to Arab states (Stepan and Robinson, 2003) and the theory of total religious rule has rarely if ever been put into practice (Haynes, 1998: 128–129). In theological terms, some scholars hold that Islam has within it concepts like consultation, consensus, the equality of all men, the rule of law, and independent reasoning, providing for an Islamic democracy (Esposito and Piscatori, 1991; Fuller, 2002).

Regardless of the theological bases of the religion and state merger, political Islam has been on the scene with its various manifestations. Islam has also been politicized as a major tool of legitimacy by political leaders (Akiner, 2000; Haynes, 1994: 67–70). Muslim majority states have the highest average levels of religious legislations compared to non-Muslim majorities (Fox, 2013). Interpretations of religious concepts also differ in the Islamism scale. To illustrate, many Muslims, who believe in Islam's guidance in political matters, interpret the concept of Jihad as a primarily personal struggle for self-improvement and not the kind of struggle that can be justified against states with decent levels of religious freedom (An-Na'im, 2002; Gopin, 2000: 82–83).

Among other transnational religious ideologies that have had a significant impact on policy-making is Evangelical Christianity, which gained increased political prominence starting from the mid-1970s. Evangelicals believe that one must go through an active conversion; that the Bible is the inspired word of God; Christ's death was a historical event necessary for salvation and that Christians must express their faith through social action (Bebbington, 1989: 4–8). Despite sharing some common premises, evangelicals and fundamentalists are regarded as two distinct groups (Ammerman, 1982). Evangelicals have "changed the US foreign policy in profound ways" (Mead, 2006). The evangelical upsurge has gained significant numbers of converts in East Asia, Latin America, and Africa (Berger, 1999; Freston, 1994) and evangelical organizations as well as leaders affected the course of conflicts, as exemplified by the Northern Ireland case (Ganiel, 2008). In the following chapters we will touch upon the influence of these groups in defining local and transnational agendas.

Transnational religious issues

Terrorism, human rights, holy places, and more

Given the extent of involvement of religious ideologies in human lives, any transnational issue can turn into a transnational religious issue. It is impossible to catalog all issues that have been influenced by religion thus far. Due to limitations of space, we will discuss the issues that have consistently been on the political agendas of state and non-state actors. Among these issues are terrorism, human rights, and holy places.

Religion has been a justification for terrorism for millennia (Rapoport, 1984) and it is arguably becoming one of the most common motivations for terrorism in the world today. A series of empirical studies show that in the 1980s religious terror became the most common form of terror. These studies also show that most, but certainly not all, terrorist groups formed during and since the 1990s are Muslim groups and that most terrorist activities from this period onward were perpetrated by these groups (Weinberg and Eubank, 1998; Weinberg et al., 2002). However, it is important to emphasize that both currently and historically religious terrorism has been perpetrated by the extremists of almost every religion.

Ethno-religious terror has been especially prominent in a number of high-profile conflicts such as the Iraq war, Afghanistan, Sri Lanka, the Arab–Israeli conflict, the "Troubles" in Northern Ireland, the Chechnyan rebellion against Russia, and the civil war in Algeria. Islamic terror groups like Al-Qaeda are responsible for high-profile attacks in the West as well as in the Islamic world.

This rise in religious terrorism is for the most part related to the increase in the levels of fundamentalism. This link has at least two elements. First, as noted earlier, fundamentalism is at least in part a reaction against modernity. Fundamentalists feel the need to alter the social and political status quo in order to bring the world into alignment with their ideology. Second, many nationalist minority movements which engage in terror as part of a self-determination campaign are linked to fundamentalist movements.

All of these issues can only be addressed through significant political and social changes. It is arguable that most fundamentalist movements are more interested in the ends than in the means; that is, there is usually no doctrinal requirement for violence in order to achieve political goals. If these goals can be accomplished through peaceful means, most fundamentalist movements would likely consider this satisfactory. However, most of their goals attract considerable opposition, to the extent that these goals often cannot be accomplished peacefully. Given this tension and the absolutist nature of their ideologies, fundamentalist movements are able to justify violence in order to achieve these goals.

Why does this violence so often manifest as terrorism? Because terrorism is likely the most effective form of violence available to these movements. Arguably, if these movements had military forces comparable to those of world powers such as the United States or were able to achieve their ends peacefully, they would not need to use terrorism. But in most cases these movements are involved in asymmetrical conflicts against state forces which have significantly more military and police power. To put it into perspective, even if a violent political movement had a budget of one billion dollars a year, this would be considerably less than the security budget of even a small state. This leaves terrorism as one of the few options available to disillusioned fundamentalist groups.

In the few cases where Muslim fundamentalists control a state, such as the cases of Afghanistan under the Taliban or Iran, their efforts to spread the Islamic revolution may also include supporting transnational terrorist organizations. Engaging in more traditional state-to-state warfare is dangerous to those states, especially since those who they consider their primary enemies have strong militaries. Given this imbalance, supporting violence through various proxy groups allows them to pursue the violent path but still insulate themselves from retaliation. Be that as it may, it is clear that this religious wave of terror is a significant factor in international relations. It has contributed to the formation or realignment of international alliances between states in order to fight it. It has facilitated the recognition that non-state actors can constitute a potent force which undermines the traditional state monopoly on the use of violence. It has also influenced the foreign policies of many states and will likely continue to do so for the foreseeable future.

There are additional transnational trends, issues, and phenomena which overlap with religion that are worthy of note. First, freedom of religious expression and human rights are becoming increasingly international issues. Human rights, in general, have become an important element of the foreign policies of many contemporary states. As noted above, several states have authorized their courts to try human rights cases even if they occur outside their borders, declaring universal jurisdiction in such matters.

The issue of religious rights is included in a number of international documents and treaties, including the 1948 UN Universal Declaration of Human Rights, the 1948 UN Convention on the Prevention of Genocide, the 1981 UN Declaration on the Elimination of All Forms of Intolerance and Discrimination based on Religion or Belief, the 1950 European Convention for the Protection of Human Rights and Fundamental Freedom, the American Convention on Human Rights, the 1969 African Charter on Human and People's Rights, and the 1990 Cairo Declaration of Human Rights in Islam, among others. The influence of religion on codification of these human rights documents – the most obvious being the Cairo Declaration of Human Rights and its complete reliance on sharia (Islamic religious law) – is becoming important in the international arena, especially since human rights violations are being considered justifications for international intervention.

Second, the issue of women's rights is becoming a source of tension between the West and the developing world. A number of states place significant restrictions on women that are incongruent with Western secular ideas of equality for women. Religion is often used to justify many of these restrictions. These tensions are similar to those over human rights described above.

Third, proselytizing constitutes a significant potential source of international tension. Numerous religious groups, most prominently Muslim and Christian groups, send representatives to states across the world. These "missionaries" seek to both find converts to their religions as well as convince members of their own religion to become more religious or switch allegiance to their particular interpretation of their religion. These efforts are often unwelcome. In 2008, 98 states placed some form of restriction on proselytizing. Many of these restrictions were specifically aimed at foreign missionaries. These states include those with Christian, Muslim, Buddhist, Hindu, and Jewish majorities and several Western democracies. Twenty-nine states (26 of which are Muslim majority states) restrict conversion away from the dominant religion (Fox, 2013).

Fourth, holy places are potential sources of international tension. One example among many is the conflict among Christians for control of Christian holy sites, competing claims to the Temple Mount, and tension between Christians and Muslims over holy sites in Nazareth. Each of these disputes has led to the political involvement of a number of foreign states. Another prominent international incident regarding holy sites was sparked by the decision of the Taliban-controlled Afghan government to destroy two giant statues of Buddha in Bamiyan, Afghanistan. In addition to Buddhist governments and scholars, there was also involvement by UNESCO and several states with Muslim majorities in the unsuccessful efforts to stop the destruction of these statues.[5]

Not all of these sources of tension are inter-religious. One such issue is the (fifth) issue of family planning. In this case the tension is between those with a more secular orientation and those with a more religious orientation, as family planning, and especially abortion, is to varying degrees restricted or banned by most interpretations of the Abrahamic religions. These issues are also framed under human rights, as we will discuss in the following chapters. Sixth, the issue of stem-cell research has also caused tension along similar secular versus religious lines. The terms of education and science are debated in the transnational public sphere. Religious communities are claiming their rights to pursue alternative forms of science and public life. This desire creates parallel ways of living in the local and transnational spheres, which may have transnational implications that can be addressed in relevant theories of international relations.

Religious identity

One of religion's many facets is identity. The concept of religious identity overlaps with most of the other potential influences of religion discussed in this chapter, but it is sufficiently important that it should be identified and discussed separately. The fact that international relations as a field is influenced by various identity issues is probably accepted by many international relations scholars but both the extent and nature of this influence are disputed.

The debate over Samuel Huntington's (1993, 1996) Clash of Civilizations theory illustrates this point well. Huntington essentially argues that the ethnic and national identities which were central to the Cold War era are becoming less relevant. In the post-Cold War era he predicts that more macro-level identities, which he calls civilizations, will become the primary form of identity which drives international relations and the primary basis for international conflict. Huntington (1993: 24) defines a civilization as:

> the highest cultural grouping of people and the broadest level of cultural identity people have short of what distinguishes humans from other species. It is defined by both common language, history, religion, customs, institutions and by the subjective self identification of people.

The concept of civilizations is essentially an amalgamation of more narrowly defined national and ethnic identities into a broader identity group based on more generally defined common traits. Furthermore, these groupings are largely religiously homogeneous. Most of the civilizations which Huntington lists – the Western, Sino-Confucian, Japanese, Islamic, Hindu, Slavic-Orthodox, Latin American, and "possibly" African civilizations – include at least some aspect of religious identity in their definition, and some are even named after religions. Thus, in essence, Huntington's clash of civilizations may be described, for the most part, as a clash of religious identities (Fox, 2004: 157–159).

This theory was among the most controversial theories of the late twentieth century in international relations. While critics of this theory were plentiful, few of these critics, other than those who argue that the world was developing a single overarching identity, openly denied that identity in general and religious identity in particular influence international relations. In fact many argued that identity would remain important at the state and sub-state level, though the focus in this context was not on religious identities per se, but rather on national and ethnic identities, or on different interpretations within the same religion (Gurr, 1994; Sandal, 2012). Thus, to the extent that religion plays a role in national and ethnic identities (Gurr, 1993: 3; Smith, 1999), these critics concede that religious identity plays a role in international politics.[6]

The implications of this potential influence of religious identity in international relations cannot be underestimated. Religious identity can influence important policy decisions. Fox (2004) demonstrates that when states intervene in domestic conflicts taking place in other states, they tend to do so overwhelmingly on behalf of minorities which are religiously similar to them. As we argued above, it is reasonable to claim that religious identity can also potentially influence international alliances.

Multiple influences of religion and international relations theory

The potential influences of religion on international relations are multiple and complex. Rather than a two-ton bear, which while large may be easy to explain, religion can be better described as a swarm of stinging bees, and we must account for each of these bees in order to fully account for religion's influence on international relations.

Thus, integrating religion's multiple aspects into existing theories cannot be accomplished through a single large alteration or reinterpretation of these theories. Rather it can only be accomplished by integrating each potential influence of religion separately. Accordingly, the discussion of Classical Realism, Neorealism, Neoliberalism, the English School, and Constructivism is organized around the multiple influences of religion delineated in this chapter. The following five chapters discuss the possibilities of integration using the seven categories described in this chapter: religious worldviews, religious legitimacy, non-state religious actors, religious states, transnational religious movements, transnational issues, and religious identity.

3   Religion and Classical Realism

Interactions within power politics

We begin the process of integrating religion into international relations theories with Classical Realism. This chapter, as is the case with the following chapters, begins with a brief discussion of the intellectual history of the theory, emphasizing what role religion played in the development of the paradigm, if any. In the case of Classical Realism, the impact of religion can be traced to the beginnings of the theory's intellectual history. After discussing the nature of this impact, we then use the categories of potential religious influences on international relations developed in the previous chapter as the basis for discussion of how religion can be reclaimed and integrated into the theory. We argue that religion is already acknowledged in some strands of Classical Realist thought, and many issues regarding religion and politics can be explored effectively through this theoretical lens.

Realism is not a monolithic school of thought or paradigm. Its various strands include their own assumptions and causal explanations. However, if one needs to come up with a relatively clear distinction in terms of categories, the Realist literature in international relations may be divided into two main schools: Classical Realism (with its own traditional and neo-variants) and Neorealism. Realism's core assumption is the existence of anarchy, which means there is no world authority that can provide guidance or checks and balances. Each sovereign state is free, in a way, to behave as it wishes. Both Classical Realists and Neorealists concur that states are the key units for analysis. States seek power in a competitive environment. Decision-makers are rational, in the sense that they have consistent and ordered preferences. In the end, they pick the utility-maximizing choice. Although Realism allows for a number of independent variables ranging from "human nature" to "distribution of capabilities," many scholars who have written on international relations theory have expressed their pessimism about the integration of culture and identity (Keohane and Nye, 1977; Lapid, 1996; Schweller, 1988: 20; Zakaria, 1999: 32–35). While not always stated explicitly, this pessimism about integration of culture clearly includes religion as well. This view may be attributed either to a relatively restricted interpretation of Realism or concerns about the intellectual coherence of this line of thought, especially as represented in its Neorealist form. Although we agree that there are limitations, we do not share this pessimism for the most part. We argue that religion is already present in the history and premises of Classical Realist thought.

Realism is not a new theoretical stream. One can trace political Realism back to ancient Greece, sixteenth-century Italian city-states, or seventeenth-century England (Lebow, 2007: 53). Thucydides (400 BCE), Niccolo Machiavelli, and Thomas Hobbes are considered among the "fathers" of the Realist paradigm. In the accounts of Thucydides (*c.*460 BCE–360 BCE), the acclaimed historian who authored the *History of the Peloponnesian War*, religious references – widely defined to cover the belief systems of ancient Greece – are frequently employed (Jordan, 1986). Even Machiavelli, the notoriously pragmatic politician and philosopher of sixteenth-century Florence, does not shy away from including religion in his treatises, albeit in an instrumental fashion. Machiavelli regarded Christianity as crucial for the stability and progress of society, but urged for a theological renewal within the religion itself (Viroli, 2010). For Machiavelli, "religion was something that demanded scrupulous attention, but its importance derived from its impact on the causes of men's actions, not from its truth" (Preus, 1979: 173). In other words, Machiavelli employed religion as a form of "independent variable" and a factor that caused men to make ultimate sacrifices.

Although he was critical of the Church of Rome, Machiavelli (1984 [1513]: 144) also regarded religion as one of the foundations of a country:

> The rulers of a republic or of a kingdom, therefore, should uphold the basic principles of the religion which they practice in, and, if this be done, it will be easy for them to keep their commonwealth religious, and, in consequence, good and united. They should also foster and encourage everything likely to be of help to this end, even though they be convinced that it is quite fallacious.

Machiavelli was frustrated with the activities of the Catholic Church and he resented the influence of this institution on the political machinery. He argued that church involvement in political life degraded Christianity more than anything else (146). However, his treatment of the role of religion in the political life of society remains one of the cornerstones of the realist prescription of "politics should not be guided by pure moral considerations." Recognizing the importance of religion, yet cautioning against its interference in the political sphere, Machiavelli theorized a pragmatic secularism.

More than a century after Machiavelli drew the framework of pragmatic politics in continental Europe, Hobbes (1985 [1651]: 168), a materialist English philosopher, dedicated a full chapter in his epoch-making work, *Leviathan,* to how religion is ingrained in human nature and how it is employed by leaders:

> And this seed of Religion, having been observed by many; some of those that have observed it, have been inclined thereby to nourish, dress and form into Laws; and to add to it of their own invention, any opinion of the causes of future events, by which they thought they should best be able to govern others, and make unto themselves the greatest use of their powers.

None of these accounts advocated that religion *should* be part of politics. Machiavelli and Hobbes were political philosophers. They both recognized that religion is an engine of power in society. Religion has legitimizing power, and it is human nature to seek guidance from the divine. In other words, Classical Realism, from its inception, has never prescribed a purely religious or moral order. However, it has always included religion as a variable, as a force capable of creating particular outcomes in the anarchic world. Realists of all time periods warned the political leaders against following moral principles, stating that such policies might come at the expense of state survival. That is, in order to redeem the religion factor in Classical Realism we first need to recognize that states often pursue policies that many Classical realists would consider suboptimal and then we need to separate out policy prescriptions from explanation.

Classical Realism, in its twentieth-century manifestation, is most clearly represented in the works of scholars like Hans J. Morgenthau, Reinhold Niebuhr, John Herz, and Arnold Wolfers. The Realist movement was a revival against post-World War I "utopianism." The exclusive focus on the goodwill and morality by American decision-makers was seen to be partly responsible for World War II. The Realists reinvigorated the tradition of power politics so that in the future, policy-makers would avoid both "passive unwillingness to use force" and "destructive and quixotic crusades" (Keohane, 1986: 8). The prevalent concern of the time was the exaggerated use of certain ideologies – including religious ones – rather than a total ignorance of what is human. Classical Realism, with its aim to attain a certain standard for reasoning and to avoid ideological rhetoric, had a normative dimension in this sense. It stood against the neglect of material interests and it opposed the overemphasis on ideological justifications for inaction or over-extension.

Another factor that explains the reluctance to investigate the religious phenomena within the framework was the unwillingness to tilt "the Westphalian deferral" (defined as "an attempt to contain and manage difference within the newly erected boundaries of states") in favor of meta-narratives that had the potential to draw attention away from states towards transnational movements; neither policy-makers nor mainstream academics stood ready to accept any movement in that direction (Blaney and Inayatullah, 2000: 32). A similar hostility towards meta-narratives of faith in politics was most clearly expressed by Morgenthau (1956: 234) when he elevated concrete national interest over vague "religious ideals":

> Thus, carrying their idols before them, the nationalistic masses of our time meet in the international arena, each group convinced that it executes the mandate of history ... and that it fulfills, a sacred mission ordained by providence, however defined. Little do they know that they meet under an empty sky from which the gods have departed.

This statement targeted the futility of employment of ambiguous ideals in a system in which the key unit (i.e., the state) existed independently of these belief systems. In this line of thought, God(s) will not favor the state that sacrifices itself in the international system; states are the only actors that can save themselves. Since state is the central political actor in Classical Realism, policies cannot be justified on the basis of pure ideology. A state's interests override any universal moral or ideological framework. Accordingly, Morgenthau argues that relying on ideologies, including religious ideologies, makes for poor policy, not that this cannot and does not occur.

A key methodological question needs to be addressed before one can formulate a convincing inter-level explanation. How does one translate individual-level needs and insecurities (e.g., the need for affiliation and belonging, the need for consistency, etc., which are also called "demand-side" variables in the economic theories of religion) to state-level variables and policies? Religion cannot be separated from culture; it occupies multiple domains and must be addressed in a "polytheic and flexible" manner (Lincoln, 2003: 5). Classical Realism actually encourages the study of morality, ethics, and religion at the individual level, or any sub-state level for that matter. However, how we can link the individual level to interest formation at the state level is not that clear-cut. This is partly what we start to do in this chapter, by looking at the links among religion, interest, and power.

Before exploring the possible linkages between religious issues and power politics, it is important to identify the extent to which non-material variables can be employed without interfering with the intellectual coherence of the theory. We therefore examine the methodological preferences of Classical Realists to identify such variables. Morgenthau (1948) joins the positivist school by asserting that political Realism believes that politics, like society in general, is governed by objective laws that have their roots in human nature. Morgenthau's political thought and his "awareness of the harshness of the social and political environment" appears to have been influenced by his background as an émigré from Nazi Germany (Mollov, 2002: xi). His understanding of science represents more of a desire to decrease the centrality of utopianism that was witnessed in the post-World War I era – a thinking that contributed to the outbreak of World War II – than an attempt to exclude non-material variables altogether. Morgenthau (1972: 9) even concedes that "the ultimate decisions that confront the scientific mind are ... not intellectual but moral in nature." His understanding of political dynamics has an inextricably human dimension. Modern man, according to Morgenthau (1972: 10), is "suspended between his aspirations, which he cannot fulfill, and his nature, which he cannot escape, [modern man] experiences the contrast between the longings of his mind and his actual condition as his personal, eminently human tragedy." Similarly, Niebuhr (1932: 48), despite his declared faith in the overall trajectory of Christianity, links rationality and morality of human life by stating that "all men cannot be expected to be spiritual any more than they can be expected to become rational." In this vein, one can say that the methodology used by the Classical Realists has been a soft-positivism that is sensitive to human nature.

What distinguishes Classical Realism from other perspectives in the realm of international relations theory literature? One answer is its focus on human nature, which may be interpreted as a causal variable or background condition depending on one's point of departure. Therefore, scholarly investigations that have human nature as either a causal variable or a background condition can accommodate religion in line with the Classical Realist tradition. Despite attempts to define politics as a science and therefore subject to objective investigation, Classical Realists take ideological issues and non-material sources of influence into account when they are assessing the challenges faced by states. The emphasis on human psychology makes it easier for Classical Realism to account for state-level and individual-level changes. The Classical Realist accounts make frequent references to the "statesman," who is expected to "negotiate treaties in its [state] name, define its objectives, choose the means of achieving them, and try to maintain, increase, and demonstrate power" (Morgenthau, 1956: 118). Such individual-level references distinguish Classical Realism from Neorealism, as the latter does not recognize the agency of the individual as clearly as the former does.

Since Classical Realists start with human nature and end up at the transnational system level, any inter-level explanation (i.e., an explanation that links aspects of human nature to society-level phenomena) is possible. This is a considerable advantage if one wants to include a multi-level concept like religion in this framework. For example, Madeleine Albright (2006: 17–32), the US Secretary of State from 1997 to 2001, draws attention to the religious worldviews of the American presidents and how they helped create an exceptionalist American political culture. Inboden (2008: 259) highlights Eisenhower's religious framing of the Cold War, noting his famous words, "when God comes in, communism has to go." Similarly, accounts of how the evangelical faith of Jimmy Carter and George Bush influenced their policies (Berggren and Rae, 2006; Black et al., 2004; Kengor, 2004; Woodward, 2002) can easily fit into the Classical Realist framework with the linking of individual level (personal faith) to foreign policy decisions. Such a linkage is not easy to establish in the Neorealist school of thought, as we will see.

It is possible to discern these individual-level/state-level linkages in most of the representative works of the Classical Realist tradition. Morgenthau, for example, asserts that "politics is governed by objective laws which have roots in human nature" as his first principle of political Realism. He then takes the "nation-state" as the main analytical level in his work. Reinhold Niebuhr, an American theologian and a leading Realist, introduced theoretical perspectives on politics based on an Augustinian understanding. Niebuhr (1932: 14) employs individual- and state-level explanations at the same time: "Every group, as every individual, has expansive desires which are rooted in the instinct of survival and soon extend beyond it. The will-to-live becomes the will-to-power." Niebuhr saw society in a perpetual state of war, a view similar to the one introduced by Thomas Hobbes in the seventeenth century. Although Niebuhr (1932: 46) prescribed moral restraint and wrote on the guiding power of the divine, he also recognized that society "will never be sufficiently intelligent to bring all power under its control." Even the most devout followers of religion are not able to cooperate to form a selfless and virtuous society.

In addition to traditional Classical Realism, there is ample space for religion-related accounts in Neoclassical Realism which "incorporates external and internal variables, updating and systematizing certain insights drawn from Classical Realist school" (Rose, 1998: 146). According to Rose, the first scholar to use the words "Neoclassical Realism," the foreign policy of a country is determined by its place in the international system but relative power capabilities influence foreign policy through unit variables. This causal process is not as straightforward as the Neorealists claim it to be. Unit-level factors, such as the perceptions of the political elite, play an important role in explaining how material inputs lead to policy outputs. Rose identifies Michael Brown, Thomas Christensen, Randall Schweller, William Wohlforth, and Fareed Zakaria as Neoclassical Realists. Although we recognize that Neoclassical Realism is a distinct perspective, we treat it along with Classical Realism due to their philosophical similarities and space limitations.

This chapter follows the framework that is introduced in the previous chapter. This does not mean that Classical Realism, in its traditional and neo-variants, is equally conducive to the treatment of each issue category. We argue that although Classical Realism does touch upon each issue category in one way or the other, it is especially suitable for explaining the religious worldviews, religious legitimacy, and religious states as variables. As we also stated in the previous chapter, there are inevitable overlaps among categories. To illustrate, an issue of religious worldviews can also be a case of non-state religious actors and transnational religious issues. These overlaps bolster our argument that there are many ways to investigate the issues of religion and politics within the intellectual tradition of Realism. The categories are not meant to provide impermeable and mutually exclusive cognitive toolboxes but, rather, a flexible classification scheme that will help us more efficiently systematize the multiple influences of religion.

Religious worldviews and Classical Realism

Within the Classical Realist framework, religious worldviews can influence the policy preferences of policy-makers in three main ways. The first way is taking religion as an intervening variable between human nature and power politics, and the second way is employing cognitive tools of foreign policy analysis to *S* explore how religious beliefs can influence political decisions. These first two ways are based on the assumption that decision-makers are inevitably informed by their religious convictions. As a third way, we posit that the worldviews of a policy-maker's constituents may constrain the policy options available to a ? *N.-m* policy-maker, sometimes regardless of her own religious beliefs. This is not *PR* inconsistent with Classical Realism. As discussed above, while many Classical Realists may believe that religious concerns "ought" not to influence policy preferences, Classical Realism does not preclude the possibility that they, in fact, can influence policy preferences. *Of CSe not-buy almost*
Also nat'l id

Human nature, religion, and the need for security

One avenue of potential religious influence is the treatment of human nature by Classical Realists, which allows for the integration of religion as an intervening variable leading to power politics. Along with Reinhold Niebuhr, Morgenthau treated "human nature" as an independent variable and as the birthplace of the desire for power and security. In this light, religion may be seen as an answer to the basic human need for belonging and guidance. It can also be an aspect of identity with repercussions for the decisions human beings take and the strivings they experience. In this manifestation religion may be treated both as a quasi-dependent variable and as an explanatory variable where policy preferences are influenced directly by religious worldviews. The extent to which people emphasize religion is shown to be correlated with the level of development in a country (Norris and Inglehart, 2004: 220). As the level of existential security decreases, the emphasis on religion grows stronger. The surge of religion in Latin America and Africa, the proliferation of religious NGOs and increased membership of religious groups, may be partly caused by this insecurity and the need to belong.

Despite this basic need to belong, human beings are not consistent throughout their "guided" lives. They focus on their material desires, sometimes at the expense of the well-being of others. In his *Moral Man and Immoral Society*, Niebuhr (1932: xx) asserted that "the easy subservience of reasons to prejudice and passion, and the consequent persistence of irrational egoism, particularly in group behavior, make social conflict an inevitability in human history, probably to its very end." George Kennan (1967: 319), the American diplomat who introduced the concept of "containment," also expressed his pessimism in equally religious terms: "I wish I could believe that the human impulses which give rise to the nightmares of totalitarianism were ones which Providence had allocated only to other peoples and to which the American people had graciously been left immune." Any variable stemming from human nature may be used to explain decisions and political trends within the Classical Realist tradition. One might think that Niebuhr and Kennan focused on the negative aspects of human nature disproportionately, such as its passions, prejudices, and weak disposition. However, it is these traits that permit totalitarian control in their extreme forms, where the individual "submits" to higher ideological aspirations. This reasoning is applicable to the political expressions and leaders of religious traditions.

Cognition and religious worldviews

A second avenue may be found through the use of cognitive variables related to religion. The scholars of religion and international relations can be encouraged by the liberal use of emotional and cognitive terminology in Classical Realism. Investigation of the cognitive variables started most visibly in the "behavioral revolution" of the 1950s and 1960s. During this period, an interest in political psychology could have allowed for the integration of religion as part of socialization and in relation to its effect on the psychology of the decision-maker. However, the difficulties associated with measurement – as experienced with psychological variables in general – and the "inappropriateness" of inquiring about an individual's religious faith marginalized religion in the behavioralist literature.

As stated above, Classical Realists, albeit employing a constellation of levels in their explanations, stick to the assumption that states are the core – if not the only – players in international politics. A state's constitution is different from an individual's. In a Niebuhrian reasoning, despite the individual possibility to attain the moral ideal, it should not be expected that human collectivities can get close to it. Individuals have beliefs and ideals; states do not. In a state-level account in which religion or ideology is treated as the *only* variable, it becomes appropriate to shift to some alternative school of thought. Using religion as an individual- or societal-level variable with influence on state behavior is different from explaining state behavior (as a sum) exclusively by an ideology. Morgenthau (1967: ix) indirectly supports this argument in the fourth edition of his *Politics among Nations* when he expresses his regrets that his conception of power was taken by some only in a material sense, whereas it also includes charismatic power.

Religion, along with other non-material factors, can be assigned value by decision-makers and, accordingly, can be included in cost-benefit calculations. Religious worldviews do not constitute obstacles to rational thinking. The calculation of costs and benefits by a religious leader would inevitably be influenced by his faith and the faith of his constituents. Furthermore, these calculations result in policies that can change the course of international politics. Especially in authoritarian states, where there are only a few (if any) checks and balances, an individual's decision-making process becomes central (Hermann and Hermann, 1989). As discussed in more detail below, in democratic societies the religious views of constituents can also influence policy, to the extent that policy-makers take the opinions of constituents into account.

It should also be noted that there is no "one" rationality, and there may well be different paths to reach the desired ends. Robert Pape (2003) shows that even suicide terrorism follows a strategic logic. Although his data is not limited to religiously motivated suicide terrorism, it still shows that an action, which would be deemed "irrational" by many, not only has the potential to provide the individual with a spiritual purpose requiring the highest form of sacrifice, but also has the power to achieve tangible political aims such as territorial gains. Rapoport (1988) similarly argues that when one's goals are guided by non-material concerns such as the desire to guide events toward a messianic era, actions that in other contexts may seem irrational become rational. This process occurs, in particular, when religious people believe that the day of deliverance is imminent and that they are soldiers whose purpose is to guide events to their conclusion. In such cases the perpetrators fight against seemingly irrational odds because the goal they wish to obtain has such an overwhelmingly high value. They also believe that they have both historical momentum and the divine on their side.

This perspective has implications for game theoretical thinking, which is explained in detail in the following chapters. Suffice it to say that faith can figure into the player's reasoning and change his path along with the desired end-points. This does not mean that games should be "irrational." Alternative rationalities are not only theoretically possible but also practically widespread in world politics. There is no obstacle to religion's informing strategic calculations in multiple ways. In a similar vein, religion, as a core value system in many individuals' lives, has influence on cognition. Wolfers (1962: 42) states that "factors external to the actor can become determinants only as they affect the mind, the heart and the will of the decision-maker." Wentz (1987), among many others, notes that we are more likely to ignore any outside information that clashes with our belief systems.

A number of foreign policy theories and tools, within the general frame-work of Classical Realist theory of international politics, are already sensitive to religion and to the constraints religion might put on our cognition. One example of this is *schemas* which are defined as "cognitive structures that represent knowledge about a concept or type of stimulus, including its attributes and the relations among these attributes" (Fiske and Taylor, 1991: 98). Schemas can be directly affected by religion. *Operational code*, another frequently used foreign policy tool, has traditionally been employed to explain the rules of conduct and the norms of behavior that were exhibited by politically influential groups (Leites, 1951, 1953) or individuals (Walker et al., 1999). Alexander George (1969: 199) divides operational code into two categories: Philosophical Beliefs (beliefs regarding the fundamental nature of politics, the nature of political conflict, and the role of the individual in history) and Instrumental Beliefs (beliefs about ends–means relationships in the context of political action). Both of these types of beliefs can be influenced by religion. Malici and Buckner (2008) use George's framework to explore the cognitive diagnostic beliefs of Mahmoud Ahmadinejad and Bashar al-Asad. Their results show that there is nothing especially irrational about either actor's foreign policy behavior, though they are informed by different experiences and worldviews.

One can also turn to leadership studies for additional insights. Kissinger (1966: 514) divides leadership into three types: the Bureaucratic Pragmatic type, the Ideological type and the Charismatic/Revolutionary type. Religious leaders, depending on the context, can be under the Ideological or the Charismatic/Revolutionary types, or they can be a mixture of both. In a Neoclassical fashion, Kissinger (1966: 513) reminds us of the importance of leadership to the decisions taken by the states:

Whatever one's view about the degree to which choices in international affairs are "objectively" determined, the decisions are made by the individuals who will be above all, conscious of the seeming multiplicity of the options. Their understanding of the nature of their choice depends on many factors, including their experience during the rise to eminence.

When systematically investigating the influence of an individual's faith on foreign policy-making, therefore, cognitive frameworks within the domain of foreign policy studies constitute useful tools.

Religious worldviews, public opinion, and decision-making

Thus far we have focused on the individual's own cognition and worldviews as they play out in political decisions. Our second consideration is the worldviews of the audience of a decision-maker. Since re-election and approval are usually the priorities of a politician, it is expected that the worldviews of the constituency matter. This phenomenon, which has transnational implications, may be investigated by using foreign policy tools that focus on political optimization. Poliheuristic decision-making theory, for example, holds that decision-making is a two-stage process. During the first stage, politically unacceptable possibilities (i.e., the options that will prevent the incumbent from re-election or continuing in office) are eliminated without consideration of other dimensions. It is only during the second stage that politicians engage in a more detailed optimization (Mintz, 2004; Sandal et al., 2011). In other words, whereas the worldviews of the constituency figure into the first stage, the worldviews of the decision-maker become especially influential in the second stage, where a choice among politically viable alternatives is required.

Religious worldviews, in this sense, are influential even in secular settings. In officially secular India, the Bharatiya Janata Party represented an exclusivist *Hindutva*, Hinduism "that overcomes the divisions of Hindu religion and society and a state that restores Ram Rajya, the ideal rule of the mythic Lord Rama" (Hardgrave, 2005). Hindu nationalists make speeches for the liberation of Lord Ram's birthplace and the phraseology is imbued with religious imagery (Varshney, 1993: 240). BJP's fierce stance led to an aggressive security policy and a faster development of nuclear weapons, not to mention harsher positions vis-à-vis Kashmir and Pakistan. The political campaign that was conducted under the banner of "Ram aur Roti"[1] ended up changing both the foreign policy framework and the material capabilities of the country. This change became possible due to the BJP's exclusive political discourse catering to the conservative Hindu worldview.

In another officially secular country, Turkey, the ruling Justice and Development party (Adalet ve Kalkınma Partisi – AK Party) came to power with its Islamic credentials. Although the party did not prove to be as "radical" as the secular circles expected, it challenged the conventional power politics wisdom from time to time, relying mostly on the Muslim public support. For example, in March 2003, the majority of the parliamentarians from the AK Party voted against a resolution authorizing the deployment of the forces of its NATO ally, the US, to Turkey to open a northern front in a war against Iraq, a fellow Muslim-majority country. Taydas and Ozdamar (2012: 13) report that the deputy prime minister of the time, Abdüllatif Şener, remembers that it was especially difficult "to convince the [AK] party's pro-Islamist deputies, who were being seriously pressured by the Islamist conservative media, intellectuals, and constituencies not to participate in the war." In another instance of redefining the national interest, Prime Minister Tayyip Erdoğan practically ended the Turkish–Israeli strategic partnership when he walked off the stage at Davos after harshly criticizing the Israeli president Shimon Peres. Although there were mixed reactions in Turkey, Erdoğan's reputation in the Middle East – with the significant exception of Israel – considerably increased due to the pro-Palestinian worldviews of the Muslim populations.

It is important to emphasize that this discussion of integrating religious worldviews into Classical Realism focuses on policy goals and not on the means for attaining those goals. Specifically we argue that material benefits are not necessarily the only source of international policy preferences. Non-material factors, including religious worldviews, can have a profound influence on policy choices. Most Realists would recommend against paying too much attention to non-material factors in decision-making but, as we demonstrate here, the Classical Realist tradition has considerable room to accept and even explain the influence of these motives. Morgenthau's and Niebuhr's broad interpretations of power and interest as well as a renewed focus on the Weberian legacy in Classical Realism is good news for scholars who are interested in using cultural variables in this framework (Barkawi, 1998; Hamilton, 1995; Pichler, 1998; Williams, 2005).

Religious legitimacy and Classical Realism

Religious legitimacy is a potent tool of persuasion in international relations and local politics. We argue that accounts of such legitimacy are compatible with Classical Realism, and in fact, religious legitimacy may be considered a form of power and influence.

Religious legitimacy as a form of power and influence

Although Classical Realism emphasizes power and interest, these concepts are used flexibly enough to permit integration of less tangible forms of power such as legitimacy and persuasion. Realism, Morgenthau (1956: 5) argues,

> does not endow its key concept of interest defined as power with a meaning that is fixed once and for all.... The kind of interest determining political action in a particular period of history depends upon the political and cultural context within which foreign policy is formulated.

Morgenthau's "interest formation" may be further explored with the help of constructivist methodologies, paying due attention to political and cultural context. Despite Morgenthau's cautions against the use of ideology at the expense of prudence and self-restraint, religious ideologies can still influence interests. More specifically, if a state relies heavily on religion for legitimacy during a period in which religion is influential in terms of bringing people together, then religion may well be tied effectively to interests. Depending on the context, moral arguments can override "strategic speculation" as Loriaux (1992) states in his analysis of Augustinian Realism.

Similar to the concept of interest, power has a flexible definition in Classical Realism. Morgenthau (1956: 8–9) contends that:

> its content and the manner of its use are determined by the political and cultural environment. Power comprises anything that establishes and maintains the control of man over man. Thus, power covers all social relationships which serve that end, from physical violence to the most subtle psychological ties by which one mind controls another.

Niebuhr (1996: 260) also argues that man can "create an endless variety of types and combinations of power, from that of pure reason to that of pure physical force." Power has a wide range, and "control" is the key concept here. As long as a social or political factor such as religion is used as a means of "control", it can directly be linked to power.

In the social science literature, there is certainly precedent for the proposition that religion is a source of social power and control. For instance, in sociology, the functionalist school of religion posits that one of religion's major functions in a society is to maintain social control and power. Karl Marx's classic argument that religion is the opiate of the masses refers to the use of religion by the governing elite in order to pacify the citizens (Pickering, 1984; Turner, 1991; Wilson, 1982). Gill (2008) similarly argues that religion can be a more efficient and less costly means of domestic control than coercion. These arguments are part of a broader set of arguments that link religious and political elites. Religious elites and institutions might support the legitimacy of the state in return for benefits from the government (Stark and Finke, 2000; Toft et al., 2011; Turner, 1991).

While these discussions of legitimacy are usually carried out in the context of domestic politics, they can also be conducted in the field of international relations. Religious organizations, wittingly or unwittingly, might endow a specific government with legitimacy. Longman (2010) argues that this was the case with the churches in Rwanda during genocide, as the early missionaries defined the divisions along racial terms and remained institutions of the power elite. The churches, Longman states, conveyed a message of "obedience, division and power" instead of "love and fellowship." The same story was true for South Africa as well. Apartheid, at least initially, had the "blessing" of the church. One can debate the extent of this influence but, given that both Apartheid and genocide in Rwanda have become transnational issues, it is crucial to question the role of religious actors – positive and negative – in the process.

Within this framework, "influence" is particularly important. Employment of religion as a "source of legitimacy" (which increases one's power by increasing one's control over fellow citizens or even the citizens of another country) is consistent with Classical Realist literature. Froese and Mencken (2009: 103–104) argue that:

> throughout the course of the Iraq War, the Bush Administration has consist-
> ently framed its war policy in decidedly religious language … [and] Bush's
> chief speech writer from 1999 to 2004, Michael Gerson, affirms that he
> inserted religious language and biblical quotes into nearly all Bush's
> speeches, literary references understood by millions of religious Americans.

On a more general level, Kelley (2005) argues that the US presidents generally use religious rhetoric to justify war. However, religious discourse is a double-edged sword; it can work both for and against a policy-maker. For example, Thaksin Shinawatra, former prime minister of Thailand, being aware of the strong Buddhist values of the society, employed religious rhetoric and made references to an influential ascetic monk and philosopher, Buddhadasa, in his political speeches (Phongpaichit and Baker, 2005:137). Ironically, it is argued that his downfall was partly due to the spiritually informed Buddhist public opinion, which expected him to live up to the Buddhist standards he highlighted in his speeches (Kitiarsa, 2006). Leaders may be held responsible for their publicly stated beliefs, and they are expected to practice what they preach.

Some scholars go to the extent of claiming that the legitimacy of governments cannot be thought independently of religion (Geertz, 1977; Gill, 1998; Koko-slakis, 1985). Niebuhr (1932: 36), while optimistic that high religions move "toward an interpretation of the divine as benevolent will," also reminds us about the possibility of the employment of religion as a "tool" by saying, "human vice and error may be clothed by religion in garments of divine magnificence." Religion is not qualitatively "good" or "bad" in the sphere of international relations; it is just a phenomenon that is used in different contexts. This understanding suggests that analyses of control mechanisms would contribute both to the Classical Realist framework and to the literature on legitimacy. This holds true for the Neoclassical tradition as well. Thomas Christensen (1996: 11) states that "national political power," defined as "the ability of state leaders to mobilize their nation's human and material resources behind security policy initiatives," constitutes "a key intervening variable between the international challenges facing the nation and the strategies adopted by the state to meet those challenges." Taliaferro and colleagues (2009) also posit that ideational factors play a crucial role in helping leaders to extract societal resources. Along those lines, Barr (2009: 68) argues that the former president of China, Jiang Zemin, promoted Confucianism as "a stabilizing factor that would provide a new rationale for the legitimacy of the regime." Hu Jintao, Jiang's successor, continued to echo Confucian themes to legitimize his policies.

In religious states, legitimacy becomes even more of a pressing issue. Saudi leaders, for example, had to seek a *fatwa* (Islamic religious edict) that would legitimize US military presence in their country against the threat of Saddam's expansionism in 1990. After the Gulf War in 1990 to 1991, Saddam Hussein also realized the value of religious legitimacy. Under the "faith movement" (*al-Hamlah al-Immaniyah*) he initiated, Saddam built new mosques and instituted increased constraints on alcohol consumption (Sidahmed, 2007). Saddam had also given himself titles like "the leader of all Muslims" and he used quotes from the Qu'ran in his speeches until he was toppled (Anderson and Stansfield, 2004). Similarly, Shahin (1998) states that in Tunisia, Algeria, and Morocco, even though sharia was not implemented in practice, the governments had invoked the symbols of Islam to suppress the religious opposition and to draw mass support around policies that would not normally be received enthusiastically by the society.

Classical Realist works have recently been under renewed focus. Patterson (2008: 3) draws attention to the relevance of Christian Realism as a "vibrant intellectual approach for evaluating political phenomena that starts with considerations of power, order, security and responsibility." There has been a lively debate about which components of Classical Realism would be useful in analyzing the Iraq War. Echoing Niebuhr, opponents of the war might point to the danger of unchecked power, while advocates could call upon the need to act "to prevent greater evil" (Elie, 2007: 86–96). Chernus (2008: 854) argues that the neoconservative call for US domination reflected the influence of Niebuhr albeit based on a selective reading, as it does not take into account "Niebuhr's stress on the limits of self-aggrandizement and his concomitant sense of irony." In a similar vein, international relations scholars note that given Morgenthau's opposition to the Vietnam War, he would most probably have opposed the Iraq War on the grounds that "spreading democracies" can easily transform into a "crusade" that is not viable in power politics terms (Mearsheimer, 2005). Niebuhr and other Classical Realists, explored at greater length, would prove to be of considerable relevance to foreign policy analysis, since mere "distribution of capabilities" does not seem to offer satisfying explanations of world politics.

Non-state religious actors and Classical Realism

Non-state religious actors are not taken as a main unit in the Classical Realist tradition. However, their influence on decision-making and interest formation is difficult to overlook. With the failure of the Western secular ideologies that have been linked to colonialism in regions like the Middle East, Africa, and South Asia, indigenous faith traditions have become popular in the political arena (Juergensmeyer, 1993, 2008). Modern communication technologies (Shupe, 1990: 22), coupled with increased opportunities for political participation of religious communities (Rubin, 1994: 22–23), enabled once-ignored faith communities to have a say in the future of the nation.

In this context, we identify two ways in which non-state religious actors may be studied from a Classical Realist perspective. The first uses the "security dilemma" concept to study relations between the non-state religious actors and to shed light on the identity-related conflicts among religions. This is especially noteworthy, since such a Classical Realist argument recognizes the rationality dimension in religious conflicts that is not very much emphasized in the primordialist literature. The second possibility of integration is through the influence of non-state religious actors on foreign and domestic policies of the states by creating alternative interests or modifying existing ones.

Security dilemma and non-state religious actors

As we previously argued, Classical Realists start with human nature and gradually build up to the state level. This allows domestic religious actors, in the form of religious institutions or religious communities, to take their place in scholarly investigations. The term "security dilemma," as explained by John Herz, is a useful concept which applies to religious actors that desire to preserve their long-held faith tradition in a competitive and anarchic world of different identities. Groups or leaders are "concerned about their security from being attacked, subjected and annihilated by other groups or individuals" and their attempt to gain more power for their security "renders the others more insecure and compels them to prepare for the worst" (Herz, 1950: 157).

Coupled with the identity-related concerns elaborated below, followers of any religion would most likely feel under threat in a competitive "market." A Catholic would feel less than fully safe in the face of a rising wave of evangelical Protestantism, especially in forms that declare the Pope as the "anti-Christ," as was the case with the Free Presbyterian Church in Northern Ireland. Jews would feel threatened by increasing Christian missionary efforts; Christians would be wary of the growing Muslim population as one will observe in Germany, France, and the Netherlands, among others. Muslims may feel threatened by the apparent dominance of Christian majority countries in the international system. This does not necessarily mean that there will be "religious wars" just because of the changing demography, but religion in some respects is a zero-sum game. One cannot be a Jew and a Muslim at the same time. If one religion gains more followers relative to other religions, it has gained influence in the larger religious market. In the face of changing numbers and levels of devotions of the followers, one can witness the insecurity and "preparing for the worst just in case" in the religious sphere. Religion is so central an issue that leaders and groups cannot behave pragmatically as easily as they would do if the contention was over another part of their identity (Laustsen and Waever, 2000: 719).

Non-state religious actors as competitors to the state

Another way non-state religious actors influence the power balance is by creating an alternative to the existing state identity. Religious minorities, by rebellion or by resisting the prevalent doctrines (religious or secular) in the public sphere, may threaten the organization of a state (Lincoln, 1985). Religious institutions can also oppose the policies of the state and withdraw their support in the event of state policies not coinciding with the interests of the religious elite (Fox, 1999a).

One example of this influence of religious actors is the transformative role of the Catholic Church in Poland and its influence in providing an alternative to communism. The Catholic Church, which had been attacked under communist rule, became a mediator between the communist government and Solidarity, the Polish non-governmental trade union which the government tried to abolish. During the turbulent 1980s, Poles from every political stripe sought refuge under the auspices of the Catholic Church, which managed to keep its moderate and pacifying position between the communists and the opposition while maintaining its staunch anti-communist position. Gradually, the communist rule was delegitimized and the Church became one of the most powerful entities in the country (Eberts, 1998: 820). Even when one defines Classical Realism in the most restricted manner, it is still not possible to discount the victory of an institution over communism – even if in a limited geography – in the Cold War history.

Consider also the role of the Dutch Reformed Church in the Apartheid system in South Africa. The segregationist policies were inspired and consolidated by the policies of the Dutch Reformed Church (DRC). The DRC was the country's established church and had a prior record of vigorously pursuing segregationist policies. In 1857, for example, a synod of the DRC introduced separate services along racial lines. This segregationist policy had been represented as "the will of God" by using various textual references from the Bible pointing to the differences among people (Esterhuyse, 1981: 34–35). The Tower of Babel story (Genesis 11: 1–9) became a "cardinal tenet of Apartheid theology" (Johnston, 1994: 187) – it was normal for people to be treated differently because they were different, and the difference in treatment was the divine will.

In 1960, the World Council of Churches (WCC), which is the broadest umbrella organization for the ecumenical movement, sponsored the first conference that protested Apartheid. The members advanced 17 resolutions emphasizing the biblical passages on equality and human rights, thus challenging the truth claims of the churches promoting separation. Not surprisingly, the DRC, in an attempt to separate itself from this inclusive line of interpretation, withdrew its membership from the WCC. Eight years later, the South African Council of Churches (SACC), the national ecumenical coordinator of the inter-church communication and a partner to WCC, issued the "Message to the People of South Africa," signed by 600 ministers and 27 churches. This statement was regarded as the strongest religious denunciation of Apartheid that had ever been issued (South African Democratic Education Trust, 2004: 679). In the same year, the WCC initiated the *Program to Combat Racism* (PCR), which translated the condemnations into practical action. Under the PCR initiative, the WCC set up a special grant program to combat racism, from which racially oppressed groups and organizations representing these groups were going to be funded. The fund was supplied not only by voluntary contributions from churches but also from local ecumenical and support groups all over the world. The WCC was also instrumental in rallying businesses and individuals against companies that kept its ties with South Africa. This protest, along with international sanctions endorsed by the WCC, cost South Africa close to $10 billion between 1984 and 1989 (Warr, 1999: 504–506). The most serious challenge to the political system and the dominant theology supporting Apartheid came in the early 1980s. The World Alliance of Reformed Churches (WARC), which has a membership of 214 churches representing 75 million Christians, made the following statement, again backed by numerous scriptural references: "Apartheid is a sin, and ... the moral and theological justification of it is a travesty of the Gospel and, in its persistent disobedience to the Word of God, a theological heresy" (quoted in De Gruchy and Villa-Vicencio, 1983: 170).

After years of international religious and secular pressure in addition to the domestic religious challenges, "Church and Society," the document issued by the DRC in 1986, acknowledged that despite the good intentions of the Church, supporting Apartheid was a "mistake." This recognition was translated into the withdrawal of legitimacy bestowed on the political actors that supported Apartheid:

> The Dutch Reformed Church is convinced that the application of Apartheid as a political and social system by which human dignity is adversely affected, and whereby one particular group is detrimentally suppressed by another, cannot be accepted on Christian-ethical grounds because it contravenes the very essence of neighborly love and righteousness and inevitably the human dignity of all involved.
>
> (Quoted in Kinghorn, 1990)

As a result of the international pressure and the U-turn in the public theology of the DRC, the domestic political outlook started to change. The public became more attentive to the voices of moderation which won a theological debate. Political change followed the change in public theology (Sandal, 2011). In September 1989, Frederik Willem de Klerk, the leader of the National Party whose motto was "Fairness, Firmness, Peace," came to power. As soon as he came to power, de Klerk ordered the release of prominent political prisoners, including Nelson Mandela, lifted the state of emergency that was declared in 1985, and repealed all Apartheid laws.

The South Africa example, along with the Poland one, demonstrates that non-state religious actors, sometimes in connection with other actors, can play significant roles in defining the political ideologies. Non-state religious actors can change the domestic and foreign policy agenda of the political actors and influence state identity and interests, all of which are important variables for the Classical Realists. This effect grows more serious when non-state religious actors become the service providers in a country where there is a political vacuum. To illustrate, Shadid (2002: 111) observes that for the Lebanese, and for the Palestinians, Hezbollah and Hamas have been associated with "clinics, legal-aid societies, schools, hospitals, dental offices or orphanages that dot the landscape where their own governments have withdrawn." Similarly, in Brazil's favelas, where the state is non-existent, Pentecostalism is said to be one of the very few things that function (Freston, 2006). Such provisions challenge the remaining legitimacy of states and secular political governance, transferring agency to non-state religious groups gradually. Non-state religious actors can influence the rise and fall of governments and this can hardly be ignored in power politics.

Religious states and Classical Realism

A religious state, defined as a state which makes its policies in accordance with the teachings and tradition of a specific religion, can have political interests that include ensuring the survival of the state, preserving and even exporting a religious doctrine. Even the civil norms of behavior in secular states develop characteristics similar to religious ones (Bellah, 1970). Arguably, the secular Westphalian state system takes its roots from the Protestant reformation (Philpott, 2000). In short, a state that defines its interests in line with a religious doctrine is not an anomaly at the system level, no matter how narrowly Classical Realism is defined. Along those lines, we argue that religious states are not necessarily more ethical or moral than their secular counterparts. Their inclusion in Classical Realist accounts, however, is crucial because religion can constitute an effective "flag" to rally around in the face of threats from outside. Especially in the Neoclassical Realist accounts, religion may be one of the missing links between the distribution of capabilities and foreign policy behavior. In addition, the theoretical tools which Classical Realists used to analyze the Soviet Union and communism may be employed for the study of the states and groups that export a particular form of religious ideology.

Religious ideology and national interest in religious states

Religious ideology can influence national interest in multiple ways. However, one should be careful about separating the analytical observations from policy prescriptions. Morgenthau (1972: 9), for example, warns decision-makers against linking politics with a moral purpose:

> The lighthearted equation between a particular nationalism and the counsels of Providence is morally indefensible, for it is that very sin of pride against which the Greek tragedians and the Biblical prophets have warned rulers and ruled. That equation is also politically pernicious, for it is liable to engender the distortion in judgment which, in the blindness of crusading frenzy, destroys nations and civilizations – in the name of moral principle, ideal, or God himself.

This statement and the others that advocate a strict separation of moral purposes and worldly politics should be understood within the context of the history of the tradition. If a Classical Realist gave advice on politics, she would surely recommend staying away from employing any moral doctrine as the basis of nationalism. However, as discussed above, this is a policy recommendation and not an argument that religion cannot be influential. There are many states that define their identity primarily by a religion either because the country indeed represents a community that is more bound by faith than any other common identity, or religion is used for instrumental purposes as a means to control citizens and maintain stability.

Religion can be an effective tool to ensure unity within a state in the face of the perceived threats from outside. Morgenthau's statement (1956: 5) that "the kind of interest determining political action in a particular period of history depends upon the political and cultural context within which foreign policy is formulated" leaves ample room for religious states and their foreign policy-making within the framework of international relations. Even religious states recognize that "loyalty to the nation comes into conflict with duties to humanity" (Morgenthau, 1945: 12) and the individual moral norms may not be the same as societal-level norms. Islam, for example, strongly discourages Muslims from going to war against other Muslims, and limits the reasons for war to self-defense and the protection of Islamic values (Abou El Fadl, 1999: 151–155; Hashmi, 1999: 162). Consider, however, the Iran–Iraq War in the 1980s among many other wars between co-religionists. Despite being a theocracy based on Shi'a principles, Iran did not hesitate to fight against the Shi'a population of Iraq. On a relevant note, religion has also been a factor in the making of alliances, which is an area we investigate in the next chapter.

National security is an ambiguous symbol. National interest and national security, "while appearing to offer guidance and a basis for broad consensus, they may be permitting everyone to label whatever policy he favors with an attractive and possibly a deceptive name" (Wolfers, 1952: 481). Walter Lippman (1943: 51) argues that "a nation is secure to the extent to which it is not in danger of having to sacrifice core values, if it wishes to avoid war, and is able, if challenged, to maintain them by victory in such a war." Therefore, not only can a threat to religion be easily interpreted as a national security issue by the political elite, but also a specific religion can be construed as a threat to the order of a state, religious or secular.

National security is not merely a function of material power. Neoclassical Realists make the case that distribution of resources is only part of the story. Zakaria (1999: 19) wrote:

> Classical Realists have written carelessly about "power maximization", leaving unclear whether states expand for material sources or as a consequence of material sources. Neoclassical Realism makes the latter assumption; increased resources give rise to greater ambitions. States are not resource-maximizers but influence-maximizers.

In connection with the religious worldviews of the elite, one can employ the Neoclassical accounts of foreign policy behavior when studying the actions of religious states. As Randall Schweller (2004: 169) argues, statecraft is a consequence of "elites' preferences and perception of the external environment" in addition to structural constraints. If a specific faith tradition is adopted as a state religion, the perception of the external environment will inevitably be influenced, if not entirely defined by this identity. Elite consensus on foreign policy decisions "concerns the degree of shared perception about some facts in the world being problems (vs. not) of a particular nature (vs. some other nature) requiring certain remedies (vs. others)" (Schweller, 2004: 170). To illustrate, Ayatollah Khomeini is said to have believed that "the existing world order should emulate his version of the Islamic state paradigm" (Ramazani, 2001: 214). Expectedly, under such conditions, political elites would make religion a core value not only to be protected, but also to be spread.

The ideological aspect of religion is not very different from the former Soviet Union and the idea of spreading communism, a topic to which Classical Realists devoted considerable attention. Consider, for example, Morgenthau's description of the world in 1952 (p. 4):

> Today, the two main power centers in the world, Washington and Moscow, are also the center of two antagonistic political philosophies which have a tendency to transform themselves into political religions. These two power centers profess and act upon two incompatible conceptions of human nature, of society, and of government, and have found it at times hard to resist the temptation to try to make the world over in the image of these conceptions.

Similar to the Cold War, in today's world, material and discursive battles are going on between deeply incompatible conceptions of governance. For example, Elie Kedourie (1992: 5) claims that there is a difference between the Western conceptions of governance and its Muslim counterparts:

> The idea of representation, of elections, of popular suffrage, of political institutions being regulated by laws laid down by a parliamentary assembly, of these laws being guarded and upheld by an independent judiciary, the ideas of the secularity of state ... all these are profoundly alien to the Muslim political tradition.

It is hard to fully agree with Kedourie's primordialist evaluations but it is also difficult to ignore how political elites portray the incompatibilities among values and governance styles. Although it is not to be expected that the very same principles are executed everywhere in the world with the same speed, the differences among the multiple understandings of governance may prove to be an issue of global contention when the political actors aim to spread their forms of governance to the rest of the world. To give a contemporary example, the American discourse of spreading democracy by any means may result in a power struggle with the Muslim communities who protest the military methods involved.

The debate on governance takes place not only among religions, but within religions as well. Sachedina (2001) distinguishes between exclusive and inclusive interpretations of Islam. Inclusive interpretations rely on a fresh take on exegesis in the light of the pressing problems of our age. These interpretations

regard all human beings as equal and they take compassion as a guiding principle, Sachedina argues. Hefner illustrates this argument with the Indonesia
example. He states that inclusivist Indonesian Islamists transformed the religio-
political landscape and "western social science, classical Islamic scholarship,
Indonesian history – these and other sources were drawn into the effort to create
a new Muslim discourse of civility and pluralism" (Hefner, 2000: 119). Sandal
(2012) also draws attention to the fact that the strongest tensions are among different interpretations of the same religion, rather than among different religions.
Given the centrality of political ideas, the speed with which the ideologies are
diffusing and the existence of significant material capabilities in general, there is
no reason why we cannot employ the Classical Realist frameworks of power and
influence to explore the clashes we are witnessing in today's world.

   To be fair to the Classical Realists of the post-World War II setting, religion
was not as much of an issue of concern as communism or fascism. Those political ideologies had a transnational dimension but they were embodied by individual states. The arms race in conventional and unconventional weapons
defined the meaning of power and threat in the 1950s and 1960s. Although
nuclear proliferation is still considered a grave threat, issues ranging from terrorism to competition over sacred territories have taken their place on the
security agenda. Religious states fit comfortably into the Realist paradigms since
they are "states." However, the fact that they command not only a narrow
national identity but also a stronger source of influence – religion – gives them
an advantage over their secular counterparts when it comes to mobilization of
both their citizens and co-religionists all over the world.

Transnational religious actors and Classical Realism

Although Classical Realism is not as steadfast as Neorealism when it comes to
the premise that "states are the main actors," still, any account that treats religion
without reference to states would need to justify such a departure from the core
tenets of Classical Realism. A shift to other mainstream frameworks – such as
Neoliberalism, Constructivism, or the solidarist branch of the English School –
may therefore be considered as an alternative to heavily state-centric paradigms
by scholars who do not want to take the "state" as a reference point. In this light,
transnational religious movements, including religious ideologies, fundamentalisms, and the views espoused by terrorist groups constitute challenging cases of
integration into Classical Realist theory. However, one can point to a number of
relevant debates that draw attention to the relevance of supranational entities and
possibly find a frame in which to place transnational religious movements.

Transnational religious movements forming alternative political units to the state

In this section, we discuss the grand ideas of religious groups that might challenge the structure of the international system, the impact of international

alliances in the form of institutions, and the alternative identities which trans-national networks provide, thereby challenging the power of the nation-state. The exponents of political Islam and evangelical Christianity as well as institutions such as the Vatican Church are among the transnational religious actors that provide alternative ideologies to nationalism.

Many transnational religious movements are working to spread their religious ideologies and to create a worldwide community of believers that behave in line with the teachings of a specific religious tradition. This can have a number of manifestations. First, this ambition can manifest itself as an effort to create a religious super-state and eventually a religious world government. In his discussion of the viability of a world government, Arnold Wolfers (1949: 187) contends that "lack of consensus among the major nations about the desirability of a world government as well as about the kind of world government today would be more likely to lead to war than to reduce enmity." Herz's security dilemma (1950) among politically active groups is also useful in explaining the competition of religious movements in the transnational sphere, as he was an exponent of a more holistic study of international relations (Sylvest, 2008).

Second, the desire for religion-based political units can have institutional manifestations. These manifestations include formal or informal alliances between states which are based upon and to some extent pursue goals influenced by their shared religious ideology. These alliances may take the form of an organization, hierarchically either horizontal or vertical. One example of horizontally organized institutions is the Organization of Islamic Cooperation (OIC), which has its own permanent delegation to the United Nations. Among the OIC's aims are to "endeavor to work for revitalizing Islam's pioneering role in the world while ensuring sustainable development progress and prosperity for the Member States; to enhance and strengthen the bond of unity and solidarity among the Muslim peoples and Member States" (OIC Charter). The OIC has been active in advocating the rights of Muslim minorities in non-Muslim majority countries like Thailand and India.

A case of interest within the framework of vertically organized institutions is the status of the Vatican City, which provides a territorial base to the Catholic Church. It has a permanent observer status in the UN and has diplomatic relations with more than 160 countries. The Catholic Church has been vocal in a number of issues in international politics. It stood against the inclusion of abortion rights language in UN documents on population and development, and it opposed the Persian Gulf War as well as the economic sanctions against Iran, Iraq, Libya, and Cuba (Reese, 1998: 3). The Holy See is also a signatory of agreements like the Nuclear Non-Proliferation Treaty and the Nuclear Test-Ban Treaty. In short, the Catholic Church, representing millions of Catholics around the world, has a say in issues of both high politics and the social sphere. True, its "army" is restricted to the Swiss Pontifical Guard at the gates of the city but if power is defined as influence, the Holy See enjoys a network that is arguably among the most powerful in the world.

Another case that is worth exploring before we move on to the third point is the role churches played in the ethno-religious conflict in the Balkans. The Serbian Orthodox Church, which was initially disappointed at the disinterest of Slobodan Milosevic in consolidating the social and the financial status of the clergy, strongly backed Serb nationalist parties in Croatia and Bosnia Herzegovina (Perica, 2004:144). The Church is geographically located in Serbia, Bosnia Herzegovina, Montenegro, the Republic of Macedonia, and Croatia, and it has been politically active in furthering policies that have been in accordance with Serbian interests. Its influence has been coupled with the public religious expressions of the Orthodox leaders in the Balkans. Radovan Karadzic and Ratko Mladic (respectively the political and military leaders of the Bosnian Serbs) "made great play of their Orthodox faith" (Bruce, 2003: 50). Coming to the awareness that the Church commands a significant influence in the region, Milosevic eventually sought to win its favor by allowing the construction of new churches and the selling of the Church newspaper *Pravoslavje* on the newsstands (Herbert, 2003: 247).

Third, transnational religious actors can create an alternative basis for identity and political organization which competes with the state. One should also note that not every citizen identifies primarily with the "nation" in the European sense. Religion can also provide the individual with a sense of belonging which is just as strong, if not more so. The most striking example is the concept of ummah (community or nation of believers) in Islam. Shahin (2008: 173) reminds us that the word "citizenship" has no equivalent in the classical Arab language and the root for citizenship/nationalism in Arabic is *watan*, which refers to a place of residence rather than a national identity. Although it is debatable to what extent ummah replaces the traditional concept of nation in the minds of all Muslims, it is clearly the basis for organization among some Muslim groups, including the extremist ones that have a claim to the governance of the Islamic world. Jemaah Islamiyah, for example, is a militant Islamist organization dedicated to the establishment of an Islamic state covering Southeast Asia guided by a strict interpretation of sharia. Similarly, but on a larger scale, Al-Qaeda's pan-Islamist ideology is joined by local organizations such as the Islamist Movement of Uzbekistan, which was once an organization that focused solely on Central Asia (Hoffman, 2004: 550). As Al-Qaeda, with its ideological allies, gains territorial bases especially in Central, South, and Southeast Asia, it becomes more rooted by making those territories de facto states. When these power transfers occur, the status of the new entities may be considered similar to that of a religious state. By virtue of their threat to the international system and the sovereignties of other states, these transnational religious actors become part of the national security concerns at the system level, which puts them on the Classical Realist agenda.

Transnational religious movements are often concerned with influencing state policy. This engagement may be viewed through their impact on individual states without giving up the understanding that their agenda is pursued in a coordinated manner across many states. For example, Evangelical Christians, who have a transnational network across continents, continue to shape the political agendas of the countries in which they are based, including several Latin American countries, the Philippines, China, and Korea. Philippine charismatic groups along with the like-minded co-religionists across the world engaged in a faith-based warfare with communism, inspired by their evangelical worldview (Brouwer et al., 1996). Ian Paisley, once the leader of the Democratic Unionist Party in Northern Ireland and an important party to the conflict which spread beyond the local borders, was also the leader of the Free Presbyterian Church. For years, Paisley attacked the Catholic Church in the newspaper he co-founded, *The Protestant Telegraph*. The case of Paisley and the conflict in Northern Ireland is an instance of fundamental evangelicalism that has regional and international repercussions.

Most of the ways through which Classical Realism accommodates transnational religious movements are linked to the state. The only serious exception is religion providing an alternative basis for organization which competes with the state, and this exception, admittedly, is difficult to reconcile with Classical Realism. Nevertheless, given that transnational religious movements give meaning to some local security issues that define the agendas of states, Classical Realists cannot afford to ignore the trajectories of ideologies that have the power to mobilize millions. As Thomas (2005: 106) argues, Zionism is a transnational idea as is Pan-Islamism, each having its own symbols and "prophets," yet both of these ideas have contributed significantly to the interest formations and power definitions of individual state actors.

The definitions of power and interest, as Classical Realists expect, have changed over time. For example, the idea of Zionism and how and when it should be implemented has been a cause of debate even among the Jewish community. There are ultraorthodox sects that still believe a Jewish state should not exist until the messiah comes to establish it. Firestone (2006) argues that there was a Jewish public theology that even condemned Zionism as "dangerous" and "threatening to the well-being of the Jewish community" by using traditional theological arguments. This religious perspective lost its strength especially after the 1967 war and gave way to another public theology that now sees it as legitimate for Israel to control the territories of the biblical Land of Israel. The power of such transnational movements leading to the establishment and the consolidation of the core units of the system (i.e., the states) is testimony to the fact that there cannot be a full picture of the power politics without an account of the link between nationalism and religion.

Herz (2003: 415) notes that the transformation of the US actions against 9/11 perpetrators into a full-scale war "against non-state actors as well as nations and regimes, have added immeasurably to the security concerns and dilemmas among countries." The role of transnational religious actors as well as their "potential" to become independent actors is becoming increasingly recognized as an influential factor in Classical Realist thought. Unlike the post-World War I world in which a state's enemy was another state, we are currently witnessing transnational actors that are represented as enemies or friends. If power and survival, the core variables in Classical Realist thought, are to be redefined in contemporary terms, transnational religious actors cannot be excluded from international relations theory.

Transnational religious issues and Classical Realism

Although it may prove to be challenging to recognize transnational actors as one of the core agents in Classical Realism, transnational issues are not beyond the scope of the tradition. The Classical Realist agenda is not necessarily confined to state-level issues. Holy places and human rights are among the issues that are easily securitized and become a matter of national interest, and thus merit an investigation under the Classical Realist framework. Admittedly, when it comes to social issues like family planning or medical/ethical debates such as the acceptability of stem cell research, Neoliberal tradition or Constructivist approaches may be much more conducive than Classical Realism. We argue that transnational issues are relevant to Classical Realist theorizing because these issues may be regarded as matters of national security that is worth defending by tools of power politics.

Human rights and power politics

In a discussion of interests and religion, Niebuhr (1954: 30) asserted: "a consistent self-interest on the part of a nation will work against its interests because it will fail to do justice to the broader and longer-term interests which are involved with the interests of nations." Niebuhr, by his emphasis on "the ethical consequences of interdependence" (1941: 2) that no state can escape from, draws attention to the impossibility of thinking of the nation and its interests in a narrow manner.

When one looks at the positions of the Classical Realists toward the Nazis, one can easily see this desire to prevent large-scale political disasters and destruction. Patterson (2007: 3) notes that both Classical Realists like Niebuhr, and the English School scholars Martin Wight and Herbert Butterfield, "defended the use of force against Nazis in terms of morality and justice without a strict Just War catechism." Although this desire to intervene on behalf of others may initially look inconsistent with the Realist approaches to foreign policy, it is not. Expansionist dictators, who inflict considerable damage on their own populations and express the intention to spread their ideologies, constitute a threat to both human rights and the stability of the state system. In such cases, human rights issues become matters of interest not only to the Classical Realists and the English School proponents but also to the Neorealists.

The ranking of issues in the agenda of a state may also differ. Since "national interest" does not have a fixed meaning in Classical Realism, a number of what are considered "transnational issues" may be points of contention for states that have different views. Nations may "seek to acquire new values at the price of greater insecurity" and goals like "liberating enslaved peoples" could bring states to the edge of war (Wolfers, 1952: 492). Religious worldviews mentioned in the first section may also get a state to pursue any agenda based on a religious ideology through the distribution of goods and services. Iran, for example, has funded Islamic groups to spread its own brand of governance and to increase its influence. The Iranian Revolutionary Guard Corps has trained Hezbollah forces and funded the group's social and philanthropic programs in Lebanon (Fuller, 2006: 142). It is also claimed that Iran provides direct state funding to Hamas and Islamic Jihad which is "performance-based" yet ends up covering a significant amount of the groups' expenses (Levitt, 2006: 173). For some, these groups are the service providers and alternatives to a failed state, whereas for others they are threats to security and stability.

Controlling sacred territories to increase power

The importance of holy places to the followers of a religion also makes acquiring or keeping sacred territories under one's control a matter of security. Many states, even the secular ones like France and Germany, have had their sacred claim to the land which shaped their national identity (Smith, 2004). Don Akenson (1992), in his comparative study of Israelis, Ulster-Scots, and Afrikaners, describe their culture as "covenantal cultures" that form a deep attachment to their territories. For such communities, the defense of these sacred lands is a matter of supreme national interest.

In some settings, the establishment narrative is based on the concepts of sacred territory and chosen people. The civil war between the Sinhalese and the Tamils in Sri Lanka was at least in part provoked by a chauvinistic interpretation of Buddhism which states that Buddha charged the Sinhalese with preserving the true Buddhism – Theravada Buddhism – and gave the Island of Lanka to the Sinhalese to create a "citadel of pure Buddhism" (Manor, 1994). Due to the presence of a significant non-Buddhist population on the island that contested these claims, deadly riots and decades of civil war ensued in Sri Lanka. The Sri Lankan government lost control over some parts of its territory to Tamil rebels but recovered it later as a result of massive military campaigns.

This interest in sacred territories, both at the state level and the individual level, embodies itself as a matter of life and death. Take the case of Jerusalem, a city that is of prime importance to Abrahamic traditions. Israel declared Jerusalem as its capital city. Even Israel's close allies, such as the US, still keep their embassies in Tel Aviv, not recognizing full Israeli sovereignty in Jerusalem. Palestinian leaders also declared Jerusalem as their "eternal" capital (Emmett, 1996). On societal and individual levels, both Jewish and Muslim extremists have used violent means to express their claims. On January 1, 1997, an off-duty Israeli soldier Noam Friedman fired his M-16 rifle into a crowded market, wounding seven Palestinians. Friedman later stated that "Abraham bought the Cave of the Patriarchs for 400 shekels of silver, and nobody will give it back" (Quoted in Miller, 1997). On July 2, 2008, a Palestinian called Hussam Dwayat drove a front-loader into a bus and several cars on Jaffa Road, Jerusalem, killing three people. Similarly, on July 22, 2008, another Palestinian, Ghassan Abu Tir, rammed a mechanical digger into a number of cars in Jerusalem, injuring ten people before being shot dead. Although the majority of Muslims and Jews do not go to those extremes, it is a fact that Jerusalem is more than a city for many. Decision-makers of any side will not give up their claims in the near future and this is a cause supported not only by locals but also by international Zionist and Islamic organizations. In Classical Realist terminology, it is a matter of supreme national interest which is to be defended at all costs. The possession of the land, by virtue of its symbolic importance, has the potential to tilt the balance of power to a significant extent.

Religious identity and Classical Realism

Addressing identity is challenging because it intersects with all the issues explored above. Religion is part of one's identity, and hence anything that has to do with religion will be directly relevant to identity. Religious identity matters in Classical Realism because it is a part of the judgments regarding who "we" and "others" are. Different faith traditions have different legacies for societies and decision-makers, and these legacies figure into the redefinitions of political identity. Second, access to political power in religion is often defined by the institutional structures of that faith tradition. Actually these structures are part of what distinguish one religious identity from another. Although institutional dimensions will be examined in Chapter 5, they are also relevant to Classical Realism since they matter in power politics as defined in this tradition.

Religious identity defining political groups

Religion figures into decisions regarding who an actor's allies and enemies are. Classical Realists recognize that one of the most important judgments which policy-makers have to make is deciding whether the other actor is a status-quo state or a revisionist state. Such a decision implies a judgment about the other's motives and "identity." Jervis points to the fact that Realism emphasizes the reciprocal relationship between identities and conflict. In addition, "social psychologists have long known that perceptions – and misperceptions – of what people have in common often grow out of conflicts as internal unity is gained by seeing others as the Other" (Jervis, 1998: 988).

International relations theory, thus far, has underestimated the importance of primordial ethnic and religious ties (Carment and James, 1997: 16–18). However, religion as it plays out in ethnic conflicts, especially as an independent variable (i.e., defining who we are and who the other is) and intervening variable (as a tool to bring people together who actually have other grievances), may be situated in a Classical Realist explanation. Instrumentalism can incorporate religion as an intervening variable but still preserve the assumption of rationality, whereas religion, used as a primordial variable, would involve emotions and passions. In a Huntingtonian fashion, the religious identities of communities also affect how others evaluate their position in the cultural advancement scale (Horowitz, 1985; Triandis, 1972). Consolidating the existence of cognitive biases that come with the identity, Tetlock (1998: 877) states that "people often prefer internal, dispositional explanations for others' conduct, even when plausible situational accounts exist." In her account of the political positions of the Muslims in Western Europe, Klausen (2005) touches upon these situational accounts when she rejects the clash of civilizations thesis. The integration of immigrant communities into Europe has become an issue of global politics, and it has often been portrayed as a matter of religion. Klausen recognizes the importance of different political inclinations in the very same religion, and she points to the multiple Muslim identities – secular-integrationist Muslims, voluntarist Euro-Muslims, traditional neo-Orthodox Muslims, and the anti-clerical Muslims. However, political leaders may not always be sensitive to this diversity and they may encourage a separation of spheres. Turner (2007) cautions that establishing such religious enclaves under multicultural policies would risk alienating the religious communities even more and may lead to "an escalation of draconian measures." Such a spiral would inevitably threaten the stability of states and create a self-fulfilling prophecy of a "clash of civilizations."

Religious identity and authority structures

Identity, in the contexts of Classical and Neoclassical Realism, is also operationalized through the authority structures of specific faith traditions. Many of the issues touched upon earlier in this chapter are influenced by religion as part of the identity of the nation or another collectivity. However, the nature of religions and the institutions prescribed in religious texts are best categorized under the identity variable. Authority structures also matter considerably in the politics of a religion. Christians and Jews, for example, have different attitudes toward political issue categorization (Miller, 1996). Zakaria (2004: 5) identifies Islam as a religion that has "no religious establishment that can declare by fiat which is the correct interpretation." He explains that the challenge with Islam in world politics is not the dominance of religious authority but the absence of it:

> The decision to oppose the state on the grounds that it is insufficiently Islamic can be exercised by anyone who wishes to do so. This much Islam shares with Protestantism. Just as a Protestant with just a little training – Jerry Falwell, Pat Robertson – can declare himself a religious leader, so also can any Muslim opine on issues of faith. In a religion without an official clergy, bin Laden has as much – or as little – authority to issue fatwas (religious orders) as does a Pakistani taxi driver in New York City.

The institutional structure and the precepts of a religion, when combined with interpretation, influence the terms of conflicts and cooperation. Since Classical Realism recognizes the influence of human nature and the quest for power, societies' turning to religion as a result of state failure can be explained with the very same realist principles that explain state behavior. True, one would be talking about the society in this instance instead of the state as an actor. However, this is not excluded in the premonitions of Morgenthau (1949: 148):

> Contemporary nationalism tends to display earmarks of expansive religion which attempts to impose its own standards and institutions upon rest of the world. The prospect of such a situation is not the unification of the world through religion but a period of religious wars, inspired by the religious fervor of nationalistic universalism and, more or less hesitatingly, supported by the traditional religions.

Such nationalism, as expressed by Morgenthau, is observed in multiple settings and defines the identity of even secular states. One example is Turkish nationalism and its widely criticized "secular" structure. Kessler (2008: 282) observes that the military, the judiciary, the educational system, and the state bureaucracy are ostensibly secular but strongly influenced by Sunni Islam. This influence, which is a remnant of the Ottoman tradition, limits the public discourse by not giving recognition to Alevis that constitute 15 percent of the population, Kessler argues. The secular nationalisms, in short, usually impose the mainstream understanding of religion onto societies and they rarely stay at an equal distance from all religious traditions.

Similarly, Japanese nationalism is intertwined with its Shinto background. One example of this interaction may be seen in the political meaning attributed to sacred places. The Yasukuni Shrine, dedicated to the spirits of those who died when fighting for Japan, has been at the center of political controversies since noted war criminals were also named among the spirits that are to be revered. O'Dwyer (2010: 148) contends that Yasukuni narrative is a distinct patriotic narrative about the past. The intersection of this patriotic narrative with faith is difficult to miss. Former Prime Minister Junichiro Koizumi's visits to the shrine had angered the Chinese and the South Koreans as it signaled an aggressive form of Japanese nationalism that was proud of its heritage, even the most violent episodes. In September 2011, Prime Minister Yoshihiko Noda stated that he would not visit the shrine, opening the way for a "mutually beneficial and strategic relationship" with China. However, occasional visits by Japanese politicians continue to spark controversy among Japan, China, and South Korea.

Religion and Classical Realism: interactions within power politics

In this chapter, we have argued that the Classical Realist framework has ample space within its theoretical construction to accommodate religious variables. Unlike Neorealism, Classical Realism has exponents in history (ranging from Machiavelli to Niebuhr) who have touched upon the issues of faith and their importance in the political sphere. The fact that Realism developed as a reaction to utopianism by no means excludes the recognition of religious considerations in the world of politics. To the contrary, in order to remain consistent with the tradition's premise of studying what is out there, Classical Realists have no option but to re-explore the existing links among power, interest, and religion. Classical Realism is clearly capable of accepting that religious worldviews can influence policy decisions while at the same time recommending that policy-makers avoid moral considerations in world politics. It can also recognize religion as a source of power in that it is a factor that can influence human behavior.

The list is not meant to be exhaustive, but we explored the main avenues by which religion can be reintegrated into the Classical Realism as an explanatory factor and how Classical Realist tradition can explain the links between religion and international relations. Although there are many possibilities of such inter-action, the most suitable avenues seem to be religious worldviews, religious legitimacy, and religious states. Given that the role of the "statesman" is recognized in the tradition, the influence of religion on cognition and perceptions, as well as the impact of religion on redefining the concepts of power and interest, are regarded as integral to studies conducted within the Classical Realist framework. In a similar vein, religion plays into the Neoclassical realist framework by constituting a possible link between material capabilities and perceptions. Especially given that religion has been at the forefront of the political agenda ranging from issues like ethnic conflicts to peacemaking since the end of the Cold War, its importance can hardly be overestimated.

4 Religion and Neorealism

Interactions within the international system

Neorealism, essentially a reformulation of Classical Realism, is a theoretical approach to the world politics that focuses on the relationships among the states in the international system. Neorealism has lent itself to heated debates due to its explanations based on material capabilities and balance of power. Kenneth Waltz, with his pioneering work *Theory of International Politics*, is regarded as the intellectual father of this theory. Robert J. Art, Joseph Grieco, John Mearsheimer, Randall Schweller, and Stephen Walt are also counted among the Neorealist scholars who shifted the focus from the individual to the international system. Although Neorealists refer to the same Political Realists in the history as do the Classical Realists, the theory in its current form is relatively new, stemming mostly from the Cold War perspective of the world politics.

Neorealism may be seen as a reaction to the "unscientific" aspects of Classical Realism. Nye (1988: 241) asserts that "the significance of Waltz's work is not in elaborating a new line of theory, but in the systematization of realism." Keohane (1986: 164) shares the same view and sees Neorealism as a "progressive problem shift," but one that preserves the core assumptions of the theory. According to Neorealists, international structure constrains the range of policy options available to the state. Only the states which take these structural constraints into account can survive. Self-sacrifice and idealism have no place in international politics. In this sense, the assumptions are similar to those employed by the Classical Realists. Indeed, Neorealists do not negate the major premises of their predecessors. They emphasize the balance of power in the system; in other words, the distribution of capabilities. All states share the same basic motives and interests. The main difference among states is their relative power and position in the international system.

Neorealists concur with the Classical Realists about the existence of anarchy. There is no overarching power or authority that can control or prescribe the behavior of states in the international system. The main actors in international politics are the sovereign states which seek power to ensure their survival. Self-help is one of the most important behavioral assumptions in Neorealism. States behave in line with their self-interests. They cannot trust other states, as those states also seek power to further their own interests. As mentioned in the previous chapter, this uncertainty leads to what Herz called a "security dilemma": States build up their own capabilities to make sure that they will not be harmed. This increase in material capabilities leads to a suspicion among other states. This perpetual uncertainty leads to a power competition.

States are interacting units that exhibit behavioral regularities and form the "system." State leaders are concerned about relative gains, and this is one of the dimensions that distinguishes Neorealism from Neoliberalism (Grieco, 1988). For Neorealists, the ranking of power in the international system is a determining factor, so cooperation may not always be in a state's interest if it is going to benefit the others more than that state itself. The international system, as a result of balancing acts and distribution of capabilities, could be dominated by one great power (unipolar), two great powers (bipolar), or more than two powers (multipolar). The workings of the international system are derivatives of the relationships among the existing or arising poles. Neorealists do not dwell much on the power struggles among small states, since they believe that these struggles or conflicts do not have the potential to change the overall distribution of power in the system.

Security is defined in strictly military terms, at least in the standard Waltzian framework (Waltz, 1979: 79–80). This is one of the reasons why religion was kept out of international relations discussions during the Cold War years. States engage in balancing behavior by trying to adjust their power capabilities internally (by increasing military spending and economic status) or externally (by making alliances) in the face of the security dilemma. Although Defensive Realists emphasize survival, Offensive Realists claim that states will seek whatever they can possibly get within the system, hegemony being their ultimate goal (Mearsheimer, 2001: 22). Moving from these understandings of security in an era dominated by concerns about nuclear warfare, Neorealists have written extensively about arms races, alliances, power transitions, and war. Culture, economics, and psychological and sociological investigations of human and community behavior were regarded as reductionist, since they focus on the behavior of the parts rather than the system. These dimensions were seen to be tangential at best to state security.

For these reasons, Neorealism has not allowed for an easy accommodation of religion, or any other non-material variable for that matter. It is the most challenging perspective in this respect among the theoretical strands of international relations. The perspectives that use individual- or society-level variables, such as the Classical Realist accounts, are looked down upon by Neorealists because these accounts explain too little by using too much detail. Although Neorealist scholars claim that their system-level theory is parsimonious, their relatively narrow focus has been widely criticized in the literature. Two of the critics, Legro and Moravcsik (1999: 53), state that Realism, especially its Neo-variant, suffers from a degeneration in which "its conceptual foundations are being 'stretched' beyond all recognition or utility"; it has become a generic commitment to the assumption of rational state behavior, despite the fact that this rational state behavior might not always be observed in practice. We argue that the exclusion of religion from international relations accounts is due more to the intellectual narrowness of "minimal realism" – that is, defined by "anarchy" and "rationality" only – than the authentic foundations of the paradigm (Legro and Moravcsik, 1999: 6). James (1993, 2002), for example, demonstrates that in a post-Cold War world, Neorealism can actually be elaborated to capture the interactions between macro and micro processes. In their evaluation of contemporary Realism, Freyberg-Inan et al. (2009: 3) state that in order for Realism to remain relevant, it should either follow an "elaborated structural realist" (James 2002) or a Neoclassical Realist route. Goddard and Nexon (2005: 47) contend that "Waltz is more 'sociological' than his critics maintain, and his analytical decisions are more sophisticated than constructivists sometimes allow." In short, Neorealism is not monolithic and, like many other perspectives, it is theory "in progress."

In this chapter we show how religion can be part of the Neorealist explanations that have long been the subject of theoretical debates. We also draw attention to the fact that Neorealism is not confined to a narrowly defined Waltzian framework. Other prominent Neorealists, such as Stephen Walt and John Mearsheimer, have recently written on contemporary issues, including the tensions between the West and the Islamic world. Such engagements show that Neorealist scholars do not by default exclude religion, and Neorealism actually has an evolving framework that can accommodate the changing realities in the international system.

Religious worldviews and Neorealism

Although Neorealism focuses on the international system level, we argue that there are three ways in which religious worldviews can play a role in the Neorealist accounts. First, religious worldviews can be part of a unit-level theory that complements the structural theory elaborated by Neorealists. In this context, unit-level theories refer to state-level and individual-level behavioral explanations. Second, religious worldviews can be part of Stephen Walt's "balance of threat" theory. Walt argues that an actor's perception of the power capabilities and intentions of the other actors is at least as important as the distribution of material capabilities. These perceptions may be influenced by the religious worldviews of the actor as well as the opponent. Third, we look at the concept of ideology developed by Neorealists to integrate religion into the theory. With the resurgence of religion that came at the expense of nationalism in many places in the world, there is no reason why religion cannot be seen as a force at least as influential as nationalism was 30 years ago.

Complementing the systemic accounts: religion in "unit-level" theories

As described above, unit-level theory is a theory that focuses on the attributes and behavior of the actor, be it a state or individual. System-level theory focuses on the international system. Even within the narrowest interpretation of Waltzian

Neorealism, it is possible to include unit-level factors, including individual worldviews, as parts of complementary accounts for Neorealist explanations. Kenneth Waltz (1988: 618) states that system-level theory is not a replacement for but an addition to the unit-level explanations of Classical Realism, which seem deficient in explaining the international affairs by themselves. Neorealism is not an omnipotent theory; it needs complementary explanations, including those on societal mechanisms and human nature. Without an explicit view of man, Neorealism cannot have any view of the human condition, and therefore becomes philosophically antiseptic (Shimko, 1992: 299). The perceived aloofness of Neorealism when it comes to human nature makes it difficult to see it as a sufficiently flexible framework to integrate faith on an individual level.

Is this really the case? Do Neorealists ignore the human dimension in its totality? Brooks (1997: 450) argues that the picture is far more complicated than it appears because the Neorealists implicitly replace the human aggression in Classical Realism with "fear." However, despite the existence of "fear" in Neorealism as a key variable, it is not meant to be used on an "individual level." Neorealism "blackboxes" the state much more than does Classical Realism (Keohane, 1986; Legro and Moravcsik, 1999). How a state can have fear or how its choices can be explained without reference to its components remains a question Neorealists face. For the purposes of this section, though, "fear" is interpreted to include the "fear of extinction" at the state level. As we explain later in the chapter, this may also take the form of "fear of extinction" as a religious state.

Although it may seem challenging to include human nature and local politics in Neorealism, scholars concur that a system-level theory cannot explain international politics all by itself. Even Waltz (1979: 48–49, 78, 87, 126) himself acknowledges that system-level theory has to be accompanied by a unit-level theory in order to obtain a full account of events. A unit-level theory would inevitably take religion into account as part of the worldview of the leader, political culture, or bureaucratic system. Saudi Arabia and the United States may assume a similar political position on an issue for very different reasons. Barack Obama (USA), Benjamin Netanyahu (Israel), King Abdullah (Saudi Arabia), Hu Jintao (China), and Atal Vitari Vajpayee (India) cannot be expected to have the same worldview that would lead them to take the same course of action under similar circumstances. Different worldviews, especially those influenced by a strong identity variable such as religion, may result in different rationalities. A unit-level theory that includes identity-related variables such as religion would provide the system-level theory with insights about the political causal mechanism and, consequently, with the possibility of falsification and the prospect of better theoretical predictions.

Democratic Peace Theory which states that democracies do not go to war with each other may be regarded as a unit-level theory. In Waltzian terms, the fact that two states are democratic does not have a determining influence on their mutual relationship, but their position in the system does. Democratic Peace Theory, however, may explain why a specific path is taken instead of others. As an example, one can explore the US–Indian nuclear deal from this perspective. In 2006, President George Bush concluded a civil nuclear energy agreement with the Prime Minister of India, Manmohan Singh. The deal was controversial. India was one of the few states that was not party to the Non-Proliferation Treaty, and thus did not qualify as a partner in nuclear technology exchanges. The agreement also marked a major shift in policy for the United States, which had imposed temporary sanctions on India in 1998 after the latter conducted nuclear weapons tests. Neorealists might explain this development as a balancing move to constitute a counterweight to China's rising influence. Unit-level explanations, however, explain why this was the path that was chosen from among other possibilities of balancing against China. Proponents of the deal argued that the deal would bring India closer to the United States at a time when the two countries are forging a strategic relationship to pursue common interests in fighting terrorism and spreading democracy (Pan and Bajoria, 2008). In other words, the fact that India is a secular democracy which fights the insurgents, most of whom, in their case, are Muslims, has undoubtedly been a factor in the partner choice of evangelical policy circles. The congruence between the threat perceptions of India's regime and Bush's own worldviews constitutes a unit-level account. This account explains why a certain path of balancing has been preferred over the others, and why Pakistan was not extended the same opportunity as India.

Nevertheless, this avenue of including religion in Neorealist accounts is not without challenges. It essentially integrates elements of Classical Realism that most Neorealists would argue are part of the non-scientific elements of Classical Realism that would better be left out of Neorealism. Especially during the Cold War, religious worldviews were regarded as secondary to the material capabilities of states. The changing outlook of world politics, however, altered the perspectives of many Neorealists who started to recognize that religion can be a separating or binding factor in alliance formations. Whether the religious worldview of a state or a politician can fully override traditional balancing concerns is another question. Yet the fact that these attributes form a credible unit-level theory is consistent with even the narrow interpretations of a conservative Waltzian Neorealism.

Threat perceptions and religion: Stephen Walt's "balance of threat" theory

The second possible avenue of integration of religion into the Neorealist explanations is through taking perceptions into account. Balancing, bandwagoning (joining a stronger power against the threat), and buck-passing (transferring the responsibility for responding to a threat to another state) are among the actions an actor can pursue in order to protect itself from a rising power. However, when a state builds up its capabilities, not all states feel equally threatened. For example, today, if the United Kingdom or Canada was to triple its weapons arsenal, this would hardly constitute a threat for the United States. If Russia or Iran was to do the same thing, the US would most probably start thinking about how to match those capabilities. In short, "who gains what" matters in the international system. Since religion is an integral part of the "who" question, it plays into the decisions about balancing. Stephen Walt (1985) calls this mechanism "balance of threat" theory and he gives four criteria that figure into the perceptions as to whether a state poses a threat or not: aggregate strength, geographical proximity, offensive capabilities, and offensive intentions. Although Walt does not focus on how much weight each category has, he argues that the Neorealist thinking is not only about capabilities but also about perceived intentions.

There are parallel debates to this understanding in Islamic Law. Takim (2007), for example, notes that in the *siyar* ("international relations" in Islamic jurisprudence) literature, there were jurists who have been proponents of "offensive realism" or "defensive realism." Takim does not use these international relations theory labels in his review, but the similarity is difficult to miss. "Offensive realists" like Abu Ishaq Shirazi distinguished between *dar al-harb* and *dar al-Islam*, and stated that Islamic states are expected to maximize the power of the Islamic governance in the international system. "Defensive realists" like Abu Hanifa advocated the view that intentions matter, and only when threatened the Islamic states should go to war. The sophisticated discussions around these issues in the Islamic legal literature show that contrary to what many may think, there already exists a rich Realist literature within religious traditions.

In defensive realism, not all criteria put forward by Walt are equally relevant in today's world. Especially in the aftermath of 9/11, one can say that geographical proximity has lost its relative importance with the increasing range of missiles and the morbid creativity of the transnational actors when it comes to overseas destruction. Similarly, the ability to project power into distant regions is more available to states than it was in the past. With the demise of the Soviet Union and the growing irrelevance of the conventional armies in the twenty-first century, policy-makers in every state find it challenging to keep track of others' capabilities. All of these developments increase the relative importance of intentions. This leads to a constant tension in the system, which is further exacerbated by the mutual suspicions based on previous experience, statements, or sometimes by a mere difference in state identities.

"Balance of threat" theory may be regarded as a constructivist twist on the narrower Waltzian realism. As we indicated in the first chapter, this is one of the reasons why we regard constructivism as a methodology as much as a theoretical approach. Constructivist approaches are found in every theory, even in Neorealism. What Walt essentially says is "agency constitutes structure" by the "articulation" of particular identities and projecting specific identities on to others (Klotz and Lynch, 2007: 75). In other words, the system is partly shaped by how states view each other, how they create identities (articulation), and how they interpret others' actions as part of specific identity categories (projection). How one situates the state in one category and sees other states as "in-group" or "out-group" is dependent upon the shared ideas both in the state and the system. Within this context religion plays a role. Those who are different from us, "the other," are often stereotyped and perceived as more dangerous and threatening than those who are more similar. This is certainly true of religious identity (Juergensmeyer, 2008: 2). Thus, religion of one's potential adversary might influence how that adversary is perceived.

It is also possible that the use of a religious ideology by an adversary may make that adversary seem irrational, intransigent and threatening. Also, a religious ideology may explicitly define who is considered an enemy and to what extent this enemy should be feared (Juergensmeyer, 2000; Rapoport, 1988). To illustrate, Mahmoud Ahmedinejad has made statements about expanding the Islamic governance and expressed his hope that the "Jewish-Zionist state occupying Jerusalem would collapse" (Cole, 2006). This has led to the construction or consolidation of the idea of Iran as a state with violent inclinations. These statements and how they have been interpreted were influenced by the post-9/11 threat perceptions, which placed radical Islam at the center of the security agenda. As a result, what kinds of weapons Iran acquires has become much more of a concern than the arsenals of other states such as India or even Pakistan.

This avenue of integration that takes Walt's balance of threat theory as a starting point also allows for integrating religious party politics and the mechanisms by which these politics can influence the distribution of capabilities within the international system. In India, the threat perceptions and the priorities of the secular Congress Party – which ruled for around 40 years – were different from its successor's, the Hindu nationalist Bharatiya Janata Party, which promoted religious laws and fueled the Hindu–Muslim conflict in the region. During the years the party was in power, the BJP's focus on Hindu nationalist ideology influenced its threat perception of Pakistan. Given the nuclear capabilities of India and Pakistan and the increasing influence of the paramilitary groups in the region, the implications of such a conflict for the international system could hardly be underestimated.

The differences in worldviews are arguably the most acute in the Middle East. The alliances and enmities in the region have always had the power to draw "poles" of the system into a worldwide conflict. Even the most moderate elements of the region are now shaped by religious worldviews. The AK Party in Turkey, with its religiously conservative party elite, has contributed to the changing strategic outlook. The shift in threat perceptions is reflected in the clashes between this conservative party elite and the secular army that was in strategic partnerships with the United States and Israel. The United States and Israel are now perceived to be more as the "other" than in the past. The fact that Turkey did not allow the United States to use its territory for the Operation Iraqi Freedom in 2003 and that it refused to participate in a multi-state military air exercise that would have included Israeli warplanes were some early examples of this shift (Taydas and Ozdamar, 2012). It also shows that even if there is a power disparity between two actors in the international system, the powerful cannot always make the others do everything it wishes. With the rise of a new wave of Islamism in Turkey – albeit still moderate when compared to its counterparts in the region – the politicians have witnessed that power balances are beginning to change in Europe and the Middle East.

Ideologies and conflict: religion as the new nationalism

A third avenue of the integration of religion is possible with the application of analytical tools that were used to investigate nationalist ideologies. As Juergens-meyer (1993) also argues persuasively in his book *The New Cold War?*, religion is the new "nationalism." Merging with ethnic identities, religious ideologies have the power to rally support for national and international causes, and to change the balance of power. Such processes have already taken place in many parts of the "third world" (Kedourie, 1971); yet they were not theorized until the dominant blocs of the Cold War also became aware of religion's influence in the political sphere.

Immediately after the end of the Cold War, John Mearsheimer (1990: 56) stated that hyper-nationalism is a powerful force that has deep roots in Europe, and that it contributed to the outbreak of past European conflicts: "Nationalism has been contained during the Cold War and it will be a force for trouble unless it is curbed." Mearsheimer, along with Walt, later came to recognize the import-ance of religion, be it in the Jewish, Christian, or Islamic world. They stated that post 9/11, "US support [for Israel] has been justified by the claim that both states are threatened by terrorist groups originating in the Arab and Muslim world." They also drew attention to the power of the American Israel Public Affairs Committee along with the Christian Zionists in defining the security agenda, and the "need to rebuild America's image in the Arab and Islamic world" (Mearshe-imer and Walt, 2006). Even in the eyes of staunch Neorealists, nationalist ideo-logies started to give way to their religious counterparts.

Currently, nationalist ideologies are renegotiated in the light of religious frameworks. Brubaker (2012) criticizes the understanding of nationalism as a distinctively secular phenomenon, stating that one can treat religion and nation-alism as analogous phenomena; religion may help in explaining the features of nationalism; religion can be part of nationalism; and there can be forms of reli-gious nationalism. Saat (2012), for example, shows how Malay identity is refashioned toward a tolerant Islam and the unwillingness of the ulama to define national identity independent of religion. Similarly, despite not having a pro-nounced religious dimension, the Arab Spring also brought religious political actors who had been excluded from the mainstream Arab political scene. Yagil Levy (2011) observes the same trend in the Israeli Defense Force and states that religious politics has started to have a tangible impact on the actions of an other-wise secular nationalist military.

Even during the times when Western academics were not sensitive to reli-gion's political potential, the power of ideologies was noted in the Neorealist literature. Stephen Van Evera, for example, explores which kinds of nationalism can cause war. Van Evera (1994: 6) defines nationalism as a political movement having individual members who give their primary loyalty to their own ethnic community, and these communities desiring their own independent state. He then moves to categorize nationalisms by exploring numerous variables, includ-ing the extent of national myth-making and how the members perceive other nationalities. His hypotheses and propositions are surprisingly suitable for religion, and religious communities as well. In the end, there are many people in the world who devote their primary loyalty to their religious community. These communities usually find a voice through sub-state actors, and they desire their own independent political arrangements in the form of a state or empire.

Van Evera's individual hypotheses are also worth considering within the context of religion. For example, he states that "if economic conditions deteriorate, publics become more receptive to scapegoat myths, hence such myths are more widely believed, hence war is more likely." Almond and colleagues (1995: 37) found the very same tendency among religious scapegoating: "In the short run, recessions, depressions, inflation, strikes, unemployment and famine may create attitudes and grievances among particular groups in the population, inclining them favorably to fundamentalist arguments, themes and practices."

Another hypothesis advanced by Van Evera is "the more severely the nationalities oppress minorities now living in their states, the greater the risk of war." The same concerns are valid for religious minorities, and for the religious doctrines of the states which these minorities are under. States which support a single religion are far more likely to engage in such discrimination (Fox, 2008) and minorities which experience religious discrimination are more likely to rebel (Fox, 2002, 2004.) In addition, religious minorities experiencing discrimination are more likely than other minorities to attract intervention on their behalf, usually by a state with which they share religious affinities (Fox, 2004).

Van Evera's hypothesis that "the more densely nationalities are intermingled, the greater the risk of war" is also worth exploring when it comes to the effect of "local" intermingling of religious groups on conflict. Although it is early to arrive at a conclusion that "local intermingling poses a greater danger than regional alliances", one can see examples of brutal ethno–religious conflicts among groups that live together closely, as seen in the cases of the Catholics and Protestants in Northern Ireland, Christians and Muslims in Nigeria, and Sinhalese and Tamils in Sri Lanka. The deadliest conflicts we see on the news today have significant dimensions of religion, especially when compared to the conflicts during the Cold War.

The religions that act as the "nationalisms" of the Cold War are not confined to Islam. Tibetan "nationalism" in China, for example, reflects a form of Buddhism with a nationalist discourse. Tibetan demonstrators in different settings shout for independence and the long life of the Dalai Lama. In the Main Temple of Dharamsala, people work on building a Tibetan way of life relying on Buddhism, and in some Buddhist monasteries, "monks and nuns make Tibetan flags, compose anti-Chinese songs and political pamphlets" (Kolas, 1996: 52). Tibetan Buddhist nationalism has been one of the top security concerns of China, which considers it a threat to state unity. Recent reports by Human Rights Watch (2011) note that there is a dramatic increase in the Chinese security expenditures. These expenditures "have been a major factor in the escalation of tensions that have led to several protests in which monks tried to set themselves on fire to bring attention to the situation." The fate of Tibetan monks and the local population is increasingly drawing attention as a human rights issue as well.

Another form of Buddhism has been engrained in Sri Lankan nationalism, which dominates the political structures of the state and does not recognize any opposition. The government of President Mahinda Rajapaksa has been the first to fully embrace the Sinhalese Buddhist nationalist ideology, suggesting that an end to Sri Lanka's Buddhist supremacy and the solution to resulting ethnic conflict is unlikely (DeVotta, 2007). Buddhist discourse has been part of the state ideology for the past two centuries. The ethnic conflict in Sri Lanka was between the Sinhalese (majority, mostly Buddhist) and the Tamils (minority, mostly Hindus). Liberation Tigers of Tamil Eelam, an organization which fought for a homeland for Tamils, has been one of the main actors in the ethnic conflict which displaced two million people and killed thousands. The conflict also involved India starting from the 1980s, especially with the insistence of an Indian state, Tamil Nadu, with its ethno-religious ties to the Tamils in Sri Lanka. India helped Tamil rebels at times, and R&AW, the Indian intelligence agency, is said to have been involved in shaping the political structure of the movement (Ramachandran, 2004; Weisman, 1987). In short, the clash of Buddhist supremacy represented by the Sri Lankan state and the violent Tamil (Hindu) resistance to the dominance of Theravada Buddhism brought two states, Sri Lanka and India, to the brink of conflict. In 2009, the Sri Lankan troops claimed to have brought an end to LTTE. Excessive reliance on military methods in the campaigns and the continuing incidents of intolerance shows that an aggressive Sri Lankan Buddhist nationalism was and still is in play.

Religious legitimacy and Neorealism

The means for integrating religious legitimacy into Neorealism are similar to those of integrating it into Classical Realism. There are two interrelated avenues for integration. The first avenue for integration rests on the fact that a number of states, especially religious ones, need religious institutions to justify their actions in the domestic and international spheres. This is a requirement for their survival and consolidation of power in the system, which comes before short-term material gains. The second way of integration is related to influence, by which states not only ensure their survival, but also engage in external balancing (in the form of alliances) to further their interests. Unless a state can enlist the support of the others and convince them of the legitimacy of its actions, the range of options becomes narrower and the possibility of success decreases. This influence may be counted as an item under Stephen Walt's "Aggregate Strength," which is one of the factors that influence threat perceptions in the Neorealist framework.

Religious legitimacy as a prerequisite for survival

Religious identity constitutes a vital part of domestic and foreign policy-making of many states, be it religious or secular. Since religion is usually an intrinsic part of existential myths that give meaning to states' actions, protecting this religious heritage may become a "must" to ensure a state's survival for at least two reasons. First, the state's legitimacy, or even its *raison d'être*, can be linked to religion. Without this heritage, a state's existence may be questioned not only by outside actors, but also by its citizens. Second, in many cases if not all, the state that is devoid of its religious element would not be the same state. In essence, should the religious element of the state be removed, the state as it is currently formulated would cease to exist. For example, as we mentioned in the previous chapter, Saudi Arabia, in the face of an existential threat from Iraq, recognized the need to have American troops on its land. Yet the policy-makers wanted to secure a fatwa to show that foreign military presence on the Islamic holy lands was not by default against Islamic Law. If this religious edict had not been sought, the legitimacy of Saudi rule would have significantly declined. This lack of legitimacy would have undermined its standing among – and effectively its ability to influence – other Islamic states.

The importance of theological sources of legitimacy is reflected in the ongoing battle of "religious edicts" in the Islamic world, one of which was a source of tension between the Saudi family and Osama Bin Laden. Bin Laden's 1998 declaration in *Al-Quds Al-Arabi* states that the United States occupied the Islamic holy lands, humiliated the Muslims, and used Saudi Arabia as a base to attack other Islamic states. These actions, according to Bin Laden, constituted a declaration of war against the Muslims. Bin Laden, and Islamic circles close to his cause, felt justified in issuing a fatwa which stated that killing Americans is a duty of Muslims until they withdraw from the Muslim lands. However, the Saudi royal family continues to see cooperation with America as a strategic asset, albeit on a smaller scale following the tensions brought about by 9/11. Again, this is not to say that the fatwas have the power to rally all the Muslims around a cause. Yet these edicts have been regarded as necessary conditions to legitimize an action in the eyes of an organization's or a state's members.

The centrality of a religious tradition in a political struggle can also increase as a conflict escalates. In the face of existential threats to a group, if faith is one of the common grounds for a community, it may become a defining and legitimizing feature. According to Seul (1999: 567), this process was seen within the Bosnian Muslim community as the conflict escalated in the Balkans. Alija Izzetbegovic, the Bosnian Muslim leader, championed "the homogenization of a Muslim ethno-religious identity" (Mojzes, 1995:142) and his political party came to be identified with Islam. Similar events occurred in Croatia and Serbia during the conflict. As the conflict intensified, religion and religious institutions became more central to politics in the Balkans.

Religious legitimacy – or the lack thereof – can also undermine a government's or leader's power. For example, Egyptian leader Anwar Sadat signed the

Egyptian–Israeli Peace Treaty in 1979 following the Camp David Accords facilitated by US President Jimmy Carter. This treaty was seen by many as a betrayal to Islam. Sadat was assassinated by a fundamentalist Islamist in 1981 and Egypt was expelled from the Arab League. In Latin America, the Catholic churches have openly challenged authoritarian rulers in some states, effectively withdrawing their support for state legitimacy. For example, in Chile, the bishops established Vicariate of Solidarity in 1976 in the face of human rights abuses of the authoritarian rule of Augusto Pinochet (Fleet and Smith, 1997: 115). Similarly, in Brazil, the National Conference of Brazilian Bishops denounced the governments' policies as "fascist" in 1968 (Mainwaring, 1986: 100–141). In other Latin American countries such as Bolivia, Guatemala, Panama, and El Salvador, the religious institutions became the hubs where the oppositions to the ruling regime met (Cleary, 1997). These examples constitute testaments to the fact that the limits of conflict and cooperation are not only defined by the distribution of capabilities, but also by the management of images and legitimacy in the world system.

In sum, in order to protect the unitary character and long-term stability of the state, political leaders often need the "blessing" of the religious institutions in their country. In the absence of this blessing, religious institutions and leaders may become the contact point for dissidents in the country as well as for rivals at the international level. Not all interactions take place through state channels. In the presence of anarchy, balancing behavior is expected to occur, as Neorealists argue, yet it can be in a disaggregated fashion. A regime that cannot secure the approval of at least the dominant religious institutions is bound to face a coalition, composed of internal and external actors, that aims to end its rule.

We have touched upon the use of religion to maintain legitimacy in the domestic sphere, primarily because it is difficult to discuss the importance of legitimacy in the international sphere without also addressing its domestic sources and implications. This domestic–international nexus may not sit well with the "black boxing" of domestic politics in Neorealism. However, the fact that some states use and need religious legitimacy to maintain their standing in the international system can be considered an element of the system's structure.

Religious legitimacy as a source of power

The way through which religious legitimacy influences international politics within Neorealism takes religious legitimacy as a potential source of power in the international system. We begin with the assumption that every state tries to gain as much influence as possible (Gilpin, 1981: 94–95). If a state loses influence in the international sphere, and other states increase their influence, the state's survival may be at stake (Gilpin, 1981: 86). By representing the actions in an acceptable way to other actors in the system, a state can tilt the balance of power in its favor. There is a growing Neorealist literature which acknowledges that there are paths which are more likely to encounter resistance from important actors in the international system than others. Religious legitimacy can influence the extent of this "resistance."

The most cited example in the discussions surrounding international legiti-macy has been the unilateral United States operation toward Iraq. A number of prominent Neorealists not only started to question American foreign policy, but unwittingly, these exponents of Neorealism widened the scope of the Neorealist framework. To illustrate, Stephen Walt (2005: 109) states:

> when foreign populations disapprove of U.S. policy and are fearful of U.S. dominance, their governments are less likely to endorse Washington's initi-atives and more likely to look for ways to hinder them. Rising anti-Americanism also increases the number of extremists who can be recruited into violent movements such as Al-Qaeda.

The Bush Administration did not heed the United Nations Security Council when launching a preventive attack against Iraq. One might argue that this unwillingness to defer to UNSC could partly be attributed to the evangelical dis-taste for multilateral organizations (Mead, 2006: 13). Regardless of the reasons however, the inability of the US forces to locate the WMD capabilities that were the stated reason for the attack damaged US credibility and undermined its legit-imacy. This situation was further exacerbated by the abuses in the Abu Ghraib prison, the correctional facility in Iraq where the Iraqi prisoners were kept. The Iraq War, according to John Mearsheimer and Stephen Walt (2003: 59), was a war the Bush Administration "chose to fight but did not have to fight" and it has the potential to lead to increased hatred toward the United States in the Islamic world.

To summarize, religious legitimacy constitutes a kind of power that has the potential to change the balances and distribution of capabilities in the system. Religion is one of the most important sources of legitimacy. It is dangerous even for the most powerful state in the system to ignore the reactions of a sizable reli-gious community.

Non-state religious actors and Neorealism

As discussed above, sub-state actors are usually not regarded as of major interest to Neorealist scholars. However, this does not mean that there is no possibility of interaction between the faith communities and the Neorealist terminology in the political sphere. In this section, we argue, first, that the competition among the ethnicities and sometimes the religious communities determines who will get to control the resources of the state. This is especially important in that non-state religious actors may then have the power to define the "threat" differently from their rivals, thus balancing in a different way. Second, the issue of lobbies and their influence in defining state interests has been an ongoing debate even among the Neorealists. There is a need to investigate mechanisms and implications of this influence for the system.

Neorealist theories of domestic conflict and their implications for religion

As religion became an increasingly prominent source of belonging, the proportion of religious conflicts has sky rocketed in the past 50 years. Toft (2007: 97) states that whereas 32 percent of civil wars involved religion in the 1940s, this percentage increased to 50 percent after 2000. In a similar vein, Fox (2012) reports that the proportion of serious domestic conflicts that may be classified as religious rose from a range of 20 percent to 30 percent in the 1960s (depending on the year in question) to a range of 55 percent to 62 percent between 2004 and 2008. Toft (2011) argues that religion can play a significant role in conflicts because "salvation" is seen as indivisible; followers of majority religions cannot signal credibly to followers of minority religions; religious actors prefer "future" to "present" and they believe that God is with them.

In the face of the resurgence of religion as one of the primary causes of conflict, including ethnic conflict, the relative disinterest of the Neorealists in bridging domestic and international levels did not prevent scholars such as Posen from using Neorealist concepts like "security dilemma" to account for ethnic conflict. According to Posen (1993), security dilemmas within states are analogous to interstate dilemmas as the collapse of multi-ethnic states leads to an "emerging anarchy." This anarchy forces different groups in the state to provide their own security and to fight for control of the state. "A group suddenly compelled to provide its own protection must ask the following questions about any neighboring group: is it a threat? How much of a threat? Will the threat grow or diminish over time?" (Posen, 1993: 27). Posen's choice of terminology is ideal if one wants to account for religious group dynamics and competition as well.

Posen (1993) also draws attention to the fact that there is no "one" anarchy, but a number of anarchies in the system. That is, if one peeks into the "black box", one often finds a Neorealist anarchic competition for power, especially in cases where governments have failed or are in a state of transition. Religious institutions and identities can play a role in these conflicts. This is how one can investigate the strength of insurgency and paramilitary movements in Iraq. The continued presence of the United States in Iraq consolidated the division of society along sectarian lines, which rendered a military success impossible. In another oil-rich country, Nigeria, the civil war between Muslims and Christians poses a serious threat to the stability of the country. Especially given the importance of the geography in terms of vital resources, such "anarchies" become a concern for Neorealists. Using an elaborated Realist framework, James and Ozdamar (2005) and Ghose and James (2005) also draw attention to how religion can internationalize domestic conflicts with a focus on Kashmir. In the post-Cold War world, it is even clearer that local conflicts with religious dimension cannot be underestimated as they have the power to change the balances in the system.

Likewise, Kaufman (1996) acknowledges the possibility of such anarchy under conditions like the lack of effective control by the government and the presence of strong ethnic groups with enough of the attributes of sovereignty. He divides ethnic conflicts, and the security dilemma, into two: Mass-led hostilities and elite-led hostilities. In the former, fear and mistrust "trigger spontaneous outbreaks of violence, activating a security dilemma which in turn exacerbates hostility and fear" (1996: 157). In the latter, "extremist elites begin or provoke violence in order to activate an ethnic security dilemma which in turn generates more violence" (1996: 158). Both mass-led and elite-led hostilities can spark religious conflicts as well.

In short, even if Neorealism cannot easily accommodate ethnicity or religion in its core framework, concepts like security dilemma, balancing, and polarity can still be employed to account for conflicts that have a religious dimension. In the end, Neorealism has a coherent literature and terminology and, whether one agrees with the key assumptions or not, Neorealist terms have been adapted to account for intra-state or transnational identity conflicts in a relatively parsimonious way. This terminology transfer implies that these terms may similarly be adopted to account for international identity conflicts.

Lobbies, religious interest groups, and Neorealism

A second matter of interest at the intersection of religious non-state actors and Neorealism is the agency of the lobbies. The case that has been discussed most fervently in public is the Israel lobby and its influence in shaping the American policies. Two prominent Neorealists, Stephen Walt and John Mearsheimer, published numerous manuscripts on the issue, one of which is a book entitled *The Israel Lobby and the U.S. Policy* (2007). The book quickly became a best-seller. In a *London Review of Books* article, Mearsheimer and Walt (2006) note that "the combination of unwavering support for Israel and the related effort to spread 'democracy' throughout the region has inflamed Arab and Islamic opinion and jeopardized not only US security but that of much of the rest of the world." They make the case that the Israel Lobby, which includes not only the American Jews but also Christian evangelicals such as Gary Bauer, Jerry Falwell, Ralph Reed, and Pat Robertson, shapes the US military spending and priorities. The fact that two staunch Neorealists arguing not only that a faith-based alliance defines the military and political agenda of a powerful state but also jeopardizes world security is a testament to the centrality of religious issues to the Neorealist agenda of the twenty-first century.

Similarly, religious parties can change the rules of the game when they come to power. This change can be in either a peaceful or a violent direction. Political parties can be based on a religious agenda (BJP) or become faith-driven in time, like U.S. Republican Party. Religious leaders either take political positions themselves or counsel religious parties. For example, ultra-orthodox political parties in Israel are guided by councils of highly regarded Rabbis. In some cases, such as the case of Rabbi Ovadia Yosef and the Shas Party, a single religious leader can define the leadership and the policy of major ultra-orthodox political parties with multiple seats in Israel's legislative body (Kamil, 2000). The rise in the number of political parties with strong religious discourse shows that there is a demand on behalf of the population to be represented by a religious party. The participation of these religious actors in the public sphere changes the prevailing secular discourse and the rules of gaining power. Kalyvas (2000: 393) argues that "religious entrepreneurs" are better able to initiate collective action and intense conflict. Centralized religious institutions are also likely to enforce compromises and promote civil peace under certain conditions.

Admittedly, when we look at the core Neorealist assumptions, we see a reliance on the nation-state, as it was defined by the Treaty of Westphalia and consolidated later with the rise of nationalism and the resistance to imperial political arrangements. This assumption, however, has been shaken many times by local politicians and their followers, whose primary loyalty is not to the nation-state but to a nation defined by religion. These local teachings came to influence people across the borders. Non-state religious actors denying the legitimacy of the nation-state reached their counterparts in other countries. In the Islamic world, teachings of Sayyid Qutb, Abu al-A'la Maududi, and Ayatollah Khomeini prioritized ummah, underscoring the artificiality and the corruption of Western political arrangements. Again, these teachings and views do not represent or influence the totality of the Muslim world, yet it shaped the threat perceptions of the United States. In September 2006, George W. Bush stated that the expectations of the "enemy" were very different from a nation-state's:

> They hope to establish a violent political utopia across the Middle East, which they call a "Caliphate" – where all would be ruled according to their hateful ideology. Osama bin Laden has called the 9/11 attacks – in his words – "a great step towards the unity of Muslims and establishing the Righteous ... Caliphate". This caliphate would be a totalitarian Islamic empire encompassing all current and former Muslim lands, stretching from Europe to North Africa, the Middle East, and Southeast Asia. We know this because al Qaeda has told us.[1]

In addition to physical and discursive battles between members of different religions, there also exist strong tensions among the members of the same religious groups. The local fundamentalists, who first challenged their own states, have their own differences when it comes to the ideal form of governance. In the case of fundamentalist Islam, as the fundamentalist groups found themselves in a war against a common enemy, be it the Soviet Union or Israel, they constrained their vision to a governance based on sharia law, leaving the details for later (Abu-Rabi, 1996). However, these local groups merge on an international level, leave behind their differences, and form transnational religious movements to challenge the state sovereignty. This may result in a system-level change, a matter of supreme interest for the Neorealists.

Religious states and Neorealism

Religious states constitute the easiest category to investigate within the Neorealist framework. Below are the main avenues for integrating the behavior of religious states into Neorealist theory: religious states as "states," religion as a factor changing policy preferences, and religion defining a state's goals.

Religious states as units in the international system

First, religious states are no different from their secular counterparts in that they strive for power and, more often than not, they increase their material capabilities to balance the capabilities of their rivals. However, unlike secular states, they also have access to religious discourse when they are rallying their allies, be it other religious states or their co-religionists who are living in other states. In this vein, we argue that a state's adherence to a faith tradition will influence its ally/enemy status for other states. As we discuss above, Walt's (1985) "balance of threat" theory, due to its implicitly constructivist terminology, can allow the introduction of religion even as an independent variable in this respect. What a state sees as a threat in another state may be defined by ideological as well as religious differences. States may lose allies and engage in balancing along religious lines in a manner similar to the way they did along ideological lines during the Cold War. Thus, like ethnicity, religion may have an influence on external balancing, or, in other words, on the alliances and rivalry patterns that have direct implications for the distribution of capabilities in the system (Davis et al., 1997). For example, Iran's relationships with the rest of the world – especially with Europe and the US – radically changed after Khomeini's revolution. The exclusive religious stance of Iran that is openly hostile to US dominance and its current alliance and strategic partnerships with a number of actors – ranging from Latin American leaders to transnational Shi'a paramilitary groups – may also be attributed to the change in political system inside Iran.

The rivalries do not have to be inter-religious; they may also be inter-denominational. For example, Saudi Arabia (Sunni) and Iran (Shi'a) regard themselves as the champions of Islamic societies. Saudi Arabia severely restricts the religious practices of Shi'a Muslims, including bans on the imports of Shi'a religious books and audiocassettes, and censorship of public speeches by clerics and scholars (Boyle and Sheen, 1997; Fox, 2008). These restrictions point to the threat perceptions of Saudi Arabia in Walt's terms. Iran is regarded as a threat to the survival and influence of Saudi Arabia, which is one of the reasons why it chooses to "ally" subtly with the United States despite the internal protests. At the time of writing this book, the allegation that Iran had plans to assassinate the Saudi ambassador to Washington led to a heightening of the existing tensions between the two states. Regardless of the accuracy of such allegations, experts surmised that such crises might not only lead to a serious division among countries with Muslim majorities, but also to the possibility that Riyadh might even take part in behind-the-scenes talks with Israel, because the Saudis see the Jewish state as a powerful counterweight to Tehran (Leigh, 2011).

Religion as a factor in changing policy preferences

A second avenue for integrating the role of religious states into a Neorealist understanding of international relations presupposes that a commitment to religion may change the policy preferences of a state in the international sphere. True, states usually strive for their survival, but leaders may see different paths leading to the desired point without compromising their ideology. For instance, Telhami (2002) claims that nothing in Neorealism precludes a theory that links moral factors and the external behavior of states. If "relative power" is regarded as an instrument for implementing a state's motives, domestic politics and ideology can be treated again both as independent and intervening variables. Governments engage in conflict over any scarce and valuable good, including political and national ideology as well as religious identity. The assumption of fixed preferences is more permissive in this sense than it seems (Legro and Moravcsik, 1999: 55). National ideology and religious identity are in the "scarce" good category in the sense that there are usually few religious traditions and too many competitors for legitimate international leadership and representation. For Saudi Arabia and Iran, international politics revolves at least in part around the leadership in the Islamic world, a position that only a limited number of actors may assume at the same time. The BJP tries to monopolize the representation of the Hindu identity, whereas the battles between the Protestants and the Catholics have historically often been over the representation of Christianity.

The presumed Realist position about the absence of morality in the realm of politics is a mere theoretical preference that should be replaced in the light of emerging challenges (Telhami, 2002). In the end, Waltz (1979: 72) notes that systems theories explain why different units behave similarly and, despite their variations, produce outcomes that fall within expected ranges. By contrast, theories at the unit level tell us why units behave differently despite their similar placement in a system. Linking Telhami's and Waltz's views on the issue, it is not impossible for scholars of international relations to devise a perspective toward religious ideology that is acceptable within the limits of Neorealism.

Moving on from an understanding of religious ideology that figures into Neorealism, one may also talk about different routes to the desired ends or, in other words, different paths of rationalities. In state-centered game theoretical thinking, each actor tries "to maximize expected value across a given set of consistently ordered objectives, given the information actually available to the actor or which he could reasonably acquire in the time available for decision" (Snyder and Diesing, 1977: 181). The issues of perception and personal bias also play into the calculation of the utility (Jervis, 1976). The game theoretical thinking, in line with the Neorealist tenets, assumes that the actors will attempt to choose the best for themselves but how they arrive at what they regard to be the best option is still a question for game theorists to work on. Be it on a state or an individual level, what an evangelical political leader regards to be the best way to follow for the state and the world may differ considerably from the path chosen by a Confucian politician.

Religion defining a state's goals

Religious states may not only prefer different paths to achieve the same end as their secular counterparts, but they might also have radically different goals. Whereas secular states cherish survival of the state as their primary goal, religious states may see the spread of their ideology as the ultimate aim of their existence. In this respect, game theory as a tool to explore decision-making should be open to diverse rationality paths, by taking the past actions of the actor and expectations of the audience into account.

Neorealists concur that a state may want to go beyond preventing power losses, and move toward enhancing their power position (Gilpin, 1981: 87; Waltz, 1979: 91–91). Robert Art (1991: 7), a prominent Neorealist, states that "grand strategy specifies the goals a state should pursue, including both security and non-security goals, and second, to delineate how military power can serve these goals." Art proceeds to count "where feasible, promoting democratic institutions and certain humanitarian values abroad" and "preservation of the independence of Israel" among the key US interests after the Cold War. The extent to which the US may be considered secular is a matter of debate. Regardless, if Neorealists see promotion of values and ideology as a matter of national interest, it is only expected that religious states will go to greater lengths to "promote" the values and ideologies upon which their states are founded. In addition, the US interest of protecting the State of Israel, intentionally or not, may be perceived as Judeo-Christian cooperation against the Islamic states and groups that are opposed to a Jewish state in the Middle East. The military alliances, not only between the US and Israel, but also among Islamic states and groups, aim at tilting the balance of power in favor of the goal they pursue.

In sum, although religious states are easier to accommodate within the Neorealist tradition, they still pose a challenge in a number of respects. We argue that these challenges are not impossible to overcome. However, this process involves opening Neorealism to alternative assumptions and tenets that may result in an expanded tree of possible actions in a game-theoretical sense. As noted above, several prominent Neorealist theorists have arguably come to this realization.

Transnational religious actors and Neorealism

One can find a place for a trans-system religion variable in Neorealism defined broadly to include the scholars who regard themselves as "Neorealists" yet who do not confine themselves to the Waltzian framework. One possibility is suggested with the security complex theory of Buzan, by which he extends the Neorealist understanding of politics. A second avenue of interaction is through the Neorealist emphasis on survival as an end. This emphasis is also warranted for religious "units," which are sometimes willing to compete with and even to challenge the unity of states.

A revised look at the international system: classical security complex theory and religion

Buzan's (1993a) framework of "Classical Security Complex Theory" (CSCT) approaches the matters of power and existence from a multi-method perspective. It divides the proposed international system of Neorealism into more manageable regional blocs with different layers of national interest. In other words, this framework is a variant of Realism that is open to new variables at different levels. Buzan et al. (1997: 12) define security complexes as "a set of states whose major security perceptions and concerns are so interlinked that their national security problems cannot reasonably be analyzed or resolved apart from one another." The theory's revised version, which focuses more evenly on military, political, economic, societal, and environmental sectors and brings non-state actors into the "security complexes," permits investigation of complex issues like terrorism and NGOs.

The linkage of the societal level with other levels in this framework makes CSCT a suitable theory for scholars who want to focus on any identity variable. This is especially true if an investigation relates to a certain region in which security concerns of the actors cannot be thought of independently from each other. This framework is based on the "deep structure" proposed by Buzan et al. (1993: 38) in their discussion of Neorealism and anarchy. Deep structure recognizes different levels of claims to sovereignty by different units which lead to a hierarchical setting. Not all states have full control over their affairs, and full sovereignty is only an "ideal" that can be attained by only a select few in the system. Put differently, the sphere of sovereignty that is shared by every actor is limited. Given this, how states end up using their capabilities is not always a direct consequence of how they are ranked in the international system in terms of their capabilities.

In the context of the Middle East, Leenders (2007) argues that Iraq, Syria, and Lebanon are interconnected in terms of military, political, economic, and social networks. In his analysis, religion plays a prominent role in all these dimensions and the conflict formation. In order to study regional conflicts, the geographical scope should actually be extended "to include Palestine, Iran, Turkey and Saudi Arabia" (Leenders, 2007: 978). CSCT, with its sensitivity to shared identity and regional power balances, would be helpful in explaining the dynamics of Middle Eastern politics and its impact on the international system.

CSCT may seem outside of the Waltzian framework at first glance and may be regarded as a complementary theory of unit behavior in Waltz's terms. Buzan et al. (1993) clarify the causality and they do not quite change the basic premises of core Neorealist thinking. As a result, the current structure of CSCT is most suitable when looking at how a specific factor (e.g., religion, ethnicity, or race) plays a role in a certain region and how it interacts with the units as well as the system. However, CSCT may not be as ideal as Neoliberalism, Constructivism, or the English School if one wants to look at the mechanisms of global governance and the diffusion of transnational ideas.

Religious movements as alternatives to the state

The second avenue for integrating religious transnational movements into a Neorealist framework involves the changing nature of threats to state survival. Waltz (1986: 127) states:

> only if survival is assured, can states safely seek such other goals as tranquility, profit and power.... They cannot let power, a possibly useful means, become the end they pursue. The goal the system encourages them to seek is security. Increased power may or may not serve that end.

A theoretical framework, which places the highest value on a state's survival, must pay attention to threats to this survival. Thirty years ago, when Waltz wrote his book defining Neorealism, the threat to the survival of a state was usually another state. However, today, at a time when the United States wages "War on Terror," even the Neorealists cannot afford to neglect how transnational religious movements – including terrorist organizations – can pose a threat to a state's survival. These organizations can even change the "balance of power" in the international system. US intelligence assessments state that Al-Qaeda is trying to develop and obtain chemical, biological, radiological, and even nuclear weapons (Meyer, 2008). In addition, the terrorist groups have the capabilities to make even the strongest states commit the action they desire. Walt (2005: 114) states:

> Terrorists win by attacking stronger side's resolve and forcing it to take actions that alienate potential supporters. Al-Qaeda and the Iraqi insurgency use terrorism because it allows them to attack vulnerable targets while avoiding confrontation with superior U.S. forces. Terrorism can also provoke the United States into overreacting in ways that could increase opposition to the U.S. presence in the Middle East. Sometimes the strategy works: terrorism helped Bin Laden drive much of the U.S. presence out of Saudi Arabia – and it may still defeat the U.S. mission in Iraq.

In this statement, Walt acknowledges that transnational religious actors have the potential to affect external balancing and the power distribution in the system. In other words, they become part of the international structure and place constraints on the actions of states by provoking fear. These transnational actors become a direct threat to the survival of states such as Pakistan – an American ally in the region – as well as Afghanistan. As Walt (2005) also states, Afghan President Hamit Karzai and the Pakistan's military leader Pervez Musharraf have received considerable US support by making the case that their states will be run by the radicals if they were to fall.

Different organizations constituting serious threats to the existence of the states also stressed their religious character. The FLN (Front de Libération Nationale) in Algeria, which played a key role in Algeria's struggle against France, was an Arab nationalist movement, yet it stressed its Islamic character. In a similar vein, EOKA (Ethniki Organosis Kyprion Agoniston), a Greek Cypriot nationalist movement that employed paramilitary activities to achieve its goals, had ties with the Greek Orthodox Church (Rapoport, 1984: 674). Hoffman (1998: 94) reports that half of the terrorist groups that were in existence in 1995 had stated religious motives. Religious groups or establishments that are strongly affiliated with religious institutions constitute an alternative to the traditional state. In a significant number of states, this claim to political power is regarded as the primary security threat, rather than one that is posed by other states. Many transnational religious groups seek to take over states or territories within states, and possibly transform them into religious states, which, as noted above, can have a considerable impact on the international system.

Along these lines, one may also interpret the resurgence of religion as a reaction to the "unipolar moment" which is regarded as a "geopolitical interlude that will give way to multipolarity between 2000–2010" (Layne, 1993: 7). Layne argues that "hegemon's unbalanced power creates an environment conducive to the emergence of new powers" and "the entry of new great powers into the international system erodes the hegemon's relative power." What differentiates today's politics from that of the past is the growing inequality among the states and an increasingly uneven distribution of capabilities (Waltz, 1999). In this case, as Grieco (1988) emphasized, relative power gains much more importance – yesterday's allies who benefited from cooperation may become tomorrow's enemies due to frustration. While these statements were for the most part intended to predict the rise of rival states, they can also encompass the rise of a counter-ideology based on religion.

To illustrate and merge the points we touched upon above, let us examine the case of United States support for the *mujahideen* struggle against the communists which took over Afghanistan in the 1970s. At the time, the United States' primary enemy was the Communist Bloc which included the USSR and its satellites. This state-based perspective, which Waltz theorized during the same time period, led the United States to militarily support Afghanistan's Islamic groups because these groups also had anti-communist agendas. Annual appropriations for Afghan aid reached US$650 million and the military assistance included Stinger surface-to-air missiles and helicopter gunships (Pach, 2006: 82). In the end, the rebels had the capabilities to defeat the Soviet forces in Afghanistan. Among the mujahideen that received this assistance was Osama Bin Laden, who was to become a prominent enemy of the US 20 years later. The US had unquestionably benefited from this deal in the 1970s and 1980s by containing the Soviet influence in South Asia. Yet, US policy-makers did not foresee that the unorganized groups who inhabited the Afghan mountains were capable of inflicting massive material damage and fear in the coming years. In retrospect, the relative gains, in terms of material capabilities and the learning/training process, favored the mujahideen.

The mujahideen have since transformed into a transnational organization which controls significant pieces of territory and is capable of posing a strategic threat to states in the world system. This organization – or more properly a constellation of affiliated and cooperating organizations – has a coherent ideology based on religion combined with the capabilities to pursue their political vision in the international system. In this context, Neorealist terms are still very much relevant and retain their explanatory power. Yet the only way they can remain central is by recognizing the importance of transnational groups in the realm of high politics. Waltz (1979: 95) states that transnational actors (by which he usually refers to the multinational corporations) matter, yet they are controlled by states:

> States are the units whose interactions form the structure of international political systems. They will long remain so. The death rate among states is remarkably low. Few states die; many firms do. Who is likely to be around 100 years from now – the United States, the Soviet Union, France, Egypt, Thailand and Uganda? Or Ford, IBM, Shell, Unilever and Massey Ferguson? I would bet on the states, perhaps even on Uganda.

Ironically, these corporations outlived the Soviet Union and Waltz lost his own bet. However, the religious transnational actors that we address here are not these multinational companies, but rather organizations which are based on faith traditions. Many of these faith traditions already pre-date the state system and have, in the past and present, been among the bases for many state governments. Given the history of religions and political structures, it is likely that religions will outlive our less than 400-year-old state system.

Transnational religious issues and Neorealism

From a Neorealist perspective that prioritizes survival and the distribution of capabilities, transnational issues such as human rights and holy places play a potential role in altering the balance among the states. Human rights are defined by different cultures and religions in different terms. This definition usually might require state action that ends up changing the balance of power. This is not to say that states intervene to save their co-religionists due solely to their primordial ties. Intervention is also a matter of securing the powerful states' status in the system. In game theoretical terms, it is a kind of signal the states use to show that their power cannot easily be challenged. In a similar vein, the control of holy places, as explained in the previous chapter, is not only a power symbol but also one of the reasons why certain states, such as Israel and Saudi Arabia, exist in their particular territories. These transnational issues have been on the security agenda of not only Westphalian states but also the units that preceded them, such as empires, and, before that, tribes and other political groupings.

Human rights changing the "balance": religious groups in action

Human rights, as construed by different faith groups, became a motivating force for a number of political movements that changed the balance of power in the system. Although at first glance this may not seem to be a category that would interest a Neorealist, human rights arguably constitute a determining force which can define the rights to which human beings are entitled regardless of the political arrangement in which they live. We examine this issue in detail in the context of the English School which prioritizes the issues of sovereignty and rights in Chapter 6, and Constructivism in Chapter 7. However, this debate is too significant to ignore in Neorealist thought, especially in light of the "promotion of values and ideologies" explained above under the category of religious states.

Human rights constitute a part of the dominant narrative which is recognized – although not necessarily practiced – in the international system. States and other institutions in the system, therefore, do not hesitate to champion these rights in order to legitimize their existence and spread their influence. Accordingly, one actor's interest in the human rights in the jurisdiction of another actor may well be a threat to the latter's survival.

A recent example of the relationship between human rights and intervention has been manifest in the critiques of human rights violations in the Middle East, and the use of human rights rhetoric by the United States in its operations in Iraq and Afghanistan. Although human rights violations were not the main reasons for the operations, military involvement in both countries was preceded by "US governmental statements professing outrage over the human rights violations perpetrated by the Taliban and Saddam Hussain and were officially justified by US claims to be engaged in spreading the blessings of democracy and human rights in the region" (Mayer, 2006: 5). Fearing any human rights-related argument against Iran right after the suicide attack that killed a number of influential commanders in the Iranian Army, Iranian Judiciary Chief Ayatollah Sadeq Larijani stated that "all officials should try to make sure that Iran continues respecting human rights in order to thwart international bodies' efforts to put pressure on the country under the pretext of standing up for human rights." In the same statement he also criticized the West for "its double standards in dealing with human rights issues, especially in regard to the report recently issued by the United Nations Human Rights Council that says the Zionist regime has violated human rights laws" (*Tehran Times*, 2009). Looking at these different statements, one can see the common pattern of linking religion and human rights with a desire to justify foreign policies.

Many faith traditions adopt their own perspective toward the rights and responsibilities of human beings. Religious institutions and groups have actively advocated this vision in the political arena, sometimes openly confronting governing political forces. For example, the demise of communism in Eastern Europe was clearly influenced by the Catholic Church, which had long been a bulwark against the Prussians, Russians, and Austro-Hungarians and, post-1960s, a defender of democracy against communism (Weigel, 1992). The Polish,

Lithuanian, and Ukranian Catholic Churches challenged the spread of communist ideologies, mostly subscribing to the Vatican II premises that emphasized individual freedoms (Mojzes, 1995: 294). The Vatican doctrine provided these local churches with a power that the political authorities did not have. Therefore, it would hardly be an exaggeration to say that the Catholic Church is among the actors that rendered the Eastern European state "sovereign" (i.e., less likely to be affected by the power changes in the system and to disintegrate) as opposed to its political leaders. The Catholic Church focused on the issues of human rights and democracy, and this focus helped to keep society and state together, contributing significantly to the survival of the state as a "unit." This was achieved by providing an anchor of legitimacy both within the inside and outside of the state.

In the intersection of prestige, power, and legitimacy: sacred territories

As noted in the previous chapter, sacred territories constitute an important source of prestige, power, and legitimacy, in addition to their primordial importance to the adherents of a tradition. Smith (2000: 805) argues that the covenantal idea of election and attachment to the territory exists in a number of societies, including Armenia, Russia, Ethiopia, Northern Ireland, South Africa, India, Iran, Israel, and even in the United States, among the Protestant revivalists. The King of Saudi Arabia has the formal title of "The Custodian of the Two Holy Mosques" *(Khaadiim al-Haramain al-Sharifain)*, which indicates responsibility for the protection of Mecca and Medina. Hassner (2002) also explains how the political struggles over a sacred territory can have transnational implications, by looking at the examples of Amritsar, Mecca, Ayodhya, and Jerusalem. After Indian officers attacked a Sikh temple during a pursuit of insurgents, Sikh riots destabilized India and threatened the unity of the state, later spreading to inter-communal rioting throughout South Asia. The struggle and competition between the Muslims and the Hindus over the Ayodhya mosque is likened to the Jewish–Muslim struggle over the Temple Mount in Jerusalem. Citing American strategists, Hassner (2002: 29) also argues that had the Jewish underground attempts at destroying the Muslim holy sites in the 1980s not been prevented, the incidents could have set off a global war, given the Soviet support for the Arab states.

When one looks at the international arena, the most common stated causes of conflicts are either territory or the violation of human rights. Both of these causes usually have a "sacred" dimension, which makes any traditional bargaining difficult, if not impossible. As elaborated in Chapter 5, human rights and holy sites are also among the cited pretexts for international intervention even when the intervention is carried out for *realpolitik* reasons. Hence, religion, as a variable that anchors traditional causes of conflict to fate and divinity, is a potential explanatory variable in Neorealist thought.

Religious identity and Neorealism

Neorealists do not fully welcome identity variables but, as stated before, their accommodation as "complementary accounts" is not discouraged, even within the limits of a narrow realism. Waltz (1959: 238) does not dismiss the importance of the first and second images – the individual and state-level explanations of world politics. "The third image [system level] described the framework of world politics, but without the first and second images there can be no knowledge of the forces that determine policy." However, there has been little emphasis on these images. Neorealist works recognize that national identities could lead to conflict, yet the Cold War Neorealist literature did not touch upon religious identities. Since the majority of contemporary conflicts include some form of religious identity, it is no longer "realistic" to analyze political events as if religious identities had no influence on conflict and cooperation.

Religious identity defining the "structure": tradition, history, and institutions

The existence of the modern nation-state takes its roots from the Treaty of Westphalia (1648), which essentially put an end to the vision of a united Christian Kingdom (Philpott, 2001). States, which are at the core of Neorealist thinking, are the products of a group of disillusioned Christian leaders who were tired of a never-ending religious discourse that justified intervention and warfare. Yet Judeo-Christian values are among the sources of the norms of statehood and sovereignty. Hurd (2004a) argues that even secular notions of state are related to the Judeo-Christian tradition.

Recognizing the changing definitions of sovereignty, Waltz (1997: 913) states that "old realists see causes as running directly from states to the outcomes.... New realists see states forming a structure by their interactions and then being strongly affected by the structure their interactions have formed." In other words, identity may be an influential aspect of state behavior in Classical Realist accounts but individual state identities do not matter in the international system *unless* they affect the interactions that form the structure. We claim that religious identity can potentially influence these interactions and consequently change the balance of power. This influence manifests itself differently in different religious traditions. The tradition, history, and institutions of a religion create a unique form of influence and interactions on a system level.

Take, for example, terrorism and its impact on the system level by creating a threat that did not occupy the agendas of policy-makers during the Cold War. As we note in our discussion of transnational movements, the religious networks that use terrorism as a tool constitute a threat to the unitary character of states and influence the material capabilities of their enemies. The likelihood of this form of violence manifesting within religious traditions varies. For instance, Rapoport (1984: 673) argues:

In Islam and Judaism, the potentialities for radical attacks on institutions are inherent in the ambiguity of unfulfilled divine promises, which no existing establishment can reconcile fully with its own dominance. Because the promises are known to every member of the religious community, the Islamic or Jewish terrorist has had a human audience not present in Hinduism. To reach this audience Islamic and Jewish terrorists must become visible and must either conquer all or be extinguished.

Obviously, no religion can be represented as inherently violent. However, some traditions are represented as having theological frameworks that more easily accommodate the use of violence than others. The extent to which such tendencies manifest in a tradition can vary along a number of social, political, and cultural factors as well as over time. Both Fox (2004: 68) and Toft (2007: 113) state that Muslims appear more often in recent religious conflicts when compared to the adherents of other religions.

On a more theoretical level, Abou Kazleh (2006), in his discussion of Islam and international relations theory, notes that although there has been a disproportionate emphasis on traditionalism and war in the Islamic politico-legal literature, the literature also gradually explores Islamic pacifism with a focus on maintaining peace even under the most difficult conditions. One cannot take these theological frameworks as static. Public theologies of peace and violence are in flux. If analyses of political violence were performed during Christianity's Reformation period, it would likely show that Christians participate in the most religious violence. Activities of Jewish terrorist groups – mentioned by Rapoport (1984) in his historical comparative analysis of terrorism in three religious traditions – have been confined to Israel, yet these groups also did not have difficulty in presenting their case in religious terms. That being said, the purpose of this discussion is not to examine the circumstances under which religious traditions tend to support violence but, rather, to demonstrate that this occurs and can have a significant impact on the international structure.

In another example, the theology of the Vatican II changed the international outlook, mostly in Eastern Europe, on the ideological struggle against communism. The liberal contents of this theology also allowed the alliances of Protestants and Catholics to challenge the political rivals. However, the public theology of governance advocated by the Catholic Church has changed over time. In the nineteenth century, Gregory XVI rejected the concept of "freedom of conscience," and liberalism was condemned in the Syllabus of Errors, a document issued by the Holy See under Pope Pius IX. The First Vatican Council, which opposed rationalism, was described as the "Council of the Counter-Enlightenment" (Küng, 2001: 168). The Catholic Church's pro-status quo stance also led to its tendency to work with some of the most authoritarian regimes of the twentieth century (Sigmund, 1987: 531). The official theology of the faith traditions, in this case Catholicism, contributed to a number of issues we touched upon above, ranging from the sources of legitimacy to the workings of local churches. In other words, the institutions, authority structures, and texts of a faith tradition lead to changing theologies. These dimensions are potential explanatory variables for a number of issues, including conflict patterns and governance.

The importance of religious identity is already implied in all of the above sections and their relevance to Neorealist thought. Religious identity, as much as the distribution of capabilities, constrains and enables the actors in the system. Communities hold their leaders responsible for the protection of their identities, sometimes at the expense of material well-being. Leaders compete to be the representative of these identities, since this would endow them with power which no other source could possibly provide. The rules of the game change depending on the texts and traditions of the religion; a Buddhist politician does not use the same means as a Jewish politician. Nor do they necessarily desire the same type of "survival."

Religion and Neorealism: interactions in the international system

Neorealism has long been criticized as the most rigid theoretical perspective in terms of the accommodation of identity-related variables. In this chapter, we argue that Neorealism is not necessarily closed to including religion, which plays into the security agendas of many states in today's world. Even the staunch Neorealists contribute to policy debates that have religious dimensions. These engagements show that religion has not been banished by the tradition. To the contrary, the Neorealist terminology is useful to explain the religious conflicts.

Some of the avenues of integration we suggest in this chapter may be seen as modifications on Neorealism. Yet, it is arguable that some modification is necessary for Neorealism to remain relevant in an era where religion clearly influences international relations. The alternative would be to scrap Neorealism altogether. We consider this option a poor one because it would, in effect, also scrap all of the understanding and insight that this body of theory has brought to the study of international relations. Thus the optimal solution is to retain the core elements of the theory and supplement them with innovative ways to use the Neorealist paradigm to understand religion and international relations.

There are limits to such modification and integration. Neorealism is not the most suitable framework when one looks at issues such as missionaries, interfaith cooperation, international development, or any soft power functions of religion. Therefore, in this chapter, the focus was mostly on the relatively narrowly defined security agenda and how states are influenced by factors related to religion. The most obvious avenues of integration are the religious states and transnational religious movements that threaten the international system. Although the latter sounds counter-intuitive at first, religions, being much "older" than states, challenge the nation-state. Neorealism remains relevant by focusing on security complexes, even if it means that the theory will continue to focus on states as the primary actors. In the end, although religious actors are not the prime actors of interest, Neorealism can still contribute to our understanding of religion in international relations.

5 Religion and (Neo)liberalism
Interactions within the market of ideas

In this chapter, we explore the interactions between religion and international relations in the context of Neoliberalism. As is the case with most bodies of international relations theory, Liberalism includes many diverse viewpoints and variants. Our arguments might include references to Liberalism in general. This is mostly because Neoliberalism derives some of its core assumptions from different liberal schools of thought. Commercial Liberalism (theories that link free trade and peace), Republican Liberalism (theories that explore democracy and peace linkages), and Sociological Liberalism (theories that analyze transnational arrangements and regional integration) are, for the most part, already embedded in Neoliberal arguments. Therefore, we leave the subtleties of differentiation to the theorists of Neoliberalism, hoping that the avenues, possibilities, and tools suggested in this chapter will guide those readers who are working on the different variants of Liberalism.

Neoliberalism arguably constitutes the biggest mainstream challenge to Neorealism. Neoliberals accept the anarchy assumption of the Neorealists but they do not share the resulting pessimism. They give considerable weight to non-state actors and their influence in the political realm. Multinational companies, banks, and non-governmental organizations are among important players. Keohane and Nye (1987: 733) note that although states are still important actors in the international arena, state autonomy is being eroded by transnational forces. They regard "interdependence" as a "relatively underdeveloped and undervalued concept" with high potential. A set of rules and institutions affects relations among states, pushing the international system toward pluralism and diversity. The central argument in this chapter is that religion, with all its dimensions, is part of the diverse agenda which Neoliberalism addresses.

Neoliberals hold that transnational contacts and coalitions have transformed national interests and attitudes (Tarzi, 2004: 120), which may also be seen as a constructivist argument. Contrary to the Neorealist emphasis on states, Neoliberals portray an international system that includes competition and cooperation among national groups and transnational institutions (Nye, 1988). Neoliberals diverge significantly from Neorealists, as the former believe in the irrelevance of brute force, absence of hierarchy among issues, and the existence of multiple channels of connection. This difference renders Neoliberalism a framework that is more conducive to exploring the interactions between religion and international relations, even when religion is not directly relevant to state survival. In Chapters 3 and 4, our focus was inevitably on the matters of survival in the international system. This emphasis on survival leaves out some essential elements of transnational political dealings. This chapter, along with Chapters 6 and 7, on the English School and Constructivism respectively, aims to bring multiple possibilities of the linkage between religion and international affairs to the fore.

Another dimension that separates Neoliberals from Neorealists is that the former emphasize absolute gains, whereas the latter focus on relative gains. Absolute gains stand for the focus on what an actor acquires without regard for the gains of others, whereas the concept of relative gains denotes the value of gains when compared to the gains of others. Neoliberalism is, for the most part, indifferent to the gains achieved by others. What matters most in Neoliberalism is the absolute gain (Grieco, 1988: 487). It is also possible that the concern for one's ranking among others may depend on the centrality of the issue to survival. Relative gains considerations are likely to be more prevalent in matters of security rather than economic affairs (Lipson, 1984: 15). This is partly the implication of the understanding of anarchy. Neorealists believe that since there is no enforcing force in international dealings, long-term commitments are not in the best interest of an actor. Neoliberals, on the other hand, recognize the existence of anarchy, yet they note that international institutions and multiple interactions among the actors decrease the tendency to cheat (Keohane and Nye, 1977: 35). Thanks to these institutions, commitments become more reliable and actors can cooperate more effectively without fear of being cheated.

Neoliberalism, by stating that transnational actors will pursue their own goals and by acknowledging the importance of issue linkage, makes space for religious organizations and groups. In other words, the system-level approach of Neorealism, which sees states as the core units in the international system, is relaxed in Neoliberal thought. Reflecting the general view of Neoliberalism, Nye (1988: 243) finds the system-unit level differentiation odd to begin with. Even if one accepts the unit-level character of a theory of foreign policy, it is difficult to see how "demographic trends, transnational flows, and military technology that affect many states" are assigned to the unit level. In this vein, Neoliberals implicitly acknowledge the fact that religious identity influences today's politics in multiple realms.

In short, with its emphasis on international institutions and norms, the Neoliberal tradition is a particularly appealing framework, especially for scholars who investigate the transnational aspects and influence of religion. It is also instructive that one of the very first academic journals that published multiple pieces representative of contemporary Neoliberalism, *International Organization,* published a special issue on "Transnational Relations and World Politics" that included a full-length article on the influence of the Roman Catholic Church in international politics (Vallier, 1971). The relevance of religion to the Neoliberal agenda, therefore, is not a novel assertion. Below, we follow up on the existing literature and explore how Neoliberal scholarship and religion can come together to account for the changing dynamics of tradition, politics, and the market in contemporary international relations.

Religious worldviews and Neoliberalism

In Neoliberalism, actors are motivated by the possibility of absolute gains and the existence of multiple linkages they can use to influence politics. Power still remains relevant, yet its meaning is not limited to hard power. The world is not necessarily a realm of conflict among states with substantial armies. One can use multiple means to gain influence over others. Along these lines we highlight three central paths through which religious worldviews may be explored in the context of the Neoliberal agenda. The first is through religious actors and their influence on regime formation and consolidation, a concept frequently employed in Neoliberal accounts. The second path of integration is situating religion and human psychology in the economic and political market. The third possibility focuses on game theory and how religious worldviews can be part of formal modeling.

Religious actors and regimes

The Neoliberal framework permits the study of an individual's worldview as it relates to international politics, even when it is not directly relevant to matters of state survival. The worldviews of political leaders, celebrities, and other prominent figures help create networks, alliances, and more importantly, *regimes* that have a lasting influence on economic and political governance. In Neoliberalism, a regime is defined as "principles, norms, rules and decision-making procedures around which actor expectations converge in a given issue area" (Krasner, 1983: 1). A regime exists when "the interaction between the parties is not unconstrained or is not based on independent decision-making" (Stein, 1982: 31).

Religious worldviews can be the basis for a regime. Juergensmeyer (1993, 2008) makes a parallel, regime-like argument within the religion and politics literature. He states that both religious and secular political ideologies are "ideologies of order." Such ideologies conceive of the political world in coherent, manageable ways, provide authority that legitimizes social and political order, and define the proper way to behave and relate to society. Snyder (2011: 9) also echoes this belief when he says that "change in religion can disorder and reorder the international system." A religious framework constitutes a regime with its own principles and rules that define the appropriate form of behavior. Religious worldviews also interact with other ideologies. Depending on the conditions, this interaction can be in the form of cooperation or competition.

An example of such a religious regime is the changing dynamics of the Catholic Church, its relationship with individual states, and its creation of a "regime" with distinctive principles, norms, and rules in the issue areas of political governance. The Catholic Church, similar to other religious authorities, provides a perspective that covers issues ranging from economic governance to personal matters such as marriage or divorce. The Vatican is both a sovereign state and an NGO that commands significant level of soft power at the same time (Ferrari, 2006). Vallier (1971: 491) draws attention to the struggle of the Catholic Church with "secular faiths" through condemnations and papal pronouncements. When the communists took over in Russia, the Church shifted to diplomacy even more, and it developed new kinds of motivational sources to be able to protect its place in the public sphere.

Individuals play a key role in establishing new rules in a regime. Within Catholicism, one can study Pope John Paul II's influence on world politics. After the fall of communism, John Paul II indicated in the 1991 cyclical *Centesimus Annus* that church teachings already express commitment to the struggle against marginalization and suffering while recognizing the right to private property. Under John Paul II, the Church advocated for human rights, especially religious rights, engaged in a fight against poverty, and opposed the use of force in international relations (Hertzke, 2009). Although Pope John Paul II rarely used the language of the "just war" doctrine, he advanced a theology of peace (Heft, 2011: 216). John Paul II also engaged "world leaders with a more explicitly geopolitical analysis" and he did not shy away from talking about political power (Appleby, 2000b: 14).

The Catholic Church has been famously called "the godmother of the non-profit sector" and it has had a significant influence on social movements (Massaro, 2008: 9). These policies date back at least to the 1968 Medellin conference (Haynes, 1998: 46–47; Philpott, 2004: 34), and they coincide with an increased Catholic support for democracy and democratization in Catholic countries (Huntington, 1991; Philpott, 2004). Gill (1998, 2008) and Guillermo (2009) argue that this support for democracy and minority rights is based on self-interest and is most prominent where Catholics are in the minority or where the poor are leaving the Catholic Church for other Christian denominations. This market-based approach is consistent with the Neoliberal frameworks.

Following on from the regime approach, one can also employ *neofunctionalism* and theories of integration to account for shifting loyalties toward a religious perspective. Haas (1958: 10) argues that "political integration is the process whereby actors shift their loyalties, expectations, and political activities toward a new center, whose institutions possess or demand jurisdiction over preexisting national states." An institution involves "persistent and connected sets of rules (formal or informal) that prescribe behavioral roles, constrain activity and shape expectations" and the general institution of religion "includes a variety of quite different specific institutions, including the Roman Catholic Church, Islam and Congregationalism" (Keohane, 1988: 383). It follows from this perspective that religion, by providing a specific and binding framework, influences individuals' worldviews and shape their expectations. This influence is clearly recognized by Neoliberals.

Obviously, Haas did not have religion as a transnational institution in mind, and indeed, religion does not have a formal "jurisdiction" over national states. However, the fact that religion is an alternative institution toward which actors shift their loyalties and expectations creates an analogous situation. The recognition of religious rules in certain areas of public life (such as inheritance and family law) (Fox, 2008, 2013) makes one question the power of the state over religion.

Contrary to regime formation approaches, neofunctionalism assumes an existing regime which has overarching authority. For example, in many Islamic states sharia already dictates state policies. In 25 of 47 Muslim majority states sharia law determines issues of personal status, and in 22 of these states separate Islamic courts interpret and enforce at least some of these laws. Even in some non-Muslim majority states such as India, sharia law determines some matters of personal status for Muslims (Fox, 2013). In Canada, over a two-year period from 2004 through 2005, an Ontario government review of religious arbitration practices produced a public debate about the prospects of sharia arbitration in Ontario family law (Goff, 2011). This idea of the separation of judicial spheres was backed by influential religious leaders of other traditions. In February 2008, the Archbishop of Canterbury, Rowan Williams, gave a series of public statements on the topic of Islamic law. Williams stated that any approach to law that ignores alternative claims on one's loyalties is "completely irrelevant." He also argued that "the application of Sharia in certain circumstances" in the United Kingdom was "unavoidable." Shortly thereafter, the government recognized five sharia courts as having authority as arbitration courts on matters including divorce, inheritance, domestic violence, and financial disputes (Hamilton, 2009; Murray, 2009).

This sharia-based regime was relatively centralized until the secular Turkish Republic which replaced the Ottoman Empire abolished the Caliphate in 1924. The Organization of the Islamic Cooperation is far from assuming such a supranational status. Yet the existence of distinctive communities of believers that seek institutional channels to achieve faith-based governance warrant a theory that can account for shifting identities in search of an alternative market or traditional political sphere. Such a line of inquiry also has the potential to shed light on the hitherto neglected dimensions of religious spill-over in political governance: Which realms of public sphere are more conducive to faith-based perspectives? How do religious actors expand their influence, where do they start, and how do they spread their actions and teachings? These queries can be carried out under the Neoliberal framework.

Religion, political psychology, and the market

A second avenue of possible integration of religious worldviews into the Neoliberal agenda is through combining religion, political psychology, and the market. Economic choices that have political consequences are not made relying solely on universal standards of rationality. To put it more boldly, Neoliberal theorists argue that no theory of international relations that is devoid of moral sentiments can account for crucial dynamics of political economy. This is also enshrined in the early political economy literature. Adam Smith linked economics, conscience, and morality in *The Theory of Moral Sentiments* as early as 1759. He concluded that political and economic structures are outcomes of natural human action rather than conscious planning. Religion, as a mental framework, has a determinative effect on what is acceptable and what is not in human interactions. Such norms constitute the basis of commerce and politics.

Put more simply, Neoliberals recognize that morality influences behavior. This, combined with the uncontroversial assertion that religion is often a significant influence on morality, establishes an obvious avenue for understanding the influence of religious worldviews on behavior. For example, McCloskey's (2006) treatment of the intimate ties between political psychology in the framework of "virtues" (prudence, justice, temperance, courage, love, faith, and hope) and economic structures provides a basis for the investigation of religion and modes of cooperation. Similarly, van Staveren (2001) develops an Aristotelian conception of economics that requires a closer look at psychology. For a viable economic life, actors need to develop certain capabilities (emotions, deliberation, commitment, and human interaction) within three main domains (freedom, justice, and care). Van Staveren's model allows for the integration of a "religion" variable into Neoliberal theory because religion speaks to all these "capabilities" and "domains." Such integration may account for the patterns of distribution, conflict, and cooperation that cannot be explained by models that employ a stricter rationality assumption inspired by neoclassical economics.

Political psychology, influenced by religious commitment, has an impact on all decisions, political and economic. For example, studies of US church members show that they are more likely to give money and time, even to secular efforts (Wuthnow, 1996: 87). Church members are also more likely to vote (Beyerlein and Chaves, 2003: 229; Wald et al., 1993: 129) and to engage in other forms of political participation such as lobbying, and attending protests (Beyerlein and Chaves, 2003: 229–230). Similarly, Abdul-Matin (2011) draws attention to the existence of a powerful and value-conscious Muslim consumer base that has started to shape market behavior. This market-defining influence of religious frameworks and communities may also be observed at the state level. For example, Madsen (2007: 77) argues that thanks to Buddhism and Confucianism, Taiwan had a smooth transition to democracy after 1987 and it flourished because these traditions were "much more conducive to generalized social solidarity than the individualistic vision of classic Western liberalism."

We can further probe these studies of religion-based behavior's influence on patterns of cooperation by using the Neoliberal queries. For those who prefer a two-way interaction model of religion and social structures, Jones' (2006) study provides a valuable point of departure. Jones states that culture – defined as patterns of beliefs, habits, values, ideals, and preferences shared by groups of people – is slow to change but is still fluid and responsive to economic, political and social forces. It affects economics and politics but then is transformed itself in return. In short, religion can affect political/economic choices; yet it is also shaped by the availability and content of viable social, political, and economic options in the public sphere.

Religion and game theoretical approaches

Moving from the point above, and as a third avenue within the worldviews and Neoliberalism framework, one can apply game theoretical models to faith-based political decision-making. Snidal (1985: 35) states that game theory presumes that actors are rational but "its empirical assumptions need assert neither that the key actors are states nor that they maximize power." Although Snidal later acknowledges that "the models of game theory can be useful for theories not involving rational actors," the rationality principle of the game-theoretical models is not necessarily at odds with religious perspectives. Game theory, as a theory of purposive behavior with a focus on the conflict of interest and potentials for cooperation, can have a twofold influence on religion and international relations. First, it can explain the patterns of cooperation between religious leaders in matters related to faith; and second, it can help in understanding the decisions of religiously informed political leaders.

First and foremost, religion, as a factor that defines one's interests and goals, directly plays into the games. Game theory does not require that actors have rational goals; it requires that actors have a defined set of preferences and goals. There is nothing to preclude religion – or any other factor, rational or irrational – from playing a role in setting those goals and preferences. Beliefs and perceptions are already recognized within the game theory literature as important factors in the military area as well as in economics. Axelrod and Keohane (1985: 229) state that in game theory, "the payoff structure that determines the mutuality of interests is not based simply upon objective factors, but is grounded upon the actors' perceptions of their own interests." In making political decisions, religion may be an influential factor. This does not mean that it takes away the rationality of decision-making. For example, Salvatore and LeVine (2005: 2) draw attention to a concept of Islamic legal philosophy, *istislah*, which involves mediating between two contending positions and finding the positive. They note how much of a difference this approach makes: "The resulting public sphere can potentially be seen as a positive-sum game, one that reflects a logic quite distinct from the scarcely plastic – if not zero-sum – notions of justice based on standards of pure reason." One's perception of "interest" can also be shaped by tradition. The religious tradition can theoretically prioritize individual, societal, or state interests among others and determine the rules of the game accordingly. Madan (2010: 182) describes such a process, stating that "in the classical Brahmanical formulation of the goals and value orientations of life, *dharma*, or morality, encompasses *artha*, that is the rational pursuit of economic and political life, and provides its legitimizing principle."

Second, game theory may be employed to investigate whether and how religious leaders decide to cooperate in a competitive market. In inter-faith initiatives and ecumenical dialogues, decisions taken by the representatives of faith traditions already reflect these dynamics, with an emphasis on reciprocity and consistency of the gestures of goodwill and tolerance. Putnam's two-level games, which reflect international decisions as results of bargaining among the decision-makers both at international and national levels, may also be adapted to religious initiatives. Putnam (1988: 434) states that at the national level, "domestic groups pursue their interests by pressuring the government to adopt favorable policies." At the international level, "national governments seek to maximize their own ability to satisfy domestic pressures, while minimizing the adverse consequences of foreign developments." Local religious groups pursue their interests by pressuring the government. Evangelical Christians and the Jewish lobby are among the faith-based groups which have worked on shaping American foreign policy (Baumgartner et al., 2008; Den Dulk, 2007; Haynes, 2009b), and Muslim groups are becoming increasingly vocal, especially in the foreign policy-making of European states (Taspinar, 2003).

We can also apply Putnam's two-level games to religious leaders' efforts to balance the demands of their community and the need to work with other religious groups. For religious leaders there may be a tension between "the demands of political activism (in which it may be desirable to *minimize* difference with potential allies) and religious recruitment (which may require the *magnification* of differences)" (Jelen, 2001: 21). This tension has been the concern of religious and even political actors, who consider joining inter-faith or ecumenical initiatives yet also fear the reaction from their own communities. Balancing the concerns about reaching the other and remaining a representative of a tradition can be mapped by game-theoretical approaches. In the end, inter-faith interactions require strategic thinking. This balancing act has arguably become less challenging in the United States as recent research suggests that the clergy are becoming more politically active. Essentially, when they meet their congregations' religious needs, the congregations are less likely to object to their clergy engaging in political activity (Djupe and Gilbert, 2008).

Religious actors aim for survival. A particular threat to a faith tradition may come from another tradition or from the establishment of a secular sphere that excludes religious doctrines. Cardinal Cahal Daly of Northern Ireland, for example, once stated that secularism is "more anonymous and more subtle than either Nazism or Communism were" as a threat to faith (quoted in *Irish Times*, 2000).[1] This common "threat" of secularism fits into the model that game theorists call "the dilemmas of common aversions," when "actors with contingent strategies do not most prefer the same outcome but do agree there is at least one outcome that all want to avoid" (Stein, 1982: 309). In other words, the leaders of two different faith traditions might cooperate to prevent a secular order from taking hold of the public sphere. Obviously, not all inter-faith arrangements aim to find faith-based solutions to replace secular arrangements. Some patterns of inter-religious cooperation fit better into other games, in which all actors prefer a given outcome, such as environmental protection or eradication of hunger.

Beyond these two primary avenues of integration, game theory has already been adapted to investigations of terrorist group behavior. Enders and Sandler (2005: 12) note that game theory is appropriate for studies of terrorism, including religious versions, for the following reasons: (1) It focuses on strategic interactions where actions are interdependent; (2) it allows the figuring of threats and promises into the communication; (3) actors are rational in terms of calculating the other's possible reaction to their actions; yet (4) they are not completely informed; and (5) bargaining is possible. For the most part these requirements are met by religious groups. In the case of suicide bombings, including those motivated by religio-political reasons, Pape (2003: 344) refers to Schelling's idea of "rationality of irrationality," in which an act that may be deemed individually irrational is "meant to demonstrate credibility to a democratic audience that still more and greater attacks are sure to come." In short, game theory is a methodological tool that is already used for the analysis of the decision-making process of religious actors.

Religious legitimacy and Neoliberalism

Neoliberalism recognizes the primacy of states in the international system and the multiplicity of actors at the same time. Legitimacy is an important parameter not only for states, but for a diversity of actors for which Neoliberalism accounts. We examine two avenues of integrating religious legitimacy into Neoliberal explanations. The first way focuses on how religion constitutes a form of *soft power*, an oft-used concept in the Neoliberal literature. The second avenue uses the concept of regimes, as noted above in the worldviews section. As we have already stated, religious actors can be influential in the creation of regimes. Here, in this section, we also argue that even non-religious regimes may need the legitimacy bestowed by the religious actors in order to be able to compete with their rivals.

Religion and soft power

"Soft power," defined as the ability to shape the preferences of others through non-military means, can be easily adapted to non-state actors. The soft power of an entity entails three resources: culture, political values, and its policy (resting on legitimacy and moral authority) (Nye, 2004: 11). Soft power, when systematically employed as a tool, can help to explain why certain religious groups (including paramilitary groups in any religion) have so much influence on their adherents. By facilitating the investigation of how groups interact with institutions and what the effects are on foreign policy behavior, such a framework can also help us explain the influence of religion in ethnic conflicts. The soft power framework informs "popular beliefs, perceptions and attitudes of particular constituencies" and it – directly or indirectly – influences the behavior of states in world politics (Thomas, 2005: 7). Haynes (2009a: 296) also expands the use of the term to cover the religious actors who pursue their own "foreign policies," in part by seeking to influence official foreign policy. The aim is to embed those specific foreign policy goals into the official agenda. "If religious actors 'get the ear' of key foreign policy-makers because of their shared religious beliefs, the former may become able to influence foreign policy outcomes through the exercise of religious soft power" (Haynes, 2008: 143). These debates do not preclude states from using religion's soft power to further their foreign policy goals.

The employment of "soft power," in short, is not new in the studies of religion and international affairs. However, given the gradually increasing power of religious ideologies in societies, it should be granted greater emphasis. Today's political battles cannot be fought only at the military level. This is acknowledged by the Neoliberals. Karim Sadjadpour, an Iran analyst from the International Crisis Group, stated:

> you've got two different trajectories, and I don't think the Americans have come to this realization. The Americans have hard power in Iraq, but the Iranians have soft power, and they are able to do things. It is a much more subtle influence than the Americans.
>
> (cited in Peterson, 2005)

Recognizing the power of ideas in the Middle Eastern context, Kemp (2005: 7) similarly states that "Iran's capacity, capability and will to influence events in Iraq are high in terms of both hard power and soft power." Iran finds itself "supporting the position of the United States by supporting elections in Iraq because such use of Iranian 'soft power' is the most practical way to ensure Iraq's Shiite majority an opportunity to dominate the country's politics."

Robert Pape (2005) already theorizes such a battle with the term "soft-balancing," which stands for actions that may not directly challenge US military preponderance but use "nonmilitary tools to delay, frustrate and undermine aggressive unilateral U.S. military policies." Pape (2005: 10) adds that "soft-balancing using international institutions, economic statecraft, and diplomatic arrangements has already been a prominent feature of the international opposition to the U.S. war against Iraq." Ironically, religious groups pay more attention to exploiting ideological resources than do established states, which often find it difficult to overcome their rigid institutional frameworks and internal divisions over policy and ideology. In this vein, Nye (2008: 101) calls attention to the US helplessness among others. He reminds us that when Al Jazeera broadcast Osama Bin Laden's first videotape on October 7, 2001, US officials sought initially to prevent both Al Jazeera and the American networks from broadcasting further messages from Bin Laden instead of coming up with a counter-tape to give to the networks.

Soft power may be an answer to Stalin's famous question, "How many divisions does the Pope have?" The Pope and many – though certainly not all – other influential religious actors have no military power but they do have soft power. They have the ability to influence opinions, attitudes, and policy preferences of both leaders and their constituents. Yet soft power is not necessarily just a replacement for military and economic power. Soft power is an option that may be used both in the absence and presence of hard power. Even leaders who have military power still frequently use their soft power to achieve a long-lasting influence on people. Chinese policy-makers recognized this "soft" power of religion, and since 2004 they have begun to establish Confucius Institutes around the world intended to promote friendly relationships with other countries. Cho and Katzenstein (2011) report that Korea also caught up with China in terms of reclaiming Confucianism as an asset. Korean groups organize worldwide events around Confucianism and Buddhism, presenting these spiritual frameworks as an alternative to the material world in which we are living.

It is also worth noting that a number of faith traditions are struggling with the "soft power" of other cultures. "Far more powerful than either fax or audiocassette have been the visual and music media, which have been reworking the lifestyles of Iranians and other Muslims" (Fischer, 2002: 63). However, not all forms of cultural products qualify as elements of soft power. Nye (2008: 95) warns that "exporting Hollywood films full of nudity and violence to conservative Muslim countries may produce repulsion rather than soft power." The compatibility among different societies and the means of soft power are recognized and currently studied by public diplomacy specialists. Fundamentalist and terrorist groups attempt to counter this challenge by the same means. For example, the Islamist group Hizb ul-Tahrir promotes technopop bands. A group of Muslim youth who are members of the group actually established a rock band known as Soldiers of Allah which perform songs that have lyrics such as "the masses join under the banner of Allah and rise up in jihad against their 'oppressors' and 'occupiers'" (Stern and Moti, 2007: 26). On a more positive note, Alim (2005: 271) draws attention to the role "hiphop has played in networking Muslims around the globe, from South Asia to South Philly, from South Africa to South Carolina."

Legitimizing and delegitimizing the regimes

As mentioned above, a religious framework may be construed as a regime by itself. A state's religion can potentially be a tool to legitimize, support, destroy, or replace another "regime." Planned changes in regimes require the destruction of existing institutions and the coordination of expectations around new focal points (Young, 1982: 280). The literature on religious opposition movements has long recognized the importance of religious legitimacy in supporting, opposing, and altering regimes (Geertz, 1977; Juergensmeyer, 1993; Lincoln, 2003).

Viewed in this light, Neoliberalism has the potential to become a platform for the study of fundamentalist organizations that employ religious rhetoric or religious institutions that seek to ally or compete with the state on various issues. The tensions between the religious circles and the governments in Egypt and Algeria before and after the Arab Spring, the uneasy relationship and competition between the state and the church in Latin America and Eastern Europe during the Cold War, and the radical Islamic groups that compete with the states in the vast geographies of South Asia are all examples of challenges to the legitimacy of the state. One can also see instances of political actors trying to denigrate their opposition by putting them into "apostate" category.

Prime Minister of Turkey Tayyip Erdoğan once called BDP (Barış ve Demokrasi Partisi, Peace and Democracy Party) members "Zoroastrians." The BDP mostly represents the Kurdish constituency, and BDP representatives had just joined the AKP members in advocating the rights of women with head-scarves (*Hurriyet Daily News*, 2011). At first glance, one might be surprised to learn that the AKP tried to undermine its "supporters" in this cause, but the reaction makes sense in the context of religious politics. Arguably, Erdoğan did not want to share this transnational advocacy role with the Kurdish repre-sentatives, and the most effective way to discredit the BDP was to question the party's religious identity.

Keohane (1989: 10) states that "institutions change as a result of human action and the changes in expectations and process that result can exert profound effects on state behavior." In this sense, Neoliberalism accommodates religion both as a dependent and an independent variable. This is not to say that political actors have unlimited power over the interpretation of religion or to deny that religious traditions have a life of their own dependent on the audience in addi-tion to political entrepreneurs. However, in any given scholarly account, it is not quite possible to capture all dimensions of religion. An attempt to achieve such a daunting task might distort the picture altogether. Therefore, it is up to the indi-vidual scholar to distinguish the role(s) played by religion as an independent, dependent, or intervening factor in a political event.

Non-state religious actors and Neoliberalism

Since Neoliberalism recognizes the multiplicity of actors in international pol-itics, it is much more conducive to the integration of non-state religious actors than is Classical Realism or Neorealism. In this section, we identify three approaches for integrating non-state religious actors into the Neoliberal agenda. The first relies on a sociological theory which focuses on religious organizations and market competition. In the sphere of religious institutions and believers, there is a demand–supply mechanism which defines the success of rivaling ideo-logies. The second focuses on how communication among faith traditions evolves with iterated "games." Inter-faith initiatives constitute the prime example of this cooperation, which can be explained by the "evolution of coop-eration." The third draws attention to the public choice literature. This approach borrows heavily from the religious organizations and market literature, yet we also focus on how society prefers one form of political/ economic arrangement over the other and how religious actors figure into this choice.

Religious organizations and market competition

Sociologists have developed a market-based theory intended to explain the extent to which people are religious. Using economic logic and terminology, this theory posits that religious "consumers" (believers) choose their religious "pro-ducers" (religious institutions) in a market-like religious economy which tends toward equilibrium. In a free market, consumers are more likely to find attractive products which results in more people consuming religion (Iannaccone, 1995; Stark and Finke, 2000; Warner, 1993). In this market, religious institutions become voluntary organizations that regulate social, political and economic behavior. Stark and Bainbridge (1985: 171) underscore the role of individual entrepreneurship in forming new religions. In a similar vein, Finke and Stark (1992) demonstrate that the spread of the Methodist and Baptist denominations in the nineteenth century was due to effective marketing strategies of the clergy which won the competition over Congregational, Presbyterian, and Episcopalian traditions. This argument draws its roots from classical economic theory. For example, Adam Smith (1965: 745) argues that religious laissez-faire is the best way to satisfy the demand for religious instruction, reduce religious conflict, and promote "pure and rational religion, free from every mixture of absurdity, imposture, or fanaticism."

One can apply a similar type of reasoning to explain the role of religious organizations in politics. For example, the actions of religious organizations may be viewed as an attempt to correct "political market failures." Keohane (1984: 85) hints at this mechanism in his explanation of regimes, with each regime desiring to become a "status maximizer" and competing with the alternative regimes in the international system. As noted above, Juergensmeyer (1993, 2008) argues that this is precisely what happens across multiple states in a competition between secular and religious ideologies. Similarly, international conflict and cooperation patterns as well as deficiencies in political and economic governance have been tied to economics of religion. For example, Avner Greif (1994) shows that "individualist" cultural beliefs, unlike their collective counterparts, result in social institutions that are conducive to anonymous exchange and initiative, and therefore stimulate long-run economic growth.

Even within the same religion, there is competition regarding the interpretation of the tradition and representation of the believers. One such example among many is the competition between moderate and fundamentalist political actors. Daniels (2007) underlines this general trend of competition in defining the borders of political, social, and economic governance between liberal Muslims and their fundamentalist rivals in Indonesia, the country with the world's largest Muslim population. In order to counter the fundamentalist interpretations of Islam, liberal intellectuals established the Liberal Islam Network (*Jaringan Islam Liberal*) in 2001, which is a forum for "different intellectuals and activists concerned with liberal interpretations of Islamic teachings to counter the fundamentalist discourse and movement" (Ali, 2005: 4). Ali asserts that the LIN's intellectual inspiration was drawn from similar liberal Islamic organizations that are now emerging as serious players in the marketplace of ideas. These organizations include Al-Qalam (South Africa), An-Nahdha al-Nahda (Tunisia), the International Institute for Islamic Thought (the United States and Malaysia), the Liberation Movement (Iran), Liberty for Muslim World (England), Progressive Dawoodi Bohras (India), Sisters in Islam (Malaysia), and Progressive Muslims (the United States).

Another possible avenue of integration is through the concept of internationalization. Internationalization

> affects the opportunities and constraints facing social and economic actors, and therefore their policy preferences – not necessarily the basic values that actors seek (power, money or virtue as they define it) but their choices about which policies will best achieve their fundamental goals.
>
> (Keohane and Milner, 1996: 4)

Even fundamentalism itself is a policy choice to maintain one's identity. Religious fundamentalism "manifests itself as a strategy, or a set of strategies, by which beleaguered believers attempt to preserve their distinctive identity as a people or group" (Marty and Appleby, 1993: 3). Fundamentalist creationism in the United States uses "film, television, video, computerized direct mail promotions to commend its cosmos as genuine science to a culture still largely impressed with claims to scientificity" (Moore, 1993: 51). Similarly, Gush Emunim, a fundamentalist Jewish organization, uses modern means of communication and education in its campaigns (Rosenak, 1993).

The evolution of cooperation in religious interactions: inter-faith initiatives

Inter-faith initiatives may also be explored through a Neoliberal lens. Axelrod's (1984) "evolution of cooperation" explains the development of social conventions and effective rules in the expectation of repeated interaction. It is a useful framework to investigate the possibilities of inter-faith dialogue and its permissibility in political theologies described above. Its emphasis on reciprocity leading to cooperation puts Axelrod's intuitively plausible and prominent framework within the mainstream of Neoliberal concept formation. Works by Lederach (1995), Appleby (2000a), and Gopin (2000) which focus on the issue of religion, culture, and conflict resolution fall under this rubric of the evolution of cooperation. These works, among others, focus on finding ways to emphasize trends in religious traditions which foster tolerance, cooperation, and understanding.

The literature on inter-faith communications has explored how this "evolution of cooperation" may be observed in successful initiatives based on experiential learning, and how trust can be built – or institutionalized – in order to facilitate future dealings (Abu Nimer, 2001). Reciprocity matters most in those dealings. In other words, "linking issues with one another in productive rather than self-defeating ways" (Axelrod and Keohane, 1985: 249) extends to religious peacebuilding as well. For most of the time, parties do not directly delve into theological issues or their respective religious myths. Inter-faith initiatives start with knowing the other as a "person" and focusing on issues of common concern, such as poverty, unemployment, or any other social matter that affects people from all faiths.

Religion and public choice

The third possibility of linkage of non-state religious actors to Neoliberalism is through applying the collective choice literature to religious institutions. The public choice literature as exemplified by the works of Arrow (1970), Olson (1965), and Buchanan and Tullock (1962) has the potential to shed light on the role of religion in the relationship between collective choices and institutional arrangements. Public choice theory assumes that individuals are guided by their perceived self-interest. They make choices in light of these interests and collective arrangements that result in bargaining among actors – including politicians – with diverse preferences.

Religious organizations are important in this context for two reasons. First, they reflect elements of society's preferences and often act as representatives for these elements. Second, the choice to join and support a religious organization is part of this process of individuals making choices based on their interests. What do I get out of membership in a religious community? What type of religious arrangement do I prefer to see in the public sphere? This type of cost–benefit calculus of joining a religious sect/community has been explored in the religion and public choice literature. Iannacconne (1992) finds that in Christian denominations the existence of greater sacrifices asked from individuals leads to the provision of greater public goods. Berman and Laitin (2008) extend this club model to account for suicide attacks. The sacrifices which religious groups ask from individuals aim to weed out potential defectors. Since most of these religious groups also provide public goods, they require sacrifices as signals of commitment. In the cases of Hamas and Hezbollah, religious radicalization and public service provision (in the form of mosques, schools, and hospitals) go hand in hand. The choice to join or remain outside is dependent on the individual's needs and preferences, and the calculation of costs, benefits, and risks of membership.

Non-state religious actors in the "spiritual marketplace" (Roof, 2001), very much like their local counterparts, try to cater to the needs of the majority in order to secure a loyal community. These actors also demand a commitment from their members. Local movements weigh the costs and benefits of affiliation with transnational movements. The benefits include funding, access to expertise and international contacts as well as association with a brand name. Costs include loss of local control and negative associations that may come with that brand name. One example of this marketing process could be the increasing willingness of the Islamist groups to affiliate themselves with the most visible fundamentalist movement, Al-Qaeda. Among these local groups are the Abu Sayyaf Group, Jemaah Islamiyah, the Islamic Army of Eden (Yemen), the Islamic Movement of Uzbekistan, the Libyan Islamic Fighting Group, and Hezbollah (Bajoria and Bruno, 2009). These affiliations help local groups carve out a niche for themselves and justify their actions. One of the prominent Al-Qaeda leaders, Ayman al-Zawahiri, was reported to have provided religious justification for the violent tactics employed by the Armed Islamic Group in Algeria (Vriens, 2009).

Egyptian Islamic Jihad extremists became affiliated with Al-Qaeda as their "market share" was threatened due to increasing suppression from the state and decreasing financial resources. The group started to receive most of its funding from Al-Qaeda in 1998, and the groups actually merged in June 2001 (Fletcher, 2008).

In some cases where minority religions are concerned, groups or individuals may prefer to be defined not by their religion but by their citizenship or geographical affiliation. One example of this choice could be the status of the Catholics in Northern Ireland. Northern Ireland had been governed by the predominantly Protestant Unionist community until 1972, when the parliament was closed due to the increasing intercommunity violence between the Unionists and Nationalists. As a response to Protestant domination, Catholics in Northern Ireland demanded "to be treated by the state without regard for their identity as Catholics ... they wanted to be seen less as Catholics, more as citizens" (Appiah, 2008: 49).

In some contexts religious identity is a defining factor in deciding who is included in a political arrangement and who is not. Institutional arrangements may reflect this pattern, as was the case in Northern Ireland. The "choice" of a segment of the public has the potential to define the division of labor and provision of services in the society. Therefore, the definition of citizenship, nationalism, and religion and how groups choose to be defined are avenues of investigation at the intersection of identity and public choice. In this example, one may argue that since religion seemed to work against the Catholics in the Northern Irish context, the Catholics continued to see the Republic of Ireland as a possible motherland mostly due to the ethno-religious identity of the state. When the concept of citizenship fails to cover multiple religious identities, members of the society that subscribe to different faith traditions may find themselves closer to another state which is able to offer a more attractive option.

When it comes to the religion-public choice literature, *vicarious religion* (Davie, 2007) is also worthy of note. Although there is a downward trend in Europe when it comes to actual religious practices such as going to churches, one cannot conclude that people do not care about the existence of religious institutions (Davie, 2007; Norris and Ingleheart, 2004). Although Europeans do not see religion as an obligatory part of their lives, they still want to know that they can attend the churches "if they choose to." Citizens may want to keep religious public goods even if they do not use them often. This also explains the reactions of the mostly secular societies to religious trends they deem threatening because of the actual religious activism observed in those trends. To illustrate, the 2009 Swiss ban on the construction of minarets received the support of 57.5 percent of the voters. The ban has been controversial, especially since it was supported by a religiously tolerant society. Eveline Widmer-Schlumpf, the Swiss Justice Minister, claimed that the ban "reflects fears among the population of Islamic fundamentalist tendencies" (quoted in Cumming-Bruce and Erlanger, 2009). In other words, the ban reflects the Swiss public choice which sees the elements of Islamic affiliation contrary to its interests. In this vein, the collective stances for or against different faith traditions, especially in the context of democracies, may be seen through the cost, benefit, and risk lens of the public choice perspective.

These local decisions are particularly relevant to international relations due to the reactions to such a public choice. Ekmeleddin Ihsanoglu, Secretary General of the Organization of the Islamic Cooperation, called the Swiss ban on minarets an "example of growing anti-Islamic incitement in Europe by the extremist, anti-immigrant, xenophobic, racist, scare-mongering ultra-right politicians who reign over common sense, wisdom and universal values" (Al Jazeera, 2009). Egypt's Grand Mufti Ali Gomaa stated that the ban was an insult to the feelings of the Muslim community in Switzerland and elsewhere – even the Vatican joined the Muslim leaders and denounced the ban as a "blow to religious freedom" (BBC News, 2009). In short, any ruling over the practices of a religious community inside a country can become an international issue. In such cases, public choice is usually limited and bound by the views of an international community that advocates "absolute gains," whereby religious communities can live and flourish side by side.

Another concept at the intersection of Neoliberal thinking and non-state religious actors is social capital. Social capital refers to "the features of social organization such as networks, norms, and social trust that facilitate coordination and cooperation for mutual benefit" (Putnam, 1995: 67). The social capital approach "embodies a fundamentally social psychological proposition about the roots of efficient government and social institutions, focusing on the socialization of individuals into collective behavior" (Skocpol and Fiorina, 1999: 13). Putnam (2000: 66) maintains that "faith communities in which people worship together are arguably the single most important repository of social capital in America." Reclaiming the international relations theory concepts in the fourteenth-century sociology literature in the Islamic world, Ahmed (2002) similarly calls attention to the focus on social cohesion ('asabiyya) in Ibn Khaldun's work. Ahmed argues that the 'asabiyya that was fueled by ethnicity, race, and nationalism in the past is now breaking down, leaving its place to the kind that binds by religion.

In short, religious groupings bind people together and they influence the patterns of cooperation by increasing trust in the community and the willingness to participate in social and economic life. Social capital, which is enriched by faith communities, can be integrated to Neoliberal perspectives that focus on ways to decrease cheating and to increase trust in transnational dealings. Social capital helps create transnational faith-based communities with the norms and social trust it implies. In the absence of any formal ties that could otherwise tie the communities together, social capital gains a special influence on the creation of highly bonded yet informal transnational religious communities. This is why evangelical communities include the concerns of the Christian communities worldwide in their agenda, Islamic actors draw attention to the plight of local Muslim communities, and Jewish organizations help their co-religionists both locally and transnationally. Social capital in this case is consolidated by the religious fraternity, and it links religious identity to collective action.

Religious states and Neoliberalism

Neoliberalism allows for a focus on economic and social issues in state-to-state interactions. It also permits studying religion as a force for understanding and reconciliation between states. Therefore, like Classical Realism and Neorealism, Neoliberalism can accommodate religious states. Contrary to the two strands of Realism, Neoliberalism is open to the investigation of the relationship between the religious states and institutions. This makes Neoliberalism significantly more conducive to the study of state–NGO interactions.

Faith-based diplomacy, state, and institutions

Neoliberals recognize the centrality of states to world politics, yet they acknowledge the influence of international institutions. States remain the main actors, yet, unlike Realists, Neoliberals are optimistic about the possibilities of cooperation. Neoliberals hold that "in a world politics constrained by state power and divergent interests, and unlikely to experience effective hierarchical governance, international institutions operating on the basis of reciprocity will be components of any lasting peace" (Keohane and Martin, 1995: 50). Therefore, both religious and secular states that are parts of religious arrangements and initiatives are of interest to Neoliberal scholars.

The concept of faith-based diplomacy builds on the faith-based conflict resolution literature (Abu Nimer, 2001; Appleby, 2000a; Gopin, 2000). Its proponents argue that religion can facilitate reconciliation between enemies, solidarity with the poor, and the overturning of unjust structures. Faith-based diplomacy emphasizes pluralism, inclusion, peacemaking through conflict resolution, social justice, forgiveness, healing collective wounds, and atonement. While much of this literature focuses on grassroots efforts, it also covers state-to-state interactions (Cox and Philpott, 2003). In her book *The Mighty and The Almighty,* the former secretary of state Madeleine Albright (2006) explains how the United States has not understood the motivations of religious states well enough. At the same time, Albright counts exemplary instances where faith played a key role in successful initiatives in American diplomacy. A famous example of faith-based peacemaking was orchestrated by President Jimmy Carter at Camp David in 1978, which would not have happened if Carter had not had the ability to "understand and appeal to the deep religious convictions of President Sadat and Prime Minister Begin," Albright argues (2006: 77).

Albright (2006: 177) also criticized the Bush Administration for its lack of recognition of religion's influence in non-Christian contexts:

> One of the many ironies of U.S. policy is that the Bush administration, for all its faith-based initiatives, is far more comfortable working with secular leaders than with those Iraqis for whom religion is central. This is true even when the religious leaders are moderate in orientation and generally accepting the U.S. goals.

Albright's (2006: 77) prescription for a more successful American diplomacy requires greater understanding of other religions by the state establishment:

> In the future, no American ambassador should be assigned to a country where religious feelings are strong unless he or she has a deep understanding of the faiths commonly practiced there. Ambassadors and their representatives, wherever they are assigned, should establish relationships with local religious leaders. The State Department should hire or train a core of specialists in religion to be deployed both in Washington and in key embassies overseas.

Faith-based diplomacy is also consistent with the Transnational Religious Movements category. In this sense, faith-based diplomacy fits perfectly into the Neoliberal framework which recognizes the need for institutions to ensure that commitments are honored. Studies of faith-based diplomacy, which aim to integrate religion into statecraft and to merge the official political channels with the spiritual ones, may be conducted from an institutionalist perspective.

Another advantage of employing the Neoliberal framework is that a state does not need to be "religious" in order for scholars to explore the faith-based initiatives and influence of Track II diplomacy in transnational dealings. One example of a religious institution facilitating diplomacy is the Vatican's role in the resolution of the dispute between Argentina and Chile in 1978 over the Beagle islands, a cluster of small islands in South America. The Vatican, which was recognized as a supreme moral authority by the populations of both states, played two key roles (Laudy, 2000: 293). First, it defused the military crisis by bringing parties to the negotiation table. Second, it crafted a six-year process that allowed the parties to build trust and grapple with sensitive issues.

Similarly, prominent religious figures often play the role of mediator in sensitive situations. One such example is the Anglican churchman Terry Waite, who was an assistant for Anglican communion affairs to the Archbishop of Canterbury. Waite negotiated hostage releases with post-revolutionary Iran, Libya, and Islamic Jihad (Lloyd, 2011: 229). Religious institutions and individuals play a crucial role in defusing crises and restoring stability, and such instances can be investigated within the Neoliberal framework.

Another major example of faith-based initiatives is the role of the evangelist Moral Rearmament Movement, now known as Initiatives of Change-International, in bringing together German Chancellor Konrad Adenauer and French Foreign Minister Robert Schuman in the aftermath of the Second World War. Johnston (2003: 18) argues that "this process effectively prepared the way for the later establishment of the European Coal and Steel Community." One might contest the extent of the influence of this movement in regional integration and the establishment of the European Union. Yet the movement provided a safe space for two rival powers in a highly sensitive environment. In short, even in interstate arrangements that are primarily secular, there can still be a religious dimension.

Transnational religious actors and Neoliberalism

Neoliberalism's recognition of non-state actors such as multinational companies and NGOs implies that it can include transnational religious networks. The concept of *transnational interactions* that is at the core of Neoliberal thought is defined as "the movement of tangible or intangible items across state boundaries when at least one actor is not an agent of a government or an intergovernmental organization" (Nye and Keohane, 1971: 5). Transnational religious movements ranging from Al-Qaeda to the Red Cross take part in these transnational interactions at least as much as the Ford Foundation. With the changing scope of governance thanks to the advances of technology, religious actors take part in global civil society, transcending the distinction between the domestic and the international. Individuals, who share the same religious conviction around the world, come together to challenge the premises of the traditional state structure. In the words of Keohane and Nye (1998: 83),

> earlier transnational flows were heavily controlled by large bureaucracies like multinational corporations and the Catholic Church. Such organizations remain important, but the dramatic cheapening of information transmission has opened the field to loosely structured network organizations and even individuals.

Religious institutions connect with each other to realize their local and transnational objectives. Although it is perhaps too early and certainly controversial to say that these movements are mature enough to provide an alternative mode of governance, they are clearly too strong and widespread to be excluded from theories of international relations. The Neoliberal framework can account for them by looking at the role of non-governmental organizations in faith-based diplomacy, the role of religious transnational civil society in politics, and finally the religious terrorist groups in the market of ideas.

NGOs and faith-based diplomacy

In addition to states which engage in faith-based initiatives, non-governmental organizations that focus on issues of spirituality can be studied in the context of Neoliberalism. Johnston (2003: 14) argues that religious actors have the upper hand in peacemaking and negotiations due to a well-established influence in the community; a reputation as an apolitical force for change based on a respected set of values; leverage to reconcile the parties; and the capability to mobilize national and international support for peace. Religious actors also have access to a number of tools that are not available to their secular counterparts, such as praying, fasting, and references to scripture.

The Catholic lay organization Sant'Egidio played a facilitating role in the talks between the governments and insurgents to end the civil war in Mozambique. The Vatican itself, especially due to the symbolism of Papal visits to conflict-ridden settings, has played a crucial role in international diplomacy. Acholi Religious Leaders Peace Initiative, Pax Christi, and World Vision, along with local religious leaders, played a critical role in facilitating the peace process in Northern Uganda that would bring an end to Lord's Resistance Army attacks on civilians (Marshall and Van Saanen, 2007: 21). There is also an increasing level of inter-faith cooperation in humanitarian activism. Recognizing the importance of representation, the International Council of Voluntary Agencies included the Islamic Relief Organization and the Islamic African Relief Agency in its networks (Lynch, 2000).

Transnational civil society and religion

Religious actors constitute a transnational civil society (Rudolph, 1997) and they take part in Transnational Advocacy Networks (Keck and Sikkink, 1998). While Classical Realism and Neorealism only permit the study of those organizations if their policies have a direct impact on a state's survival or foreign policy, Neoliberalism has no such constraint. Neoliberalism recognizes multiple linkages in the international public sphere.

Faith-based non-governmental organizations have been especially influential in rural settings around the world, where spirituality, faith, and connecting to the sacred in nature are integral parts of people's lives (Narayan et al., 2000: 222). The largest alliance of Catholic Development Agencies, Coopération Internationale pour le Développement et la Solidarité, has a budget of more than US$950 million. Other Christian development agencies including APRODEV, and World Vision International, each have budgets of hundreds of millions of dollars (Clark 2003: 134).

The activities of these non-governmental organizations ranged from educational initiatives to fighting climate change. The World Council of Churches brought together members of faith-based communities with its 'A Spiritual Declaration on Climate Change' (2005). Similarly, in 2006, close to 100 evangelical leaders drafted "Climate Change: An Evangelical Call to Action" (Toly, 2009: 411). In addition to religious organizations, religious movements filled in the gaps in the developing world. Pentecostalism has growing numbers of adherents in Brazil, Nigeria, Guatemala, Chile, Korea, China, and the Philippines, providing the disillusioned populations in particular with social projects and a personal religion that emphasizes hope and inspiration.

Transnational religious actors also spread their ideology through organizational initiatives or missionary activities. The World Muslim League (based in Saudi Arabia), The World Islamic Call (based in Libya), and the African Muslim agency (based in Kuwait) fund local schools which promote conservative strands in Islam such as Wahhabism and Salafism. A Turkish version of the formation and consolidation of Islamic educational networks is carried out by the Gulen Movement, especially in Central Asia. Unlike its conservative counterparts, the Gulen Movement has not challenged the modernization process but has tried to raise a new form of Islamic consciousness that has roots in the Turkish and

Ottoman experience (Yavuz, 2003: 21). Similarly, the Catholic Church sponsors more than 172,800 educational institutions around the world and operates approximately 105,100 social welfare institutions (Weigel, 1999). The expansion of such social and educational religious networks inevitably brings a concomitant desire to create a religious political and economic sphere. This desire and its manifestations can be investigated through a Neoliberal lens.

Religious terrorist groups and the market

Finally, terrorist groups may be regarded as organizations that aim primarily for survival in a competitive market space of ideologies and movements. That is, Neoliberalist thought can examine them and their agenda in the context of transnational actors. Stern and Modi (2007: 22) state that "the inputs of the terrorist product are not unlike the inputs of products manufactured by corporate firms in that both include capital, labor and a branding or 'mission'." They have control over certain sectors to finance themselves. They compete and cooperate with each other in an attempt to maintain their financial power and reputation. Each terrorist group has its own channels of financing. There are established links among drug smuggling, fraudulent sale of petty goods, and generation of revenue for groups ranging from FARC (Revolutionary Armed Forces of Colombia) to Al-Qaeda (Biersteker and Eckert, 2007: 5). Afghanistan's poppy crops, which the United Nations says constitute as much as 86 percent of the world's opium supply, are widely considered a major source of terrorist funding (Kaplan, 2006). These mechanisms have direct relevance to international politics.

Another point of interest is the effect terrorism has on the economies of its target countries. Terrorist attacks negatively affect financial markets and the local industries. This phenomenon is not limited to religious terrorism. However, given that a number of religious terrorist organizations voiced their desires to bring down the economies of target countries, the issue is relevant to the studies of religion and international politics. Enders and Sandler (2005: 2) note that protective actions taken by rich countries shifted the targets to less developed countries that cannot afford those protections, such as Egypt, Indonesia, Morocco, and Kenya. However, given the multiple linkages among the states, the link between terrorism and the damage to the global economy cannot be underestimated.

Transnational religious issues and Neoliberalism

Unlike the accounts of Classical Realism and Neorealism, Neoliberalism is open to the discussions of economics and social issues due to their impact on the market. Therefore, when we focus on a transnational issue that cannot be accommodated in conventional security frameworks, Neoliberalism is a more suitable theoretical perspective. Admittedly, the universe of transnational issues cannot be fully captured in this section. We believe that the issues we identify – Economic Development, Human Rights, Scientific Research, and Missionary

Activities – are the ones that occupy a significant portion of the scholarly agenda and they serve to demonstrate how other issues can be accommodated within this framework.

Religion and economic development

Economic development is one of the main transnational issues in which religious actors took interest. For a long time, "materialistic determinism" and "secular reductionism" did not allow faith and spirituality to play a role in explaining institutional behavior (Luttwak, 1994). In the post-Cold War public sphere, with the help of NGOs, international development started to be analyzed from a faith-based perspective. The World Faith Development Dialogue (WFDD) was established in 1999 as a charity organization. In 1997, the World Bank established a small "Directorate on Faith" within the Bank. Although the World Bank has kept its distance from actual faith-based initiatives, the World Development Reports paid special attention to the participation of faith institutions and leaders in poverty-reduction strategies. Cooperation among the faith and development institutions in Guatemala, Ethiopia, and Tanzania under the leadership of WFDD and the World Bank showed that spirituality was an integral dimension of transnational efforts to provide education and health services (Marshall and Van Saanen, 2007: 10).

The Millenium Development Goals, which were declared by the United Nations General Assembly in 2000, have been seen as a contract with spiritual significance (Marshall and Keough, 2004: 4). These goals focused on environmental sustainability, gender equality, maternal health, global partnership, universal education, ending poverty and hunger, as well as combating AIDS/HIV. These targets are issue areas that religious NGOs had already been emphasizing in developing regions.

When investigating development issues and the religious discourse surrounding them, one should also note the symbolic significance of the Jubilee 2000 movement, composed of 40 countries that rallied for the cancellation of the third world debt. The name was derived from Leviticus (25:10): "You shall thus consecrate the fiftieth year and proclaim a release through the land to all its inhabitants. It shall be a jubilee for you, and each of you shall return to his own property, and each of you shall return to his family." British Chancellor of the Exchequer of the time, Gordon Brown, described the Jubilee movement as the most important church-led initiative since John Wesley and William Wilberforce's campaign to outlaw slavery in the eighteenth century (reported in Wallis, 2005: 271). This demonstrates that religion can also constitute a forum for those protesting the inequalities in the existing market system. More recently, Friedlander (2011), a Muslim chaplain, has noted the importance of the support of the religious actors in the Occupy Wall Street movement, a series of demonstrations protesting social and economic equality. It is indeed difficult to underestimate the power of religious organizations in rallying disenfranchised citizens and providing the protest movements with religious legitimacy.

The link between religion and development may also be an intrinsic one. Recent research, inspired in part by Weber's classic Protestant Ethic argument, suggests that religious denomination, religious belief, and religious practices all influence economic performance and economic choices (Barro and McCleary, 2003; Hillman, 2007; Kuran, 2004; McCleary and Barro, 2006; Scheve and Stasavage, 2006). Similarly, economic development targets embedded in religious doctrines usually bring an environmental-friendly approach and a focus on the protection of resources. Saniotis (2011), for example, emphasizes the Islamic view that nature is sacred, human beings are stewards of nature, and, even in times of war, close attention should be paid to protecting natural resources. Environmentalism exists in all traditions, and even secular environmentalists have started to tap into these religious resources (Gottlieb, 2006: 90). In fact, today's secular environmental and human rights movements exhibit similar characteristics to religious movements and they usually have religious foundations (Benthall, 2008). In sum, issues of development and environment will inevitably link to dynamics of religious politics, and Neoliberal scholars need to take this connection into account.

Religion and human rights

Human rights also have long been at the forefront of the international agenda. Although views on the concept of human rights vary from one faith tradition to another, religious activism has surrounded the initiatives and discourse on human rights. For example, Evangelical Christians in the United States rallied for effective human rights monitoring and advocacy in the framework of American foreign policy by establishing "unlikely alliances" with Jewish and Christian organizations as well as secular entities (Hertzke, 2004).

While one might think that human rights should be among the issues upon which most religions agree, this is not always the case. There are controversial human rights issues which lead to heated debates across different traditions. One example of this is abortion. Is abortion a woman's right to control her body, or is it a violation of the rights of an unborn? Although this may not at first glance seem to be an international issue, activism on the issue is clearly transnational. In the Cairo conference, which aimed to discuss all methods of population control and to devise a more female-friendly definition of human rights, the Catholic Church used its status as permanent observer to delay the discussion of reproductive rights and to mobilize sympathetic states (including Saudi Arabia and Sudan) against voluntary choice in family planning. This behavior led to frustration among other states to the extent that Egypt's population minister at the time, Maher Mahran, stated that "we respect the Vatican. We respect the Pope. But if they are not going to negotiate, why did they come?" (reported in Crossette, 1994). In addition to inter-faith alliances, there are also implications of this issue for violence. In her book on religious terrorism, Stern (2003) counts racist "Identity Christians" and extreme anti-abortionists among those who have used terrorism to further their cause. In short, abortion has been a politically and

religiously loaded subject both in local and international agendas. These clashing definitions of human rights and their implications for politics and the market
can be investigated within Neoliberalism.

Religion and ethics of scientific research

The role of religion in defining the borders of scientific – mostly medical –
research may seem somewhat remote from the Neoliberal agenda of international
relations. However, the transnational activism that surrounds the religious voice
on scientific issues suggests otherwise for at least two reasons. First, international religious actors cooperate to change the prevalent norms by forming a
transnational activist network (Keck and Sikkink, 1998) and overriding state
interests. In a Pew Forum poll conducted in 2005, approximately half (52
percent) of the opponents of stem cell research said their religious beliefs are the
biggest influence on their thinking.[2] Den Dulk (2007: 225) also reports that
"President Bush's 15 billion dollars to combat the global AIDS epidemic was
met with the demands by evangelical leaders to earmark a third of the funds for
abstinence education." Second, any constraint put on any line of research would
inevitably influence what is available in the market. That is, religious groups rallying around the stem cell research, evolution, or any other scientific debate have
a market-defining function.

One of the most controversial cases depicting the tension between the scientific community and the religious actors has been stem cell research and cloning.
Banchoff (2011, 2008: 281) draws attention to the diversity of ethical and religious opinions on the issue. While the Catholic Church and evangelical Protestant community are strict opponents of stem cell research, the Jewish
community, for the most part, is favorable to it, albeit with a limited public
policy impact. The Islamic approach is also permissive, yet there is no central
authority to declare this stance. The closest the Islamic community came to an
official perspective on this issue was a 2003 fatwa that permitted therapeutic
cloning, not awarding the early embryos the status that is given to human subjects (Walters, 2004: 19). With the UN-led meetings and conventions on cloning
and stem cell research, these issues created a political sphere for religious actors,
especially the Christian ones, which allied with states and other transnational
organizations.

The power of religious actors over education has also been the subject of
political debates. Members of the Creation Research Society, through their
descriptive and historically oriented publications, try to advance the creationist
agenda to replace the Darwinian understanding of evolution. The Institute for
Creation Research, a think-tank based on the campus of the right-wing Christian
Heritage College, had secured more than US$1 million by the 1980s (Moore,
1993: 49). The tension between the tenets of contemporary science and biblical
literalism led to a variety of questions such as the ability of a student to reconcile
the university's guidelines and deeply held religious beliefs. To illustrate,
Michael Dini, a professor of biology education at Texas Tech University, was

threatened with a federal investigation for not writing recommendation letters for anyone who would not offer "a scientific answer" to questions about how the human species originated (Dean, 2007). Given the transnational dimension of knowledge production and the impact of science on the market, these qualifications and trends are difficult to overlook in the Neoliberal framework.

Missionary activities

Another possible study of interest that is in the intersection of transnational issues and transnational religious actors is missionary activities. Some 350,000 Americans undertook missionary activities through major Protestant missionary agencies in 2001, eight times the number in 1996 (Moreau, 2004). Since missions are not discussed within the framework of "civil society," it has been difficult to find an appropriate scholarly framework to examine the issue (Gifford, 1998). What kinds of transnational linkages do missions provide? Given that they are transnational actors, how do they contribute to patterns of cooperation and development? How do the main actors, states, deal with their soft power in the marketplace of ideas? These are only some of the questions through which missionary activities can be integrated into an institutionalist framework.

Missionary activities, especially by Muslims and Christians, have caused considerable controversy. The issue is central to the discussions about religion, state and international relations since political authorities are often intolerant toward conversion and proselytizing efforts by others. As noted in Chapter 2, many states, including several Western democracies, place limitations on missionaries and proselytizing. Officials of the Orthodox Church of Russia have supported the restrictions on proselytizing by non-Orthodox religions. These officials pointed to the inability to compete with proselytizing currents in terms of the "Orthodox Church's lack of capacity, given the residual effects of the Soviet experience, to match the transnational resources that Catholic and Protestant groups can bring" (Prodromou, 2004:71). Nearly every Middle Eastern state prohibits proselytizing by non-Muslims. At the same time, missionary efforts have been seen as part of the "human rights" agenda and an integral dimension of the freedom to practice one's faith. Evangelical Christians lobbied for sanctioning abusive regimes, "thereby freeing Christians to practice their faith" and "opening doors to mission and relief efforts" (Den Dulk, 2007: 224). Woodberry (2012) argues that Protestant missionaries constituted "a crucial catalyst initiating the development and spread of religious liberty, mass education, mass printing, newspapers, voluntary organizations, and colonial reforms, thereby creating the conditions that made stable democracy more likely." These different understandings and approaches inevitably lead to tension between religious groups and states.

On another note, the extent of missionary activities throughout the developing world and the rise in the missionary participation in welfare provisions since the 1970s forced some policy-makers and scholars to question the relationship between a Neoliberal world order and the NGOs styled after missionary charities. Manji and O'Coill (2002) argue that missionary activities have been traditionally employed as a tool of social control of populations who were prone to anti-colonial movements. Missions, along with local NGOs, are indeed replacing the state machinery in a number of developing countries. Hearn (2002: 35) calls this process the "NGOisation of societies," which is a process that has involved foreign missions. The New Policy Agenda, which was the embodiment of Neoliberal economics, required that the state should withdraw from the public sphere to the fullest extent possible (Edwards and Hulme, 1995). In the developing world, this gap was filled by NGOs, churches, and missions. Missions are increasingly becoming part of the "multiple actors" of Neoliberalism by helping to create institutions and regimes.

Islamic charities and groups also engage in active spreading of various strands of Islam across the world. Some Sunni scholars "call upon Muslim immigrants to legitimize their presence in non-Muslim lands by acting as ideal Muslims; to build Muslim institutions such as mosques and charity organizations; to serve the political interests of Muslims worldwide; and to proselytize" (Shavit and Wiesenbach, 2009). Kroessin and Mohamed (2008) argue that Saudi charities which promote conservative ideologies have been wrongly stereotyped in the West, and that their commitment to religious ideologies is no different from those of similar Western organizations that also spread their own value systems. One may indeed argue that the market space of ideologies is competitive. The level of activism in Islam is gradually increasing in response to the Christian missionary efforts and vice versa. However, missionary activities are often seen as an infringement of sovereignty, a type of soft power that the state is not equipped to compete with. When it comes to issues of conversion there are no absolute gains, but only relative gains for religious actors.

Religious identity and Neoliberalism

One may argue that the issues discussed under the titles above may all be counted under the identity dimension as well. Worldviews are influenced by identity. Although multiple factors, like gender, family background, and social and economic status figure into the worldview of an individual, religion generally has a specific impact that can override other influences (Seul, 1999). Religious actors and movements, including states and NGOs, are distinguished from others by their emphasis on the centrality of faith dimension to their identity. In short, religious identity has a bearing in all of the sections above. However, identity, in terms of defining oneself and "the other," deserves special mention as a separate category. Similar to the effects of other elements of identity, the primary influence of religious identity is that it can help determine with whom one cooperates and competes. This section looks in particular at these patterns from different perspectives. Whereas the first line of enquiry focuses on *who* is "preferable" in social interactions, the second line focuses on *what* is preferable and what distinguishes one religious identity from others.

Religious identities defining the partner

Religious identity is an influential variable when choosing political and economic partners. Just as religious kinship can influence one's choice of allies and enemies in the politics of survival, it can also influence selection criteria in parallel spheres such as economic and social activities. Religious fundamentalism in the US has been linked with prejudice against blacks, women, homosexuals, and communists (Kirkpatrick, 1993; Laythe et al,, 2002). Beyond local politics, there are also faith groups that are eager to participate in foreign policy decisions. American evangelicals, for example, were called "powerful internationalists" because of their activism in "poverty, AIDS, sex trafficking, climate change, prison abuses, malaria and genocide in Darfur."[3] As they developed theologies of global engagement, Evangelicals started to become involved in power politics and building issue-based coalitions (den Dulk, 2007: 218). Although there is a diversity of opinions within the group, Evangelicals are reported to hold more negative views of Islam than other US Christians (Baumgartner et al., 2008). Similarly, support for political Islam has been linked to anti-American attitudes (Mostafa and Al-Hamdi, 2007). Thus, it is not only religious identity which influences with whom we are more likely to cooperate. The subgroups within a religion and the strength of one's belief also have an influence.

Ammerman (1994: 150) states that for fundamentalists, "all other knowledge, all other rules for living are placed in submission to the images of the world found in sacred texts and traditions." Although fundamentalists react to a modernization that comes at the expense of their own communal-traditional identity, they usually cannot escape state regulation (Marty and Appleby, 1991: 4). Along those lines, fundamentalist groups of all religions strive to create a public sphere for themselves where they deal mostly with each other. Even observant yet non-fundamentalist communities might be excluded. One example of this desire for separate spheres of communication is "kosher" search motors and facebook. Although the search motor (Koogle) no longer seems to be active, the kosher facebook, Faceglat, creates a space for religious Jews to interact within their own space. The founder, Yaakov Swisa (cited in Nahshoni, 2011), states that Faceglat also blocks indecent advertisements, and tracks the use of bad language and inappropriate content across the site.

The school system that was established by the Christian fundamentalists in the United States as an alternative to public schooling provides another example. Students from these schools succeed in standardized tests; yet they score poorly in evaluations based on critical judgment, which is a combination that directs these students to service jobs (Rose, 1998). This desire to limit interactions to those that are similar to oneself in the local sphere implies a similar desire to seek allies similar to oneself in the international sphere.

Religious identity also plays an influential – if not definitive – role in issues of regional integration. One of the most challenging cases in this respect has been Turkey's membership in the European Union. Although the official discourse for not granting membership to Turkey – a secular Muslim majority country – has focused on human rights issues, relationships with Greece, and the resolution of the Cyprus problem, many policy-makers and scholars articulated the argument of the European Union's being a "Christian Club" unwilling to admit a Muslim-majority country (Bac, 1998: 245). Even the Prime Minister of Turkey, Recep Tayyip Erdoğan, indicated that through Turkey's membership into the European Union "we will be contributing to the reconciliation of civilizations and the EU will prove that it is not a Christian club" (*Independent*, December 13, 2004). In short, religious identity may not be the only influence on regional arrangements but it has undoubtedly been a factor.

Religious identities defining the issues and terms of cooperation

Religious identity can be influential in defining the issues and terms of cooperation. Every faith tradition has its own sources of peace-building, warfare, cooperation, and competition in the public sphere. These sources and the culture that accompanies them shape the agenda and communication styles in the political, economic, and social spheres. Religion has an influence on the culture of communication. This is one of the reasons why public diplomacy initiatives consider religious literacy to be one of their core goals to achieve among policy circles.

Cultural differences accompanied by or enshrined in religious differences influence modes of communication and cooperation. Polkinghorn and Byrne (2001) in a study of individual behavior find that Jews, Christians, and Muslims have different conflict-management styles. To give a linguistic example, Abu Nimer (1998: 109) reports that participants in inter-faith initiatives noted that the usage of "I" (ana) in Arabic is regarded as inappropriate in public dealings, and the person who refers to himself/herself would be regarded as self-centered and individualistic.

In addition, what is regarded as integral to the identity may be expressed in political and economic life, which may, in turn, affect the level of adaptability or development in a society. Powell and Rickard (2010), for example, find that countries with Islamic legal traditions have lower average levels of total trade when compared to their secular counterparts. Similarly, Kuran (2004) argues that several aspects of Islamic law have slowed down economic growth in Muslim countries. Islamic laws of inheritance have inhibited capital accumulation. In addition, a combination of the absence in Islamic law of the concept of a corporation, the weaknesses of civil society, and the *waqf* (Islamic charitable foundation) system locked vast resources into unproductive organizations for the delivery of social services. All of these institutions arguably led to the human capital deficiencies and institutional stagnation evident in the Middle East. However, these findings are not uncontested. Norris and Inglehart (2004: 167–168) find that Muslims have the strongest work ethic of any religious denomination. Other studies find that economic growth is higher in countries with larger Muslim populations (Noland, 2007; Sala-i-Martin et al., 2004).

Unlike some strands of Protestantism which emphasize individual entrepreneurship, Islamic economic literature focuses more on collective arrangements and economic justice, even when it comes at the expense of the economic adaptation and competition that is required of societies, especially in the post-industrial revolution world. The implications of this focus are still debated. The relationship between Protestantism and the capitalist system has been widely recognized thanks to the legacy of Weber's (1905) *The Protestant Ethic and the Spirit of Capitalism*. Despite its popularity, the Weberian thesis has been challenged numerous times with the argument that the capitalist institutions actually preceded the Protestant reformation (Samuelsson, 1993; Tawney, 1926).

When it comes to issues of war and peace, most religions have diverging perspectives depending on the issue. Attitudes toward war and peace can shift over time within a religious tradition. That being said, some traditions have distinguished themselves from others by their consistent practices and theologies. This differentiation almost led to the creation of a niche for these religious groups in world affairs. One of the prominent examples of such a link between religious identity and a universally recognized niche is the case of Quakers and mediation practices. Quakers, also known as The Religious Society of Friends, are renowned for their social activism and pacifism. They believe that there is no justification for the use of arms even when someone is confronted with evil. Traditionally, this basic premise has led the Quaker organizations like the American Friends Service Committee to play the role of mediators in conflicts including the Israeli–Palestinian case (Gallagher, 2007; Lamy, 2011).

In short, although religious identities are already implied in all the categories that have been explored above, we need to re-emphasize that they give meaning to who we are and contribute to the boundaries of communities. Each religious community has its own modes and preferences when it comes to political interactions. These multiple preferences and linkages have implications that are within the scope of the Neoliberal paradigm.

Religion and (Neo)Liberalism: interactions within the market

In this chapter we investigated the linkages between religion and Neoliberalism. Due to Neoliberalism's relative flexibility in the diversity of actors, it is especially open to the study of transnational religious actors and non-state religious actors. Unlike Classical Realism and Neorealism, Neoliberalism emphasizes that due to the multiple linkages among actors, it is not realistic to separate security from economics or social issues. This makes possible the study of interactions between religion and economic development, human rights, and even the ethics of scientific research within the Neoliberal framework.

Neoliberalism also allows a number of approaches to the study of religion and international affairs. Religious identities may be explored through constructivist methodologies while preferences and decision-making mechanisms can benefit from game-theoretical approaches. Since there is considerable overlap between Neoliberal studies and economics, most Neoliberal studies of religion and politics would also benefit from methodologies and terminology employed by the economists.

6 Religion and the English School
Interactions within international society

The English School, also known as the International Society School or British Institutionalism, is a perspective located at the intersection between Realism and the utopian Liberal worldview in international relations. While recognizing that anarchy is a reality of international relations, the English School theorists see the states as parts of an "international society" that shares basic norms and understandings. The English School borrows from the Realist theory; yet it follows a distinct trajectory that builds on international legal norms in a constructivist fashion. These norms lay the basis for the interactions in an international society. Despite having a long intellectual history, the theorists of this perspective did not put themselves into a separate analytical category until relatively recently; the first reference to the English School was made by Roy Jones in 1981.

The organizing concept in the English School, "international society," may be defined as the "habitual intercourse of independent communities, beginning in the Christendom of Western Europe and gradually extending throughout the world" (Wight, 1966: 96). Hedley Bull (1977: 13), a prominent English School theorist, holds that:

> a society of states exists when a group of states, conscious of certain common interests and common values, form a society in the sense that they conceive themselves to be bound by a common set of rules in their relationships with one another, and share in the working of common institutions.

In short, the English School perspective accentuates the commonalities and possibilities of cooperation within the boundaries of an agreed-upon system whereas Realism focuses on competition for survival and power.

International society, as a concept, goes back to Hugo Grotius, a seventeenth-century Dutch theologian and jurist. Grotius is regarded as one of the founders of contemporary international law. Given that international law has theological origins, religion is already a part of the English School perspective. Among the prominent theorists of the English School are E.H. Carr, J.A.W. Manning, Martin Wight, Hedley Bull, Gerrit Gong, Adam Watson, John Vincent, and James Mayall. These scholars of the English School focus mainly on issues of human rights, moral roots and implications of international interactions, intervention, international order, and justice. This emphasis renders the English School one of the most suitable frameworks for the analysis of religion, international legal frameworks, and world orders.

The English School has often been regarded as a "via media" (middle way) between power politics and cosmopolitanism. Martin Wight's three traditions – Revolutionism, Rationalism, and Realism – have helped theorists situate the English School among contemporary international relations perspectives. In Wight's reformulation of international relations theories, religion plays an influential role. The first category, the Revolutionists, believe in "the moral unity of the society of states" (Wight, 1992: 8) and among them are the religious Revolutionists of the seventeenth century. The second category, the Rationalists, believe that reason is "superior to and independent of sense perceptions" and that it guides human beings in their political interactions. Highlighting the theological history of rationalism, Wight (1992: 13) notes that:

> Aquinas is a rationalist when compared to Augustine, because Augustine asserted the primacy of faith over reason, while St. Thomas asserted that faith and reason were two specifically different kinds of assent, and religion and science two distinct species of knowledge, and therefore the objects of science cannot be the objects of faith.

The third category, Realism, is a "a conscious break away from the theologico-ethical Rationalism dominant in the Middle Ages and equally from the latent Revolutionism which ran back to the origins of Christianity" (Wight, 1992: 17). Wight even argues that parts of Hobbes' Leviathan constitute an attack on the Roman Catholic Church and "its universal suzerainty over sovereign states." With their emphasis on facts rather than obligations, the Realists tried to put a distance between their thought and the theological bases of political interactions.

Wight's three categories provided the English School with a map, but there are still discussions about the English School's location and centrality in this scheme. Bull (1977: 41–42) says that none of the three categories can depict the state of world affairs fully and these traditions are not to be used at the expense of one another. Jackson (1996: 213) similarly asserts that the English School is inclusive of all three views, yet "rationalism" is "at the heart of this relationship." Regardless of the place of the English School, the religious roots of all the categories point to the impossibility of separating the religious and the political. This is even true of Realism, given that it was a reaction to the employment of theological premises in politics.

The tension between justice and order has been at the forefront of the English School agenda. This debate also raises the question of "units of investigation" in international relations. Although states are the main units in the English School framework, there is also an intellectual trend toward recognizing individuals as the units of interest and human rights as the main concern. International Society theorists hold that "every member of the world's population is conceived as possessing equal rights as human beings – human rights – regardless of the country they happen to live in. But they also see human rights at the present time as still subordinate to the rights of sovereign states" (Jackson, 1995: 111).

If *order* is the governing principle, then it is to be expected that sovereignty will be the primary value in international society. If *justice* comes first, however, then individuals' rights should take precedence over sovereignty in most cases. This division in perspectives resulted in two central strands within the English School: the pluralists and the solidarists. Whereas the former emphasize the importance of sovereignty and the principle of non-intervention, the latter advocate a greater focus on human rights. This division may also be seen as representing the subgroupings under the world order. For example, Linklater (1998) divides the world order into three spheres: a pluralist society of states where states do not share common interests or values; a solidarist society of states where states share common moral principles and values; and finally an embryonic post-Westphalian community centered on Europe where societies "establish closer forms of political cooperation to integrate shared ethical norms into the structure of social and political life." As we discuss below, this debate has important implications for the role of religion and ethics in international affairs.

Religious worldviews and the English School

The English School has largely focused on the possibilities of belonging to a world society and the universal morality shared by all human beings. Shared worldviews define the structure of international relations. English School scholars have also expressed the view that international society and the worldviews it takes as departure points have been predominantly European. International society formed along the religious lines at a time when the Ottoman Empire refused to participate – or was not welcomed – in the establishment of today's European system (Watson, 1987: 78). Although the English School framework has mostly been influenced by the Judeo-Christian tradition, it is possible to argue that other religious traditions have also had an impact on contemporary debates on the human condition and perspectives within this theoretical framework. These other religious traditions may be found within the shared moral traditions that English School theorists posit to be dominant in international society. They may also be seen as seeking to alter or challenge the dominant moral regime.

We examine two ways in which the English School tradition can analyze religious worldviews. The first focuses on the study of morality and ethics as a field of investigation, and how these shape attitudes toward international society. The second is through studying the interactions between different value systems and worldviews.

The study of ethics as a field of investigation

Some English School theorists claim that ethics and morality can be objectively studied, since each of them is a system of rules which influences the worldviews of policy-makers. Pointing to the possibilities of using positivist methodologies, Bull (1979: 180) averred that "the moral issues that arise in world politics are always capable of being subjected to rational investigation.... Much moral argument is about the definition of the rules and their logical relationships to one another." That is, morality, which is considered in the realm of the emotional and spiritual, can be explained by logic.

Arguably, the rational analysis of ethics and morality brought religion into positivist international relations. The question of how religion shapes ethics which, in turn, shapes worldviews falls within the English School. One such contemporary example is the "ethics of immigration reform" in American politics, which has been discussed within a Christian framework. Douglas (2010) reports:

> Arguing for a comprehensive immigration package with a guest-worker program, Richard Land, the president of the Southern Baptist Convention's Ethics and Religious Liberty Commission, quoted from Matthew, Leviticus and Micah in pressing for action on the estimated 11 million illegal immigrants currently living in the U.S.

Ethics advocacy based on scripture is not limited to the religious leaders. Lamar Smith, a Republican representative from Texas, explained his position to the House Judiciary Subcommittee on Immigration, Citizenship, Refugees, Border Security and International Law with a quote from Romans 13:1–7 that justified strict enforcement of existing federal immigration laws: "Let every person be subject to governing authorities" (reported in Douglas, 2010). Such advocacy based on religious discourse is seen in most political settings around the world.

Appleby (2008) shows that ethical convictions played a central role in the Catholic lay movement Sant'Egidio's activities in Africa, Buddhist human rights activism in Cambodia, as well as across various Sunni and Shi'ite groups in the Middle East. Vinjamuri and Boesenecker (2008) investigate how religious ethics leads to a particular conception of peace, especially in transitional justice in the form of truth commissions and war crime trials, using cases ranging from South Africa to East Timor. That the World Bank has recently started cooperating with religious actors on the ground, albeit on a small scale, similarly shows that religious ethics fills the gaps which a secular agenda cannot fill.

Even when it is not publicly acceptable to conduct religious discussions on policy issues, ethics can be the discursive vehicle that mediates the religious dimension in the political sphere. That is, the study of ethics as a separate field of investigation in international politics can open many doors even in contexts where the study of religion and politics may create challenges.

Tensions among religious worldviews in international society

The contemporary understanding of world order could be interpreted as a predominantly Christian one, yet this has not always been the case. Wight (1992: 8)

counted seventeenth-century religious Revolutionism among the influential perspectives toward the world order. At that time, the Protestants and the Catholics
were frustrated with the existing corrupt world order.

> The Protestant Revolutionism found its classic expression in the Calvinists,
> the Catholic in the Jesuits.... It is well known how the political philosophy
> of the Calvinists and the Jesuits developed along similar lines, and how each
> approximated to the other, with theories of power based on popular consent,
> of the right of resistance against royal governments and of tyrannicide.
>
> (Wight, 1992: 8)

These religious perspectives toward politics flourished at a time of tension when
there were questions about the lines along which world politics should be
constructed.

When compared to Classical Realism, Neorealism, and Neoliberalism, the
English School has considerable potential to systematically account for the tensions and clashes between different worldviews as expressed by value systems
and legal frameworks. Although Bernard Lewis (1964: 115) once noted that
"foreign policy is a European concept" that does not have a counterpart in the
Islamic tradition, studies of contemporary interpretations of law and international
relations prove otherwise. For example, Piscatori (1986) underscores a long
history of diplomacy between Islamic actors and the consistent set of policies
developed within Islamic states and empires not only toward non-Muslims, but
also toward different power centers in the Islamic nation, ummah. However,
throughout their interactions with the others, religious communities might
emphasize different values. Mazrui (1990: 22) asserts that the U.N. Charter has
the Christian message of peace and love, whereas the Islamic ethical framework
rests on justice. Although certain international norms that are embedded in the
framework of international organizations may look too commonsensical, they
are not perceived as such around the world. Different actors have different
understandings of world order, which they similarly perceive as natural and
commonsensical. To illustrate, for Ayatollah Khomeini, revolution in Iran was
only the first phase of a world Islamic Revolution. According to Khomeini, the
Revolution was to be spread by non-violent means because it was "self-evident"
and thus did not require enforcement (Hashmi, 1996: 23).

With its emphasis on ethics, law, and morality, the English School is also an
ideal framework to compare visions and theories of human behavior and moral
precepts. The core assumptions of the English School, very much like Classical
Realism, have been expressed in religious terms. Butterfield (1950: 51), for
example, noted that "Providence produces a world in which man can live and
gradually improve their external conditions, in spite of sin." This assumption not
only shows the optimism the English School holds for the possibility of an international order; it also allows for the theological interpretations for political attitudes. Wight (1936: 20) similarly called attention to the breach of ethics in the
public sphere by saying that "it is a sin to kill a man, but it is no less a sin to

keep him alive in the British prisons in India, the concentration camps in Russia, the ghetto of Germany or in the perpetual misery of unemployment." Scott Thomas maintains that Wight's anti-imperial stance and his focus on development issues make his work "an important point of departure for studying Europe's relations with the Islamic world today." Therefore, this line of study would also benefit the critical studies of international development and colonialism.

In the end, the colonial experience has had a tremendous impact on the perceptions, fears, and attitudes of the developing world. For example, Shahin (2007: 70) asserts that "many leading [Egyptian] Islamists have explicitly declared their commitment to democracy, but they frequently distinguish between democracy as a system of values and democracy as a policy instrument." Islamists tend to think that "the West has betrayed the modern humane ideals in its connection with the Muslim world, and the betrayal is best exemplified by colonialism and its lingering political and economic impacts" (Mentak, 2009: 119). The English School can offer more insights than Realism and Neo-liberalism with regard to colonialism and its impact on worldviews.

Many consider the English School a useful framework which can integrate multiple religions and moralities into political frameworks without degrading them as "irrational" or "irrelevant". Tibi (2000: 844) argues that to understand the relationship between religion and political order, a philosophical approach like Bull's is pivotal. Islamism, Tibi explains, "being the expression of Islamic revival should be conceptualized as mainly political rather than religious; the Islamic concept of order indicates precisely an ideological conviction rather than a religious belief, and presents a radical challenge to world order." As indicated above under "the study of ethics as a field of investigation," public manifestations of religion are taken seriously in the English School, without being represented as deviant or irrelevant.

In this vein, one may even argue that there are multiple sets of norms and visions of "international society" that pose a challenge to the existing west-centric system and the secular universalist understanding that foresees one universal civilization. Religious movements that set different rules and norms for international society are parts of the globalization trends that "show nothing so clearly as the continual reinterpretation of the cultural program of modernity; the construction of multiple modernities; attempts by various groups and movements to reappropriate and redefine the discourse of modernity in their own terms" (Eisenstadt, 2000b: 24). Reinterpreting these multiple modernities, Casanova (2011) indicates that the term may be used as an analytical framework that combines some of the universalist claims of cosmopolitanism with the recognition of the relevance of faith traditions in the emerging global order. Barnett (2011: 110) goes to the extent of stating that liberal cosmopolitanism itself may be regarded as a faith tradition, as belief in the divine, and transcendental values do not necessarily depend on the existence of a God. One can study these "multiple international societies," ideological patterns, and the possibility of a faith-sensitive cosmopolitanism under the auspices of the English School framework.

Zhang (2003) confirms this view in his work on how the English School, with its philosophical background and premises, became popular in China.

In Chapter 5, we stated that international organizations focusing on development have started to explore religious alternatives which might provide insights that escape secular frameworks. There are similar instances of secular institutions seeking alternative religious-legal interpretations or solutions to international problems. Muhammed Bejaoui, judge of the International Criminal Court, investigated the alternative readings of the 1980 to 1988 Gulf War and the possible solutions that could be derived from Islamic and international law. In the end however, Bejaoui stated that "one arrives at virtually same legal analysis of the 1980–1988 Gulf War whatever 'key' be used, whether that of public international law or that of Islamic law" (cited in Westbrook, 1993: 831). The effort shows that there are multiple legal frameworks which derive from religious worldviews, and which prove relevant to the discussions of current events. Comparative legal studies that reflect diverse religious worldviews, therefore, may be carried out under the English School umbrella.

In short, the English School framework does not marginalize religious worldviews and encourages their integration into public policy discussions. English School theorists see ethics and morality as relevant phenomena to international politics and recognize that religion is an essential source of ethics and morality. Using historical and sociological methods, the English School has studied compatibility and competition among religious worldviews as well as the implications of these intersections.

Religious legitimacy and the English School

Before examining how religious legitimacy may be situated within the English School framework, one should explore how the tradition defines legitimacy as a concept. Legitimacy is at the core of the English School to an extent that is not observed in other schools of thought such as Realism and Neoliberalism. Wight (1977:153) defines international legitimacy as "the collective judgment of international society about rightful membership of the family of nations." Similarly, Philpott (2001: 15) notes that "international constitutions prescribe the legitimate polities of an international society. A legitimate polity is simply one that the members of a society recognize as properly participating in the society." Vincent and Wilson (1993: 129) stress that "the principle of non-intervention no longer sums up the morality of the states" and further develop the concept of international legitimacy, consolidating its links with morality.

The English School framework considers international morality and legitimacy to be "the product of dominant nations or groups of nations" (Carr, 1946: 111). This constructivist understanding of legitimacy also implies that the dominant states' majority religion can potentially shape the expectations of other states which may not adhere to the same religious traditions. As explained below, the rules of legitimacy and the definition of morality have been intertwined, especially within the Christian tradition. Yet this does not mean that other religions are excluded altogether from contemporary interpretations of the English School.

We identify three main ways of thinking about religious legitimacy in this theoretical strand. The first is through the general norms of legitimacy and diplomatic culture that may have religious roots but have cross-cultural validity. These rules and norms of legitimacy, such as non-intervention, may be widely accepted yet are changing over time. The second is the way the West-centric order is regarded by the groups which object to this order and devise their own norms of legitimacy. The third approach is a region-based approach to international legitimacy, which reflects religious identity and worldviews within itself.

Diplomatic culture and religion

From an English School perspective, acceptable rules of conduct, even the precepts of morality that may be employed in the international sphere, are produced and reproduced by the states that dominate the system. Not all cultures and states have an equal voice in the establishment of international norms. Nardin (1999: 20) emphasizes the dialectics of international order, noting that "international society is not merely regulated by international law but constituted by it." The states that have an upper hand in the legislation of international law also define what is and what is not acceptable in international politics. The English School is at a crossroads when it comes to the recognition of multiple cultures and their potential contributions to the formation of an international society.

Even if not openly expressed, the English School's conception of religious legitimacy has relied on a Christian understanding of proper state behavior and diplomatic culture. This understanding may be observed in the core institutions of legitimacy in international society. Donnelly (1998: 21) says that "international legitimacy and full membership in international society must rest in part on standards of just, humane or civilized behavior." By the eighteenth century, international society had embraced four institutions that prescribed such behavior: international law, legitimacy, diplomatic dialogue, and use of force (Watson, 1992: 202–208).

One might argue that these four institutions, including legitimacy, have been theorized and defined primarily within the Judeo-Christian literature. Yet, these institutions have also been debated in other traditions and cultures. In other words, although each country has its particular tradition, one may argue that there is still a universal discourse to which even the most religious policy-makers resort when legitimizing their positions. For example, Jung (2001: 467) states that in Iran, "we can observe the struggle of an increasingly fragmented regime in which the competing forces try to justify their claims in an Islamic discourse about democracy, individual rights and the rule of law." Similarly, an increasing number of human rights organizations in the Islamic world, like the Egyptian Organization of Human Rights and Kowani (Indonesia), bring religious identity and the concept of human rights together. Islamists, like their counterparts in other religions, are increasingly using human rights discourse as human rights "have become part of a global lingua franca for advancing claims" (Chase, 2011: 71). In other words, the discourse on religious legitimacy is usually based on different interpretations of the same concepts (such as human rights and democracy), rather than on entirely different institutions.

Diplomatic culture also remains at the core of the English School framework's understanding of legitimacy. Bull (1977: 304) defines diplomatic culture as "the common stock of ideas and values possessed by the official representatives of states." The existence of such a culture does not guarantee that states will abide by it. Wiseman (2005) contends that with its 2003 invasion of Iraq, the United States "transgressed five norms of diplomatic culture that is widely accepted: the use of force only as a last resort, transparency, continuous dialogue, multilateralism and civility." The US tried to rationalize these transgressions with the claim that Iraq had WMDs and it had ties with Al-Qaeda. This discursive process shows that framing a threat under "clash of civilizations" which has the potential to threaten the international order may lead to a redefinition of norms in international society.

As we mentioned in the earlier chapters, references to God during the wars against Afghanistan and Iraq show that religious legitimacy has played an important role in justifying operations against Muslim majority countries. However, Bush was careful to be as inclusive as possible in his religious discourse. Barnes makes the following observations about Bush's discourse:

> While he readily invokes God, he carefully avoids mention of Jesus Christ, and he calls for tolerance of all faiths. His comments have been confined to four specific areas: comforting people in grief, citing faith's ability to improve lives, commenting on the mysterious ways of providence, and mentioning God's concern for humanity.[1]

Such a discourse may be interpreted as part of a desire to conform to the norms of international legitimacy which is expected to be devoid of specific religious imagery. One may argue that in the Westphalian order, no matter how "Christian" the norms are, religion cannot be openly employed as a cause of action. Even Western diplomatic culture, while recognizing a common stock of ideas at its center, is not tolerant of an exclusively Christian discourse. Recognizing this inclusive culture, President Barack Obama made numerous references to God in his inaugural address, yet stated that the Americans were "a nation of Christians and Muslims, Jews and Hindus and non-believers." By doing so, Obama "expanded substantially the diversity of faith and (right of conscience) that had been pronounced by his predecessors" (Slack, 2009: 788). This embrace of diversity is expected to be accompanied by a more sophisticated understanding of diplomacy. Farr (2008: 15) highlights the religious issues surrounding the US, ranging from the surge of religion in China to the changing dynamics of the Islamic world. He argues that US diplomacy should "treat faith as much as it does politics or economics." The English School provides policy-makers and scholars with a framework to integrate religion analytically into secular foreign policies.

Alternative understandings of legitimacy and international order

As would be expected, not every state or group has been satisfied with the contemporary norms of international society. The "revolt" of different traditions against an international order that has been defined in Christian terms raised debates among the English School scholars. The demarcation of "rogue states" and the regime change within them is actually a result of the changing norms and tensions within international society (Clark, 2005: 27). What is and what is not legitimate is being redefined, especially in the post-9/11 framework. This has led to a considerable level of concern among the English School theorists about the continuation of a stable international society. Dunne (2003: 316) reminds us of Hedley Bull's caution that "revolt against the West" and the great powers' free maneuvers can jeopardize the international order, and he cites four norm changes in the system: the emergence of a highly permissive understanding of self-defense; the acceptability of pre-emptive action even in the absence of an imminent threat; extending one justification for the use of force to others; and regarding domestic law as more important than international law. Even the Western world has started to reconsider the viability of traditional norms such as sovereignty and self-defense.

The debates on the acceptability of intervention have also been at the center of the English School perspective. While solidarists regarded human rights abuses as legitimate causes of intervention, pluralists prioritized "international order" and respect toward sovereignty. The latter believe that states have a duty not to intervene in each other's affairs (Bull, 1966: 63). The debates surrounding the legitimacy of intervention and the protection of human rights came to fore especially with the invasion of Iraq and the incidents associated with Abu Ghraib prison. The Muslim Public Affairs Council (2004) in the United States reported:

> The abuse of Iraqi prisoners in Abu Ghraib prison represents a growing trend in our culture that demonizes and dehumanizes Arabs and Muslims in general. This destructive attitude, which is creeping ever closer to the mainstream of American thought, authorizes and legitimates these appalling abuses. It suggests that the west, which is simply good, is at war with the Arab and Islamic worlds, which are simply bad, and stigmatizes Arab Americans and American Muslims. It conflates innocents with criminals, moderates with extremists, and progressives with fundamentalists, casting an entire culture and an entire faith as "the enemy."

The prison abuses raised questions of legitimacy that were intertwined with religious worldviews. Although Baathist Iraq under Saddam could not be regarded as a full-fledged Islamic state, the religious dimension started to dominate the agenda from the early stages of the operation. Even before the operation, there were officials who legitimized interventions or wars in religious terms. Lt. Gen. William J. Boykin, deputy undersecretary of defense for intelligence, stated that Islamic extremists hate the United States "because we're a Christian nation, because our foundation and our roots are Judeo-Christians.... And the enemy is a guy named Satan." When describing a US Army battle against a Muslim warlord in Somalia in 1993, Boykin had similarly stated that "I knew my God was bigger than his. I knew that my God was a real God and his was an idol" (quoted in Vries, 2003). In short, competing understandings of world order have shaped legitimization processes through public discourse in multiple settings across the world. Combined with military operations, these discourses arguably initiate a competition between the Christian world order and the others.

Religions and regional international societies

A region-based analysis of international society and legitimacy can accommodate religion. Different regions have different understandings of international norms; "the organization of regions, the capacity of regions to generate and promote ideas of global order, and the claim of different regions to be represented more fully and more equally are likely to play a central role in the coming struggle for global political legitimacy" (Hurrell, 2007: 146). Although multiple religious traditions are usually represented in the same region, one can make the case that region-centric accounts will reflect dominant religious values in that region. As Mayall (1995: 169) notes,

> the boundary between these separate regional worlds was seldom unambiguous, let alone impermeable; sometimes conflict across the line was deeply embedded – as in South-East Europe where the division between the Orthodox and Catholic worlds and between Christendom and Islam is often described by analogy to a geological "faultline".

Therefore, the region-based perspectives of the English School reflect distinct religious identities, worldviews, and understandings of legitimacy.

Although it might be counted under Realism or "the Copenhagen School," Buzan's theorization of the "sectors" can also benefit the English School framework as much as it does Realism. Buzan et al. (1997) distinguish among military, political, societal, economic, and environmental sectors, and how these sectors intersect in "regional security complexes." When explaining the cooperation patterns in Northern Europe, Etzioni (1965: 221) states that "there is no region in Europe and few exist in the world where culture, tradition, language, ethnic origin, political structure, and religion – all 'background' and identifying elements – are as similar as they are in the Nordic region." Such a region-based approach will inevitably include religion, and at the same time it would be more sensitive to different interpretations of the same religion. For example, the Middle Eastern understanding of Islam and the Southeast Asian public theologies are different due to varying parameters of political culture. The leader of Nah-datul Ulama and the first elected president of Indonesia, Abdurrahman Wahid, saw Islamic political legislation as a Middle Eastern tradition that is alien to Indonesia and advocated separation of religion and politics (in Esposito and Voll, 2000). No religion is a monolith and theological differences across regions cannot be underestimated. Although religion may indeed influence all five sectors, in any security complex it would be a major societal force that defines the borders of what is and what is not acceptable.

In summary, the English School can be employed to study the link between religion and legitimacy. How norms of legitimacy are created and consolidated is related to international understandings of morality. As noted above, the English School tradition already makes frequent references to the influence of religion on how legitimacy is interpreted.

Non-state religious actors and the English School

Within the English School perspective states remain the primary actors; yet the influence of the non-state religious actors is recognized. There are two central ways in which non-state religious actors can be included in the English School accounts: first, through the impact of religious institutions on political tradition, and second, through studying religious organizations that challenge the current state of international society.

Religious institutions and international society

The English School tradition recognizes that the propagation of norms and ideas has been facilitated by non-state religious actors. That is, as we discussed in more detail in the chapters on Classical Realism and Neorealism, religious actors often influence what is considered legitimate and moral. In so doing they can influence which policy options are considered viable by policy-makers. Within the English School context this may be seen as religious institutions influencing the norms of international society.

The Rationalist tradition, "the broad middle road of European thinking," has been developed by the Catholic Church, Jewish, and Arab thinkers as well as Protestants (Wight, 1992: 14). Philpott (2000) clarifies that the Reformation was a central cause in the consolidation of the modern state system. Being born out of religious dynamics, contemporary patterns of conflict and cooperation still reflect institutional preferences. Vallier's (1971) review of the Catholic Church's influence on world politics may also be investigated through the international society lens. The Catholic Church and its relationships with its local networks directly affect "domestic political developments, intergroup conflict or alliance, and cultural and symbolic meanings" (Vallier, 1971:490). This kind of a church–state relationship and the desire of the religious actors to have a say in the affairs of political institutions may be seen even in the context of apparently secular issues and contexts. Jansen (2000: 104) argues that "as well as practical collaboration, the churches and religious communities want to establish dialogue with the European Commission on the meaning, spiritual direction and ethical dimension of European unification and the policies developed in this context." Accordingly, studies that investigate the link between religious organizations and political authority fit well into the English School framework.

Religious leaders in a country or region can also lead a moral discourse on politics, especially when the credibility of the political leaders is at question. Among many such cases is the influence of the Anglican Church in sub-Saharan Africa. The Synod of Bishops of the Anglican Church of Southern Africa, representing Angola, Lesotho, Mozambique, Namibia, South Africa, Swaziland, St. Helena, and Tristan da Cunha, called on the national leaders to covenant with them "in a process of moral, spiritual, and economic regeneration, in which we seek to model our lives and our societies more closely on God's principles and purposes for humanity" (Ashworth, 2010). The synod also heavily criticized the President of South Africa, Jacob Zuma: "Democratic values are non-existent, greed is unbridled, and the recent revelations about President Zuma's sexual misconduct do not bode well for South Africa's future" (Ashworth, 2010). In such cases, religious institutions and leaders, be it churches, mosques, or any authority on religious matters, can link issues of personal morality to state morality and redefine state interests from a religious perspective.

Religious terrorist groups and international law

Bull (1977: 268–270) acknowledges that non-state actors exercise violence, which he calls "private international violence." Many terrorist organizations have a radically different vision of the world. They challenge the established norms of international order and the dominance of the West-centric state system. Mendelsohn (2009: 305), in his analysis of how international organizations respond to terror from an English School perspective, reminds us that jihadis "reject the principle of sovereignty" and "reject international law as antithetical to Islam." Mendelsohn also argues that following 9/11, a regime to prevent terrorism financing was established, which is consistent with the premises of the International Society; states come together to counter a threat which emanates from groups that do not recognize international law, and therefore are not vulnerable to sanctions or threats of exclusion from international society.

The difference in vision and the violent criticism of the political status quo have been increasingly manifested through multiple religious traditions. Sikh groups such as Babbar Khalsa and Dal Khalsa have sought an independent Sikh state called Khalistan (Land of the Pure) using multiple tactics, including bombings and assassinations. The 1985 bombing of an Air India plane which resulted in 328 fatalities has been attributed to Sikh terrorist groups. Terrorist groups that derive their principles from new religious movements, such as Aum Shinrikyo in Japan, have regarded themselves outside of the legal framework. Aum Shinrikyo, a cult that has members worldwide, carried out the deadly Sarin attack in

1995 in Japan. The group's leader, Shoko Asahara, was "inspired" by Christianity and Buddhism in devising his own interpretation of Armageddon and world order. These groups reject the currently dominant conception of international society in one way or the other. They all have their alternative visions of world order. The investigations that study these alternative interpretations and the influence of these extremist groups on the international society may be placed within an English School framework.

Religious states and the English School

Since the English School recognizes the importance of states and the role of "morality" in politics, religious states can comfortably fit into the framework. We identify three important paths to investigate religious states under the English School perspective. The first is the concept of moralities and state duties. The second is the influence of politics on religious norms and vice versa. The third is the study of religious states' desire for recognition in international society.

States and morality

The English School framework is based on a shared understanding of the duties of a state not only toward other states, but also toward the people. Religious doctrine influences how religious states conceive of their duties toward other states and people. Even in non-religious contexts, Carr (1946: 152) hypothesizes that morality shapes the conduct of state: "So long as statesmen, and others who influence the conduct of international affairs, agree in thinking that the state has duties, and allow this view to guide their action, this hypothesis remains effective." As discussed in more detail in Chapter 2, religion can often influence a statesman's conception of morality.

In the case of religious states, the influence of religion on this sense of "duty" becomes more obvious. For example, when discussing the threats that the Islamic Republic of Iran is facing, Iranian president Ahmedinejad stated that "firstly, they talked about change in the Iranian nation and the Islamic Republic, but later when they felt that they cannot do that, they proposed containment of the Revolution and imposition of restrictions on the Iranian nation." He later described Iran's active presence on the international scene a "task" and "duty" (Fars News Agency, 2010). Although resort to the divine may be observed even in the discourse of secular leaders, religious states remain the core actors that do not shy away from linking issues of law, morality, and faith. They attempt to change the rules of international society while trying not to lose their existing connections with it. Political leaders in religious states, in an attempt to justify a course of action, resort to moral discourse on a state level. In a meeting on nuclear weapons with his South Korean counterpart, for example, Israeli president Shimon Peres used similar religious discourse, calling Ahmedinejad "the world's greatest corrupter of morality" (Sofer, 2010).

Combined with the worldviews and legitimacy categories, religious states employ morality and matters of faith more comfortably in their discourse than do their secular counterparts.

Legal frameworks in religious states

Religious actors, especially within the context of religious states, reproduce legal understanding by interpreting religious law. On the one hand, religious legal frameworks can constitute a challenge to the unitary state concept. In his analysis of the Islamization of law in Indonesia, Salim (2008: 71) states that the Ministry of Religious Affairs gave relative autonomy to each religion, which later became a challenge for the state. On the other hand, religion might be intertwined with legitimacy. Religion legitimizes the state and the state gives legitimacy to a particular understanding of religion. Abdullahi An-Na'im (1990: 185) states that despite being derived from the Qu'ran and Sunna, sharia is not divine because it is the construction of Muslim jurists. Given that political and religious elites are very close to each other – and sometimes they are the same people – the interpretation of religion in a religious state is bound to be influenced by the politics of that state. To illustrate, Ahmed Tayeb, head of Al Azhar (one of the most influential institution in Sunni Islam) at the time, was a member of the Egyptian ruling National Democratic Party's (NDP) Policies Committee, which was chaired by the Egyptian president's son and possible presidential candidate then, Gamal Mubarak (Hassan, 2010).

The English School framework is also suitable for discussions on defining a religious state. Hindu nationalists have not agreed on a definition of a proper Hindu state, neither have their Jewish, Christian, or Muslim counterparts. The clash of different understandings of an Islamic state, for example, came under increasing scrutiny with the Arab Spring. Scholars and policy-makers see the Saudi model as unviable and even regard such integration of religion and state as a violation of Islamic law. Rachid Gannouchi, a prominent Tunisian Islamist in charge of the al-Nahda Party, asked,

> why are we put in the same place as a model that is far from our thought, like the Taliban or the Saudi model, while there are other successful Islamic models that are close to us, like the Turkish, the Malaysian and the Indonesian models, models that combine Islam and modernity?
>
> (Shadid and Kirkpatrick, 2011)

Libyan and Egyptian Islamists are similarly vying to define a contemporary Islamic state.

Convergence of religious law and international legal discourse occurs in multiple settings. For example, Hashmi (1999: 158) argues that most Muslims accept international law on behavior in war as compatible with Islamic rules, and are even influenced by them to the extent that the few remaining incompatible aspects of Islamic law are considered obsolete. Jewish discourse on the laws of war is more recent as it became a practical issue only with the independence of the State of Israel. While this discourse is still evolving, it is beginning to have a significant influence on the behavior of the Israeli Defense Force and, to a lesser extent, Israeli foreign policy (Cohen, 2005). These dynamics demonstrate that not only does religion influence politics, but also political norms can influence religious interpretation. The English School framework is conducive to the investigation of these two-way interactions.

Religious states and membership in international society

The fact that religious states are influenced by a religious doctrine does not necessarily mean that they do not seek to conform, or at least appear to conform, to widely accepted norms and rules in international society. Unlike many transnational religious actors, religious states' conduct of diplomacy is influenced by secular Western norms. Religious states care about how they are recognized and treated by other states. Sharp (2003: 482) explains how the ambassador-designate of the Islamic Emirate of Afghanistan to the Islamic Republic of Pakistan, Mullah Zaeef, operated as a link between the Islamic vision of the world and western international society. Employing the English School perspective, Sharp shows how the Taliban worked for international recognition as the legitimate government of Afghanistan. Sharp (2003: 486) also demonstrates that as an actor in this quest, Zaeef even sought American support for the Taliban's legitimacy, especially after the praise received by the group from the US due to the ban on poppy cultivation. In short, when investigating how a religious state conducts its formal diplomacy, the English School perspective can be advantageous when compared to Realism or Neoliberalism due to its emphasis on the legal dimensions of recognition.

Transnational religious actors and the English School

Transnational institutions, although not quite at the core of the pluralist accounts, are already integrated into international society perspectives. These studies of international movements and institutions may be perceived as a challenge to the state-based English School, but this is not necessarily the case. For example, Ralph (2005: 43) argues that the Rome Statute and International Criminal Court do not run counter to the international society perspective. To the contrary, they step in where states are unwilling or unable to carry out their duties. Ralph adds that the existence of these institutions show "the legitimacy of a world society that transcends the society of sovereign states." Being based on a legal framework, the English School has been accommodating toward transnational arrangements in order to remain relevant in today's world.

The transnational arrangements that have found their way into the English School are not limited to secular institutions and movements. Although many secular institutions have been seen as a natural part of international society, religious movements pose a special challenge in that they may not be willing to confine themselves to areas where states are unable to carry out their duties. Nevertheless, we identify two paths which can integrate transnational religious movements into the English School accounts: (1) through reinterpretation of international society in terms of ideational power; and (2) through critical theological analyses of the international order.

Religious movements as part of international society

Religious movements influence the legal and social norms in the system. Especially with the revolution in communication that recognizes no borders, states are not the sole defining actors of legal, political, or economic frameworks. The theorists of the English School recognized the power of such changes earlier in the twentieth century. Even Carr (1946: 229), an English School scholar who is also regarded as a Realist, acknowledged the transient nature of states when he said, "few things are permanent in history and it would be rash to assume that the territorial unit of power is one of them." Although the state has been the main actor in the English School perspective for some time, this focus has never been as steadfast as it was in the Realist schools of thought.

Religious movements can change norms through their ideational power, which can be more influential than military power. Brown (1995: 157) argues that "the only durable cement of nations cannot be coerced or purchased. Over the long haul, it is ideas that bind more than chains or bank accounts." Brown's ideational communities include Muslims, Catholics, and Jews, although he recognizes other possibilities such as pan-Arabism or Black ideology, which also have religious roots. Religions do not recognize national borders as natural (Mendelsohn, 2005: 55). The ideational communities created by religious traditions form a transnational network that can complement or override state-based arrangements.

The ideational influence of religious movements over legal frameworks and value systems may also be framed under the "soft power" concept, which intersects with the Neoliberal framework. Thomas (1999: 30), for example, uses the concept of soft power to argue that "transnational actors represent ideas whose time has come, ideas which increasingly shape the values and norms of the international system." Writing specifically on the English School, Thomas also reminds us that given the current outlook of the system, "international society" should be extended to account for the transnational activities of the Vatican, the World Council of Churches (WCC), and other social groupings which shape norms on indigenous people, human rights, environment, and development. For example, the WCC is leading numerous initiatives to alleviate poverty, protect the environment, and combat HIV transmission, all issues that extend beyond state borders. The WCC was also influential in forming a united voice against Apartheid. The Alliance of Religions and Conservation works with the UN and brings together the religious leaders of multiple faith traditions to create an environmental agenda. Church networks throughout Latin America have significantly influenced both development agendas and human rights regimes. In all, religious movements and institutions have been major players in setting up the rules for international society.

As would be expected, not all religious actors – even if they belong to the same faith tradition – share the same agenda. McDuie-Ra and Rees (2010: 29) argue that informal religious actors in the South are further marginalized when mainstream religious actors are integrated into international financial institutions. This marginalization leads to the exclusion of "the possibilities of transformative change and development alternatives." Such marginalization can be minimized by including scholars of religious studies in political discussions. Omer (2011: 29) argues that the scholars of religious studies are in a position to critically engage in debates on conflict transformation and peace-building. But similar to McDuie-Ra and Rees, she cautions that critical scrutiny "needs to be supplemented by a thorough exploration (and at times excavation and appropriation) of counter-hegemonic narratives, subaltern experiences, and minority opinions."

Religious movements and narratives can emerge as a protest against dominant political and religious strands. In some contexts, such as Africa and Latin America, movements like liberation theology came into being partly as a response to the domination theology of the colonizers. In parts of Asia, Christianity developed through indigenous communities – in Korea, for example, where the "main aggressor" was Buddhist Japan, Minjung theology (a version of liberation theology) is embedded in the contestation of Japanese dominance in the nineteenth century (Pieris, 2007: 264). These sophisticated theological treatments that are sensitive to different public theologies and alternative understandings may be studied under the English School.

Criticism of international society and alternative world orders

Although religious movements can complement existing state-based arrangements without necessarily challenging them, not all religious movements are willing to be "accommodated" in the existing system. The existence of revisionist religious movements that foresee alternative world orders is a challenge to the state system and pluralist international society perspectives.

Islamic groups have been among the most active networks to express views of an alternative world order and to implement these visions. Expressing an alternative world order does not require violence, but it is a clear challenge to the world order put forward by the English School. Tibi (2000: 845) believes that some Muslims foresee an entirely different world order, a *Nizam Islami* (Islamic system), which is different from a caliphate because it does not distinguish between the Sunni and the Shia. He argues that supporters of political Islam believe they will achieve world peace under the banner of Islam: "As the precursor of political Islam, Sayyid Qutb proposed international peace requires the establishment of hakimiyyat Allah (God's rule) on global grounds. This is an articulation of an Islamic internationalism with a bid for a related 'just' international order." Shani (2008) similarly discusses two conceptions of universality that the Western international relations theory has ignored. One is the *Umma* constructed by the Islamist discourse that is simultaneously critical of imposed elite secularism and the neofundamentalism of Salafis. The other is *Khalsa Panth*, the Sikh transnational community of believers. The absence of the latter from the critical international relations literature may be attributed to the colonial encounters, which divided Sikhism into the "twin narratives of" nationalism and world religion.

Similarly, the Christian Identity movement that is based on white supremacism advocates a world order centered on Europeans, very much against the underlying principles of the contemporary English School perspective. Millenarian groups, such as Aum Shinrikyo, have theologies that are based on a forthcoming battle and a purified world order. The Lord's Resistance Army in Uganda is another example of such apocalyptic groups. Its leader, Joseph Kony, claimed to be waging war on God's direct orders. These groups form networks across borders that constitute a challenge to international society as it is understood today.

This set of challengers to the existing international society highlights a significant theme that recurs throughout the discussion of religion in the English School. The English School posits that shared norms and morals shape the international system into something more ordered than the chaotic perspective of Realism. This system is defined largely by Western and Christian norms and morals but there is a recognition that other perspectives, including religious ones, interact with and influence this system. However, there is an implied recognition of a more radical alternative – that the currently dominant norms and morals are not accepted by everyone. This highlights the possibility that at some time in the future, a new international society based on different norms and morals will rise.

A religion-dominated perspective is certainly a viable candidate for such an alternative international society, as religions generally contain a set of norms and morals that can be the basis for this system. For example, arguably the Catholic Church dominated such an international society in Europe before the Reformation. It is unlikely that any such network will successfully replace the existing international society in the foreseeable future. However, these networks will likely influence it and cause it to evolve over time.

Transnational religious issues and the English School

The English School framework is a particularly suitable framework to study issues of human rights and intervention. Religion and its influence on the framing of individuals' rights fit perfectly into the English School perspective. Should states stay out of the human rights issues of other countries, assuming that each tradition has its own definition of individuals' rights and responsibilities? Or, do states have a responsibility toward human beings in other countries and traditions? These questions have been at the forefront of policy debates.

As noted earlier, the English School's solidarist and pluralist perspectives see these issues differently. Solidarists hold that "states that massively violate human rights should forfeit their right to be treated as legitimate sovereigns, thereby morally entitling other states to use force to stop the oppression" (Wheeler, 2001: 13). In other words, "states should satisfy certain basic requirements of decency before they qualify for the protection which the principle of non-intervention provides" (Vincent and Watson, 1993: 126). Issues of human rights have also been directly tied to legitimacy and membership in the international system:

> Human Rights now play a part in the decision about the legitimacy of a state in international society, about whether what it is or what it does is sanctioned or authorized by law or right. It is not now enough for a state to be, and to be recognized as, sovereign. Nor is it enough for it to be a nation-state in accordance with the principle of self-determination.
>
> (Vincent, 1986: 130)

Given the centrality of human rights in the English School, any policy decision or investigation that connects religion to human rights may be studied within this perspective. Quite a number of policy-makers have dealt with transnational human rights issues. Citizens also demand that their representatives intervene in sensitive situations abroad that have a human rights dimension. Barack Obama and his administration addressed a number of religion-related human rights concerns. These concerns range from the sentencing of the founder of the heterodox Islamic sect Al-Qiyadah Al-Islamiyah, Abdul Salam under Indonesia's blasphemy laws to the charging of 833 people under Pakistan's blasphemy laws from 1986 to 2006 (Stahnke, 2010). Similarly, Sayed Perwiz Kambakhsh, the young journalist who was sentenced to death for downloading an article about the rights of women in Islam, was secretly pardoned, partly thanks to foreign governments that had interceded with the Afghan authorities on his behalf (Reporters Without Borders, 2009). Scholars of both international relations and theology have drawn attention to the necessity of promoting religious freedoms as part of the foreign policy agenda (see Farr, 2008; Miles, 2004).

This framework can also address concerns of the Muslim citizens in the West such as the issues of profiling and discrimination against Muslims which have been at the forefront of debates in a number of countries. Ibrahim (2011) compares Muslim representation in the US and the UK. He concludes that although the UK has created space for the voices of Muslim citizens, the US still has a long way to go. Such debates of citizenship and human rights, which have important implications for transnational politics, may be conducted within the English School framework.

When discussing the issues of human rights, there is a need to address the definitions and qualifications of "rights" and "duties" within different religious frameworks. What constitutes an individual's right and what is regarded as a responsibility toward the divine are not clear-cut questions. For example, Tibi (1994: 289) notes that "in Islam, Muslims, as believers, have duties vis-à-vis the community (ummah), but no individual rights in the sense of entitlements." Tibi states that this is not going to change anytime soon, given that established scholarly institutions such as Al-Azhar or the Islamic Council (based in London) support Islamization programs which view human rights that fall short of embracing the standards of international human rights law.

At the same time, what one sees as a duty may be seen as a "breach of right" by the other. For example, in Denmark, a state that has traditionally been seen as "internationalist," there have been "heated exchanges about women, Islam and the wearing of the veil" due to the religious traditions of immigrants (Lawler, 2007: 115). Similarly, various religious traditions understand and frame issues of reproductive rights and abortion differently. As noted in Chapter 5, at the Cairo conference, which was a platform to discuss all methods of population control and introduce a more female-friendly definition of human rights, the Catholic Church used its status as permanent observer to delay the discussion of reproductive rights and to mobilize sympathetic states (including Saudi Arabia and Sudan) against voluntary choice in family planning. These legal discussions regarding religious rights and duties as well as their intersection with secular understandings of human rights can be systematized by English School theorists.

For some states, especially the religious ones, blasphemy, conversion, or inappropriate dress can constitute a crime against the divine. This raises a number of issues, including proselytizing and "protecting the unborn," which have been framed as a function of the duties toward the divine. Since there is no "universally accepted standard for judging the internal arrangements of states" (Brown, 2000: 99), the Western understanding and promotion of human rights may be seen as partial and intolerant. In addition to this issue of the imposition of Western value systems in non-Western contexts, there is also an issue of perceived Western hypocrisy regarding its own values. In the eyes of many in the Middle East and the Gulf region, the Abu Ghraib incidents, for example, have been cases of not only major human rights abuse but instances of Western hypocrisy when it comes to human rights (Wander, 2009).

In conclusion, the English School perspective is especially relevant where international law and religion intersect. This intersection is practically inevitable in the issue of human rights. This is why human rights constitute the primary linkage between the English School and transnational issues of religious origin.

Religious identity and the English School

There are three important possibilities for integrating religious identity into international relations theory which have not yet been addressed. The first involves the potential of international society to bring together different religious traditions by emphasizing commonalities rather than clashes. The second is the relationship among modernization, trajectories of development, and religion. The third is through the links among just war, religion, and international society. This third possibility is especially relevant, since just war doctrine has important religious and legal elements that link it to cooperation and conflict patterns within the framework of the English School.

Universally shared moral premises and the possibility of a common identity

The English School approach is a convenient framework for the studies of inter-faith initiatives and analyses of common practices across religious traditions. The concept of international society has the potential to bring different cultures together by pointing out their overlapping understandings of political issues. Reflecting on these overlaps, Bull (1979: 180) states the implications of natural law for international society: "There are certain moral premises that are shared universally, or near universally – that moral rules protecting life, property and sanctity of agreements, for example, are respected in all societies, including international society." The English School, despite having developed in the Western world, is open to the voices of non-Western actors.

Bull (1977: 317) argues that "like the world international society, the cosmopolitan culture on which it depends may need to absorb non-Western elements to a much greater degree if it is to be genuinely universal and provide a foundation for a universal international society." This flexibility of the English School opens the way for the integration of development studies that have a religious dimension. In short, the English School is a platform for those who study the possibility of a cosmopolitan identity and world order that have elements of all faith traditions and emphasizes commonalities more than differences. In this manner, the English School can accommodate studies of inter-faith cooperation that aim to find solutions to common challenges.

Modernity, development, and international relations

Debates on modernity may also be conducted within the English School framework. Scott Thomas (1999: 33) notes that "the consequences of religion for international society are connected to the debates, dialogues and conflicts over identity and meaning of modernity within domestic societies." Thomas (2003: 23) also recognizes that the English School "examines the emergence of international society through the prism of historical sociology is better equipped to deal with religion, culture, and civilization" when compared to other theories that start with the Western modernity assumption. In this vein, he analyzes the contribution of Alasdair MacIntyre, who stated that there is no rationality independent of tradition.

The questions of modernity, uneven levels of development, and the differences in regional institutions raise challenges. Hurrell (2007: 137–138) discusses these challenges of "identity based pluralism" and draws attention to the importance of "regions" in international society. The unity that is hoped for in the English School is not without its challenges, and Hurrell sees the relationship among regions with different values as an ongoing negotiation. In Asad's (2003: 13) words, modernity is "a series of interlinked projects" which institutionalize principles like "constitutionalism, moral autonomy, democracy, human rights, civil equality, industry, consumerism, freedom of the market and secularism."

These principles predominantly reflect Western interests. From this perspective, international society may also be seen as part of this interest-driven project. In other words, an international society that has its roots in the Western world leads to international undertakings that subordinate Eastern traditions. Colonialism may be seen as an implication of such a project. Hashmi (1996: 17) states that the Islamic revival is not comprehensible if divorced from the colonial experience; the existence of a strong and imposing international society anchored to Christian tradition creates an "other." The English School provides a particularly useful framework to study these developmental trajectories and political movements that stemmed from a particular understanding of international society.

It is possible to interpret the Islamic revival or any other revival in the Eastern faith traditions as a reaction to a dominant Judeo-Christian international society. Nevertheless, some assert that these revival movements are open to taking their place on the table without compromising the core of their religious identities. Esposito and Voll (2000), for example, argue that there are figures in Islamic revival who have emphasized the possibility of a two-way interaction between Islam and other traditions. Among these figures they count Malaysian politician Anwar Ibrahim, former president of Iran Mohammad Khatami, and former President of Indonesia Abdurrahman Wahid. Although there are debates to what extent different values may be brought together to form an international society, the recognition of these tensions and exchanges makes the English School a viable theoretical strand for studies of religion, modernity, and development.

Just war traditions and religion

Other culture- and norm-based explanations regarding religion may also be investigated by using the legal terminology of the English School. The concept of "just war," for example, is the result of the interaction between the religious and legal communities. The term is divided analytically into two main categories: *jus ad bellum* (the right reasons for going to war) and *jus in bello* (the right means used in war). Walzer (2000: 21) clarifies the distinction as follows:

> The moral reality of war is divided into two parts. War is always judged twice, first with reference to the reasons states have for fighting, secondly with reference to the means they adopt. The first kind of judgment is adjectival in character: we say that a particular war is just or unjust. The second is adverbial: we say that the war is being fought justly or unjustly.

Just war has its origins in theological justifications and precepts for war. In his review of the just war tradition, Rengger (2002: 354) states that pacifism was "virtually unheard of prior to the coming of Christianity." The just war tradition was established and refined mostly "in the period between the writings of Ambrose and Augustine in late antiquity and those of late scholastics like Suárez and Vitoria and Protestant natural lawyers like Grotius; in other words, roughly between the fifth and the seventeenth centuries" (Rengger, 2002: 354). Kennedy (1999: 6) also states that until theologians such as Vitoria and Suarez objected to religious wars and emphasized just causes in natural law terms, wars against non-Christians had been categorized as just. Within the realm of the English School, Wight (1977: 34) studied the question "have all state-systems entertained some notion of holy war in their external relations? Or is it a product of the Judeo-Christian–Islamic tradition?" The acceptability of war was studied by Grotius with detailed references to the Old and New Testaments (Harris, 1993: 735).

Just war tradition may have its roots in religious thought but it is frequently invoked by policy-makers and academics in the twenty-first century. Although the "religion" aspect of the just war tradition has been neglected in the secular debates of ethics and warfare, there have also been attempts to highlight its religious origins and how this background can enrich contemporary discussions. As part of this effort, the Church of England and the Catholic Bishops' Conference of England and Wales sponsored a symposium in March 2005 to discuss the place of just war thinking in the "War on Terror." The symposium brought academics and theologians together and resulted in a book, *The Price of Peace* (2007).

Just war has not only been used as a framework to evaluate the ethics and morality of the means of war, but it has also been "updated" with the new techniques and actors that are introduced to the scene of war. In other words, "just war" is not a static concept, and its meaning changes in response to world events and technological developments ranging from nuclear weapons to unmanned aerial vehicles. To illustrate, the employment of private military companies such as Aegis, Blackwater, Control Risks Group, Erinys, Vinnell, and KBR has initiated an evaluation of whether such entities are consistent with the just war doctrine. In this context, Pattison (2008:160) notes that "it is important to update our moral thinking about the justice of war to ensure that we have the normative architecture available to us to respond to the issues that the privatization of military force raises."

Williams and Caldwell (2006) argue that *jus post bellum* (justice after war) should be added as a key dimension of just war to the existing criteria of *jus ad bellum* and *jus in bello* for a complete framework that would inform policies and judgments regarding war. Terrorism also complicates the application of just war principles. Crawford (2003:18) criticizes the Bush Administration's counterterrorism policy, arguing that "when values of the self are defined broadly and the nature of terrorist tactics and mobilization strategies is taken into account, the distinctions blur between offense and defense, war and peace, combatants and noncombatants." These changes have best been captured by English School theorists, who have been sensitive both to the legal and sociological debates surrounding the just war.

One of the most used and misused concepts, *jihad* (Arabic word for "struggle"), also falls under the just war framework. Although some academic and policy circles have associated jihad with extremism and even terrorism, the concept is sophisticated and delineates what is acceptable in the realm of war. By giving specific quotes from the Qu'ran, Silverman (2002: 91) shows that the concept of jihad addresses the criteria of just war including right intention, proportionality, and war as the last resort. Silverman also demonstrates that terrorist acts occur when "Islamically motivated actors, both groups and individuals, play fast and loose with Islamic norms." Kennedy (1999: 11) emphasizes that Islamic *jus ad bellum* traditions – just cause, right intent, proper authority, and discrimination in the use of force – are strikingly similar to Christian traditions, while in the expression of *jus in bello* principles, Islamic writings and traditions are "somewhat mixed." Perhaps due to the universality of the *jus ad bellum* principles especially toward one's co-religionists (which did not warrant extended investigation), the *jus in bello* literature has been discussed more extensively in Islam. It is also important to remember that different Islamic traditions have different approaches toward jihad. The Ahmadiyya community, which can be traced back to nineteenth-century India, has a relatively pacifist stance toward world affairs. The leader of the community, Mirza Ghulam Ahmad, believed that jihad could not be waged by violence. Instead, he advocated "jihad of the pen," resolving conflicts through debates (Currie, 2011).

In the legal sphere there are sophisticated debates surrounding jihad, and this is one of the reasons why the English School would be more ideal than any other framework in the investigation of the concept. Abou El Fadl (1999: 150) notes:

> for the most part, Muslim jurists do not focus on considerations related to jus ad bellum or the justness of waging war against non-Muslims. Rather, the overwhelming majority of their attention is focused on jus in bello or rules related to the conduct of war. There is no doubt that Muslim jurists do equate just war with religious war.

There are also many scholars who question the assumption that the precepts of just war were introduced by Christian communities. Boisard (1980: 442) argues that the medieval Christian-Islamic encounters led the former to adopt the just war principles of the latter: "Westerners, who had scarcely any code of warfare, found that their enemies had extremely elaborate rules of conduct, whether concerning the declaration of war of damaging the enemy." Similarly, Silverman (2002: 91) claims that one of the reasons that jihad and martyrdom "strike such a chord in the West is that it clearly reminds Westerners of a religious crusade."

The concept of just war can be redefined in time and its interpretations may vary. Identities are fluid; the religious and political connotations attached to them are no exceptions. In this light, Hashmi (1999: 180) investigates the just war concept in light of the works of three influential modern Muslim scholars – Mawdudi, al-Zuhayli, and Hamidullah – and concludes that:

> With regard to the grounds for war, all three emphasize the rationale of defense: defense of one's self and one's nation, defense of others suffering persecution and killing, and defense of the right to call people to God's

message. All three go to great lengths to describe the early Islamic expansion as motivated by this last type of legitimate war – not by the desire to impose Islamic faith upon non-Muslims. All three leave the import of this type of war for modern times rather ambiguous. With regard to jus in bello, all three enjoin discrimination between combatants and noncombatants, and the avoidance of excessive destruction or cruel forms of military action. They all emphasize that wars should be fought with the goal of saving life as much as possible, and that killing in war is a means to repelling the original affront, not the goal itself.

Hashmi (1999: 173) also makes reference to al-Zuhayli's interpretation that Muslims should not be the first to use weapons of mass destruction and they should use them only as a deterrent. However, he reminds us that there still is a gap in the literature about the systematical investigation of Islamic principles regarding terrorism, guerrilla insurgency, and weapons of mass destruction. Emphasizing Islamic pacifism, Iftikhar (2011) argues that the post-Osama era will be marked by non-violent grassroots pro-democracy movements as Muslim communities are now aware that violence does not bring solutions. The investigation of such conceptual links and trends, which can shed light on the diffusion of norms in international society, would enrich both the English School itself and the literature on identities, including religion.

Religion and the English School: interactions in international society

The English School framework shares theoretical premises with the Realist and Neoliberal schools of thought. However, it has carved itself a niche in the international relations theory map with its emphasis on international society and the binding nature of an agreed-upon legal framework. Although English School theorists have noted the importance of the state as a unit of investigation, this "pluralist" view has come to be challenged within the School by "solidarist" scholars who argue that human beings should be at the center of theory and public policies.

In this chapter, we show that there are multiple ways to integrate religion into the English School. In fact many English School theorists have already done so, though in most cases not as part of any systematic effort to understand religion's role in international relations. The ethics and morality of foreign policy decisions are regarded as natural "variables" in the English School; they are seen as logical and conducive to rational investigation. The emphasis on diplomatic culture and membership of an international society allow discussions of what brings together states and groups that have conflicting interests. At the same time, although stemming mostly from Judeo-Christian roots, the English School is an ideal framework to discuss international law, alternative world orders, and the competing visions of international society held by contemporary religious actors. Although the traditional unit of investigation has been the state, the internal debates between the pluralists and solidarists show that this is changing. In short, given the religious roots of the framework and its openness to include ethical and moral considerations, the English School is a theoretical strand that is receptive to the inclusion of the religious dimensions of international relations and foreign policy.

7   Religion and Constructivism
Interactions, ideas, and identities

International relations scholars are still debating whether Constructivism is a theory, a method or an overall interpretive approach, and what kind of intersection it has with other theories (Jackson and Nexon, 2004). Even among those who accept that Constructivism is a theory, there is still discussion about what kind of a theory it is. Adler (1997a: 323) argues that, unlike Realism and Liberalism, it is not a theory of politics per se, but "a social theory that has crucial practical implications for IR Theory." Risse (2002) states that one can see oneself as a liberal or realist Constructivist.

As we have noted in the introductory chapter, we take Constructivism both as a theory and a methodology. In each theory we have covered thus far, there are constructivist methodologies that emphasize the power of ideas, norms, and perceptions. However, there are also significant numbers of scholars whose work cannot simply be placed under Realism, Liberalism, or the English School. In this chapter we cover this line of inquiry by taking Constructivism as theory.

Constructivism, as a word, was employed by Nicholas Onuf (1989) and furthered as a theory by scholars like Alexander Wendt, Friedrich Kratochwil, and Ted Hopf, among others. Although states were arguably the main "agents" in the early years of mainstream Constructivism, the literature has since embraced a wide range of actors including non-state entities and transnational organizations. What distinguishes Constructivism from other theoretical approaches to international relations is its emphasis on the construction of identities and interests of the actors, rather than taking them as given. Realists and Neoliberals have rarely problematized identity features and discourses. As a Constructivist, Hopf (1998: 193) notes that especially gender, sexuality, race, and religion have not received as much attention as nationalism and ethnicity. Constructivism has also been a critique of the materialist approaches that failed to predict the end of the Cold War.

In addition to this focus on identity, Constructivists see international structure as shaped by norms, rules, and law, in addition to material factors. In other words, stable meanings form structures and institutions (Klotz and Lynch, 2007: 24). Agents and structure mutually transform each other in an ever-changing world. Constructivists argue that "material resources only acquire meaning for human action through the structure of shared knowledge in which they are

, 1995: 73). Anarchy and sovereignty are social constructions
time.

is another key concept in the Constructivist approach. It sig-
ns are more than the sum of individual beliefs. Intersubjec-
give meaning to international relations and the expectations
nple of intersubjective understandings is the increasing consensus that surrounds the importance of human security. States that blatantly
transgress basic human rights are reproached in the international scene. In most
cases, the debates surrounding human rights violations clash with the agreed-
upon norms regarding the importance of state sovereignty. Every actor agrees
with the fact that what happened in Darfur constitutes a serious violation of the
civilian population's rights. Not every actor, however, agrees that states or transnational organizations have the right to intervene in the affairs of a sovereign
state, no matter how cruel that state is to its own people. One might argue that
the norms of sovereignty are challenged considerably, yet there is still no consensus over whether political actors should prioritize human rights over state
sovereignty.

Constructivism is not without its critics. Zehfuss (2001: 316) argues that
Wendt himself is not very consistent about identities, stating that he takes them
sometimes as constructed and sometimes as given. Walt (1998: 41), a Neorealist,
sees constructivist theories as highly diverse but notes that the common feature
of all the strands is the focus on "the capacity of discourse to shape how political
actors define themselves and their interests, and thus modify their behavior."
Yet, defining variables in a Constructivist research agenda may prove to be much
more challenging than identifying factors in a more materialist approach.
"Shared meanings," "principled beliefs," and even "identity" can be difficult to
label in a given case. In that sense, the extent to which Constructivism is positivist is still a matter of debate. However, Constructivism is also a criticism of reducing international relations to variables. There is more to international structure
than bipolarity or balance of power, and we construct the world we live in
through our discourse.

It is also a question how much of a "progress" Constructivism constitutes as a
separate line of theory. True, Neorealists in particular defined core tenets through
material capabilities, but even in this definition they did it "in a vocabulary that
reveals the meaning these objects acquire from the social relationships and
understandings in which they are embedded" (Dessler, 1999: 27). One of the oft-
used examples is the balance of threat theory furthered by Walt (1985). By
stating that it is not only about material resources but also about perceptions,
Walt takes a "Constructivist" step in Neorealism. Concepts such as balancing
(matching the power of the rival state through alliance or increasing material
capabilities) or bandwagoning (joining a stronger coalition) are also embedded
in social contexts that Neorealists do not reject. The major contribution of Constructivism as a theory, however, has been to bring this "context" to the fore and
inquire about the implications of existent understandings in multiple settings.
Yes, Neorealism recognizes that it is not only material capabilities but about

perceptions – yet how do we construct these threat perceptions? How do we decide who is a friend or foe? And obviously, as it relates to our subject matter, how does religion play into our constructions of international relations?

As with all theories, Constructivism has its divisions within itself. We will not go into the subtleties of subcategories, yet suffice it to say that Constructivism harbors both positivist and post-positivist scholars under its umbrella. Alexander Wendt (1995: 75), one of the fathers of contemporary Constructivist international relations theory, posits that "Constructivists are modernists who fully endorse the scientific project of falsifying theories against evidence." Adler (1997a: 321), on the other hand, sees Constructivism as the "middle ground" between positivist/materialist philosophies of science and a relativist philosophy/interpretivist sociology of knowledge used by postmodernists and critical theorists.

Richard Price and Christian Reus-Smit (1998: 259) argue that conventional Constructivism "has its intellectual roots in critical theory," and that conventional and critical Constructivists ought to collaborate to produce "a more empirically based form of critical scholarship," while also gaining "crucial insights into the sociology of moral community in world politics." This mutual relationship inevitably implies that Constructivism and certain strands of critical theory are intertwined, no matter how conservatively Constructivism is defined. In that sense, we also touch upon elements of critical theory in this chapter.

The study of religion, relying on tradition and discourse, follows a Constructivist logic. Therefore, it is expected that the investigation of religious phenomena in international relations can be easily conducted within the Constructivist framework. This investigation would inevitably start with the critique of core concepts such as religion itself, secularism, and political actors. As Hurd (2004a) notes, even the separation of the category of "religion" from politics is a politicized decision that is not to be taken for granted. Weber (1963), one of the forefathers of Constructivist theory, famously refused to define religion himself, situating it within a sociopolitical context rather than imposing it as a concept on the political and economic spheres. Questions related to the situation of religion in international politics, the critique of established norms surrounding faith issues, as well as how religion and politics transform each other are among questions that Constructivists can answer more easily than Neorealists or Neoliberals. In the following sections we provide examples and suggest avenues of Constructivist research that can include religion-related elements.

Religious worldviews and Constructivism

Constructivism takes into account how individuals shape their lives through their habits, thoughts, values, and discourses. We have already covered the importance of cognition and perceptions in the preceding chapters. In this section we review two ways in which the Constructivist literature has handled individual-level views on religion and the influence of these views in the public sphere. First, Constructivists take seriously how individuals, as agents, form opinions.

Second, these opinions are translated into action (discourse), and then have an impact on our understandings of international relations.

Construction of habits and thoughts

Religious beliefs influence the emotions, habits, and thoughts of individuals. These influences are often included in anthropological definitions of faith. For example, Singh (2006: 381) defines faith as "a translatable and mobile set of bodily practices, habits, modes of dress and social organization, the direction of thought, forms of leisure, the training of desire, a conception of good life, affective and cultural tendencies." A cross pendant, a kippah, a turban, or a headscarf is a way of signaling religious faith in public; temples, synagogues, mosques, churches, and shrines bring faith communities together and create a space for interaction among "believers." Even for people who do not count themselves as a member of a specific faith community, beliefs and thoughts about the afterlife, the purpose of life, and other religions have an effect on behavior. Some cover their shoulders upon entering a church, intending to respect the "sacredness" of a location, or use words like "God," "blessing," or "angel" in daily discourse; others form stereotypes – positive or negative – about the members of a faith group. In short, it is highly unlikely that one's mode of life and thoughts escape faith-related issues and practices altogether.

The Constructivist literature also features the role of emotions and their interaction with decisions. Emotions interfere with decisions and our construction of the world. Nussbaum (2001: 4) describes emotions as "appraisals or value judgments which ascribe to things and persons outside the person's own control great importance for that person's own flourishing." Recent studies prove that religion informs the individual experience and valuation of emotions (Kim-Prieto and Diener, 2009). The fact that emotions weigh in decision-making has also been used by policy-makers to legitimize their positions, and religion only increases the power of such discourse. To illustrate, Ross (2006: 213) argues that the American response to 9/11 has been shaped by affective states, and "catchy slogans, casual body language and ambiguous forms of religious discourse."

Religious stereotypes, or the stereotypes common among the members of a faith group, are among topics of interest to a constructivist. Hopf (2010: 542) argues that "stereotypes fill in information about the other actor that is missing from her actual behavior and make ambiguous evidence unambiguously supportive of the habitual categorization. Habits and emotions are close associates; they are both automatic, not reflective." Habits help us to maintain "ontological security" and satisfy our need "to have a predictable sense of self" (Mitzen, 2006). Bilewicz and Kreminski (2010) link deprivation to higher levels of stereotyping of Jews and scapegoating in Poland. In the American context, voters stereotype candidates based on candidate religion and use this stereotyped information to help them make an electoral decision (McDermott, 2007). Some studies link intensity of religiousness to overall prosocial personality traits (Saroglou et al., 2004), whereas fundamentalism (regardless of the religious tradition) has been linked to a discriminatory and unhelpful attitude toward out-group members (Jackson and Esses, 1997). These stereotypes also shape the expectations of the target group. Ghumman and Jackson (2010) find that in America, Muslim women who wear the hijab had lower expectations of receiving a job offer than Muslim women who do not.

Personal experience, including traumas, also contributes to worldviews (see Edkins, 2003). Fierke (2004: 476) notes that genocide, and particularly the experience of Jews in the German concentration camps, is another example of "intentional action that resulted in a collapse of meaning and safety." These traumas inevitably contribute to the construction of stereotypes and the demarcation of a stronger in-group/out-group separation. Religion, at times, can be part of these traumas. When it is, even if a conflict did not start out as a religious one, it will quickly assume that dimension if the sides belong to different religious groups. Traumas can also lead to exaggerated expectations about the other's plots and visions. To illustrate, in a large post-war survey in Bosnia, which, as expected, reflected war traumas of every side, McIntosh and Abele (1996) found that four out of five Bosnian Serbs believe that Muslim citizens aim to establish an Islamic state, whereas only 5 percent of Muslims considered this as a goal.

The study of beliefs and thoughts may seem to create challenges for the Constructivist research program, as it is hardly possible to measure emotions or thoughts. In this sense, the manifestations are more important for the Constructivists than the inner thoughts themselves. In other words, "constructivists are not interested in the beliefs actors hold so much as the beliefs actors share. Beliefs must be expressed, if not codified and recorded, to be shared" (Farrell, 2002: 60). Accordingly, methodological tools that trace these discursive manifestations, such as discourse and content analysis, are widely used by Constructivist scholars.

Religious narratives, social practices, and the public sphere

Kratochwil (2005: 115) reminds us that "religion provides us with an important focus for analyzing the context of agents and structures through the constitution of communities and of the 'self', precisely because the 'other' is often 'God'". Religious discourse and roles proposed through different public theologies reflect this demarcation, and set the terms of the relationship between the self and the other (the divine). Individuals may also relate to the public sphere through discourse and roles that may be colored by their religious leanings. How a devout Christian man gives meaning to his life is not the same as how a Hindu woman makes sense out of what is happening in the world. Religious worldviews influence social practices and discourse, even satisfaction with life. Lim and Putnam (2010) report that religious people are more satisfied with their lives because they attend religious services regularly and develop social networks among themselves. Todd (2010) traces the change in religious identity and social practices in post-conflict Northern Ireland; she states that individuals tap into their religious traditions to overcome the cognitive dissonance that occurred as a result of changing institutions.

Understandably, Constructivism, as an approach to the international public sphere, is more concerned with the expressions and manifestations of world-views rather than the psychological mechanisms that lie behind decisions. The term subjectivity, for example, "refers to the role of social practices, rather than psychological processes, in constituting individuals and groups" (Klotz and Lynch, 2007: 47). How do religious groups define themselves in the public sphere? Which social practices bring them together? How do they transform the international structure, and how does structure enable or constrain their prac-tices? Religion, in the end, provides the individual with a knowledge framework. Adler (1997b: 325) defines knowledge-based practices as "the outcome of inter-acting individuals who act purposively on the basis of their personal ideas, beliefs, judgments and interpretations." Such practices inevitably affect political decisions. We have mentioned under Classical Realism that religious actors may even form epistemic communities to make a change in local or international pol-itics (Sandal, 2011). To give an example, Philpott (2012) explains how religious actors and worldviews are ingrained in the concept of "restorative justice," which is much discussed in truth commissions and conciliation efforts worldwide.

Narratives are also important in conveying religious worldviews to following generations. Klotz and Lynch (2007: 45) maintain that "narratives highlight the agency of particular individuals or groups by telling a story with a plot and main characters." Worldviews, religious or not, are influenced by narratives created by politicians, religious leaders, or even regular people; in return, narratives can be transformed by contemporary public discourse. Brown and Theodossopoulos (2002) illustrate how Byzantine and Orthodox narratives prevail in the world-views of the Greeks with regard to international relations. Similarly, Marsden (2011: 328) draws attention to the "city on a hill" image (from Matthew 5:14) and "manifest destiny" that has become "deeply ingrained within the American psyche." Sandal (2013) illustrates how in the minds of Turkish citizens and offi-cials, the ideal citizen is constructed as Sunni, emphasizing the difficulties of challenging the religious narratives that are rooted in the worldviews of regular citizens. As these examples show, national and communal narratives may carry strong religious overtones; through education, upbringing, and other social inter-actions, prevalent narratives and discourses shape worldviews.

Religious legitimacy and Constructivism

Very much relevant to the relationship between worldviews and religion, reli-gious legitimacy within the Constructivist framework defines which decisions or policies may be validated in which communities and through what means. In this vein, we look at different types of communities that are constructed through shared practices and are influenced by the religion component. As a second cat-egory, we touch upon discourses of legitimacy as they relate to religion – in other words, narratives and discourses used to convince a group of people that an action is warranted.

Communities of legitimacy

The influence of discourses depends on shared understandings within a community. Each community, be it religious or secular, has its rules, norms, and institutions that define what is acceptable and what is not. As Ruggie (1998: 12) argues, norms exist "by virtue of all the relevant actors agreeing that they exist." Even the state itself is the product of these agreements and the act of "surrendering private judgment" (Blau, 1963: 307), and therefore its status as ultimate arbiter of the public sphere cannot be taken for granted. Moving on from this constitution, Wendt (2003: 504, 513) clarifies that violence and coercion cannot be the sole source of legitimacy, and, contrary to prevalent Western understandings, monarchies, communist states, and dictatorships could be seen as legitimate by their subjects; "if people are denied something of fundamental importance to themselves their acceptance of a regime is likely to be half-hearted and dependent on coercion, which even Hobbes recognized was a less efficient and stable basis for order than legitimacy." As we have argued previously, this also means that religious entities challenging the secular state – transnational or local – should not come across as unexpected, since not every group or community recognizes the superiority of state power over other alternatives, such as tribe or religious groupings. Juergensmeyer (2010: 268) shows how religious traditions offer and practice alternatives; "in Thailand, for example, the king must be a monk before assuming political power." Religious nationalism, therefore, is not new, yet its tension with secular ideologies becomes increasingly more pronounced.

Similar to the understanding of an all-powerful state, Western conceptions of democracy or international relations also cannot be generalized to the entire world. Even if Huntington's (1993, 1996) "clash of civilizations" sounds too primordial and deterministic to be used as an analytical concept, there may be a clash of understandings and values even within the same country. The prescriptions prepared by American policy circles may create tension in other parts of the world. Pointing to these biases in policy-making, Oren (1995) reminds us that the selection of criteria for one of the oft-used normative theories in international relations, "Democratic Peace," was constructed within an American cultural framework, and these standards are not agreed upon even among the so-called Western actors. American international relations theory also influences the role conceptions of what the US should do. As Wendt (1987: 360) states, "the 'balancer' in a balance of power system or a core state in the capitalist world economy, has certain powers, responsibilities, and interests which it possesses only in virtue of its social structural position." This is no different in other cultures and contexts. Each country or political grouping (including religious ones) has its vision of how the world should be and what its roles are – these conceptions form the basis of legitimacy within the relevant communities.

The role of religion in the construction of alternative political groupings and in the transformation of understandings has been hotly debated in international relations. Habermas (2006: 159) states that "under the circumstances of the secularization of knowledge, the neutralization of state authority, and of the generalized freedom of religion, religion has had to give up this claim to interpretive monopoly and to a comprehensive organization of life." From that perspective, the secular state is a very contemporary construction and its meaning is renegotiated every day. Religious transnational or local groupings claim to provide a safe space and identity for their followers, and they form communities of legitimacy and control. The importance of similar communities (starting with Anderson's depiction of nations as "imagined communities") has been emphasized in the Constructivist literature. Karl Deutsch (1957) introduced the concept of "security community" where there is a "real assurance that the members of that community will not fight each other physically, but will settle their disputes in some other way." Adler and Barnett (1996) later developed the concept without leaving the state as the constituent agent in these communities. Adler notes that security communities are "socially constructed" and "rest on shared practical knowledge of the peaceful resolution of conflicts." These collective identities provide states and individuals with stable meanings and create a specific standard of legitimacy. Agents create their concepts and ideas that are in line with these constructed belongings. Religious communities also constitute such a "cognitive region" with their own set of authorities, rules, and norms. Hall and Biersteker (2002: 4) note that transnational organizations, including religious ones, are recognized as legitimate by a larger public (that often includes states themselves) as authors of policies, practices, rules, and norms.

Political theology is another concept at the intersection of religion and politics. It is defined as "the set of ideas that a religious body holds about legitimate political authority" (Philpott, 2007; Shah and Philpott, 2011; Toft et al., 2011). Due to the absence of a generic definition of religion, how religious communities relate their beliefs to their public and political life gains a special meaning when it comes to conflict and cooperation. According to Philpott, the difference in political theologies as well as the institutional relationship differentiation, defined as the degree of mutual autonomy between religious bodies and state institutions, has the potential to explain the political ambivalence of religion. Even historical institutionalist analysis explains the state policies by looking at the institutions and ideas that shape the political culture (Pierson and Skocpol, 2002). Accordingly, the role of religious tradition and institutions in the formation and consolidation of state practices falls under the Constructivist research agenda.

One challenge for the modern state has been to coopt its religious elements into a public sphere that it can control. There are debates in disciplines such as sociology, theology, and political science over how to integrate multiple views into a genuinely democratic political arrangement that is recognized as legitimate by all parties. In this spirit, Mouffe (2006: 318) suggests the model of "agonistic pluralism" which "asserts the prime task of democratic politics is not to eliminate passions or relegate them to the private sphere in order to establish a rational consensus in the public sphere. It is, rather, to attempt to mobilize those passions toward democratic designs." Brettschneider (2010: 207) offers another model, stating that "when conflicts emerge between existing religious views and the freestanding public values central to legitimacy, the state should work to transform religious belief" without resorting to coercion. These are only two models among others that attempt to accommodate religious communities into a sphere they consider legitimate. These constructions and possibilities may best be explored under the Constructivist framework in international relations.

Discourses of legitimacy in religion and politics

Once the audience is established, the rhetorical tools and strategies to persuade actors about a policy or decision come into play. We have already demonstrated that religion is an important source of legitimacy that is used even by secular actors at times. In all religious traditions there is ample space for interpretation. When contemporary events or challenges are not handled by recognized clergy or politicians, others may step in to promote more inclusive or exclusive theologies. Illustrating such occurrences, Kratochwil (2005: 129) draws attention to how quickly the Yugoslav conflicts gained ethno-religious undertones:

> In the absence of spiritual guidance by a respected and effective clergy, and in the face of a weakened "living tradition" of religion in cult and practice, radical leaders are able to tap directly into the destructive part of the ambivalent sacred experience.

Many see religion as an established meaning that they can rely on as an identity marker, yet it can also be malleable in the hands of charismatic leaders. Such usage, however, can be problematic even when it is used to promote peace. Smith (2008) argues that even when religious discourse champions democracy, "it discourages and delegitimates democratic dissent and fails to provide the religious guidance it promises." Employing religious rhetoric can also alienate those who do not share the same values.

Religious discourse is especially important, as it represents the "operationalization" of the agent's motives and understandings. Therefore, what actors say is more of interest to constructivists than their actual motives. Political actors need to be reasonably consistent because when they follow certain rhetoric, they cannot credibly use another one that is inconsistent with the original rhetoric. This is why democratic countries are held responsible for policies which might interfere with the democratic character of that state. Krebs and Jackson (2007) show that rhetorical contestation affects policy outcomes when they look at the discourse surrounding citizenship rights of Druzes in the democratic Jewish state. Kraus (2009) reports that many Washington-based advocacy groups use religious language to influence the public agenda. This presence of religious legitimacy in public discourse also creates borders and standards in daily politics, and consolidates or transforms understandings in the international sphere. Religion becomes an integral part of mainstream political discourse to maintain consistency with the existent documents and understandings.

Inevitably, religious actors have little choice when it comes to discourses of legitimacy. In order to keep group members satisfied, these actors need to continuously justify their actions on religious terms, and sometimes show their choices to be superior when compared to secular options, or those presented by their own or another religious tradition. Looking at Islamists in Lebanon and Yemen, Yadav (2010) argues that presenting religious justifications publicly is crucial for legitimacy. These domestic issues have important international repercussions as they are part of the immigration, revolutions, democratization, and intervention literatures. How religious rhetoric is used, how it reframes the political issues, and how religious legitimation transforms over time are questions examined by Constructivist scholars.

Non-state religious actors and Constructivism

Non-state religious actors, including local places of worship and political parties that have religious agendas, may have different interests, practices, and rules from those of secular actors. The influence of this religious component on the constitution of such actors is of interest to scholars working on organizational identities. The mutual constitution of religious actors and public attitudes is also a fruitful research area that attracts a growing number of scholars from multiple disciplines. In this section, we review these two possibilities.

Organizational culture and religious actors

Every organization, religious or not, has its own operating procedures. In his Constructivist theorization of habit, Hopf (2010: 547) states that institutionalized settings are "likely sites for the operation of the logic of habit because of their associated routines, standard operating procedures, and relative isolation from competing ideological structures." Constructivist scholars study the social roles produced by these organizational cultures and habits. Michael Barnett (2002), for example, integrated his professional observations into his study of how working as a bureaucrat at the United Nations can lead to an indifference to events in failed states, even during genocides. Jeffrey Checkel (2005) explores the socializing role of institutions in Europe, investigating the conditions under which socialization leads to new roles and interests. The insights of these and many other studies in the Constructivist tradition can be useful when we study religious organizations. How do they socialize their members? Which new roles are internalized by the followers of an organization?

Local religious organizations are usually among the first places an individual experiences religious socialization. They also assign an identity to newcomers. Wendt (1992a: 399) defines institutionalization as "a process of internalizing new identities and interests, not something occurring outside them and affecting only behavior; socialization is a cognitive process, not just a behavioral one." This socializing role of institutions, including places of worships and schools, has been taken seriously by religious actors. Asik (2012) shows how Islamic groups in Egypt have sought to capture the religious discourse and control religious socialization through mass education since the 1970s. Despite this, religious socialization is usually represented in the literature as leading to parochial values. Levitt (2008) demonstrates that an understanding of "religious global citizenship" is possible through her work based on the study of Indian Hindus, Pakistani Muslims, Irish Catholics, and Brazilian Protestant immigrants living in the United States.

In political theology, the socializing role of non-state religious actors and their functions in the public sphere have long been at the center of myriad debates. Johann Baptist Metz and Jurgen Moltmann (1995) discuss the possibilities of reordering and restructuring the public sphere through political theology, emphasizing the desire to envision the Church as an institution of freedom and the rejection of its "bourgeois privatization." Religious practices, even modes of clothing, can also lead to the negotiation of the image of religious institutions in public life. For example, the freedom to wear religious clothing has recently been under increased scrutiny, largely because states see it as a political symbol, representing the confrontation of local and transnational religious actors. Benhabib (2010: 465) avers that "the wearing of the headscarf itself has politicized them [women] in all three countries [France, Germany, and Turkey] and has transformed some of them from being 'docile objects' into increasingly confrontational subjects." This clash between local religious meanings and established state authority challenges social orders.

Mutual constitution of religious actors and public attitudes

Non-state religious actors transform and are transformed by public attitudes. These agents sometimes play a more subtle role in shaping public life, and at other times their influence and interactions with other actors become more pronounced. The timing of the "resurgence" of religious actors, how they communicate and realize their agendas, and how they replicate or challenge themselves, remain important queries that have no clear-cut answers. However, one obvious manifestation is the negotiation of nationalisms (Norman, 2006) through the deconstruction and reconstruction of the established institutions of the state, not only by rival nationalist groups but also by religious actors who may have different allegiances and visions of social space.

At the same time, religious actors may represent other nationalities; sometimes the religious actors become the representative actor of a national cause. This may be seen in many conflict settings including Sri Lanka, Northern Ireland, and Kashmir. These intertwined identities may also be studied as "nested nationalities" (Miller, 2000). Furthermore, Kymlicka (2011: 292) notes the existence of post-national integration of immigrants who live in particular neighborhoods, attend particular schools, and play in particular parks, and all of these are nationally marked. In this context, long-term immigrants associate themselves with a national group, such as Poles moving into Catholic neighborhoods and Estonians preferring Protestant neighborhoods.

Non-state religious institutions usually have an influence on certain segments of the community. Karyotis and Patrikios (2010), for example, point to the relative strength of religious over political messages about immigration, especially among churchgoers in Greece. This is one of the reasons behind the persistence of anti-immigration attitudes, and the authors claim that the embeddedness of these messages does not bode well for constructive policy change and the desecuritization of immigration. Drawing from his research conducted in Lebanon, Corstange (2012: 117) emphasizes the importance of two different discourses in the construction of religious and nationalist identities: Sectarian discourse "that expresses ethnocentrism and devalues pluralist governance"; and ecumenical discourse "that endorses pluralist institutions and articulates an appeal for religious ideals to guide the ordering of the public sphere." The resulting situation is a battle of public theologies and narratives, each contesting the validity of the other.

In addition to non-state religious actors' power to shape politics, there is also the question of when and how these desires to engage political space manifest. This is a question already posed in Constructivism. Hurd (2007: 659) argues that the tension between religious and secular discourses may be explained with the help of Constructivism. She posits that "most attempts to explain the Islamic resurgence in Turkey reveal more about secularist epistemology than they do about the revival itself." In other words, the "resurgence" of a religion may be due to the failure of the existing norms and meanings to deliver on expectations. Religious agents adapt to existing structures as much as they challenge them.

Secular actors also do not have a fixed definition of social order. Turam (2006: 6) claims that the rise of religious politics in Turkey and its transition to a more moderate pro-Islamic politics was made possible not only by Erdogan and other Islamic actors, but also by the seculars who moved from intolerant forms of laicism to a moderate secularism. Analyzing religious parties in Israel and Turkey, Sultan Tepe (2012: 483) similarly argues that "it is the discursive practices instigated by the political and religious leadership that opens the religious ideologies up to different interpretations, not the inadvertent changes of institutional constraints or elite bargaining."

The attitudes of non-state religious actors can also change over time. A pro-human rights group can reverse its policies when it comes to another community. To illustrate, in Burma, the Buddhists associated with civil disobedience and struggle for democracy rallied to block humanitarian aid for the Muslim Rohingya community. Burma's president Thein Sein even urged neighboring Bangladesh to accommodate this segment of the population. The attitude of the state and the monks was received with shock in the international arena. Such changes in discursive practices and their manifestations in the social space are natural topics of interest for Constructivists.

Religious states and Constructivism

As indicated above, even the concept of state is a relatively recent construction. How does religion become an important part of a state's official ideology? How do religious ideology and a secular idea of state work together? In this section we reiterate that "state" does not have a fixed meaning and its functions may be deconstructed and reconstructed in time. We also address the changing character of religious states.

(Religious) state as a temporal construction

Since the majority of Constructivists do not take the state "as given," there have been significant debates over how it should be conceptualized. As Biersteker and Weber (1996) remark, people can challenge even deeply institutionalized constructs like sovereignty. Wendt (1999: 21) claims that states are persons. In his view, anthropomorphization "is not merely an analytical convenience, but essential to predicting and explaining [the state's] behavior, just as folk psychology is essential to explaining human behavior." Responding to this conceptualization, Luoma-aho (2009: 306) posits that the central ideas structuring the discourses of international relations, especially those concerning agency, have a theological origin and "human-like models are frequently chosen to interpret ambiguous phenomena, and generalization and systematization of this choice is the cognitive basis of religion." In a way, she construes the way we understand international relations as "religion," with us, the scholars, trying to make sense out of a story we created.

The flexible meaning of the state and anarchy is recognized by Wendt (1992a: 185) in one of his most-cited statements: "a world in which identities and interests are learned and sustained by intersubjectively grounded practice, by what states think and do, is one in which 'anarchy is what states make of it' ." In order to justify their existence, states situate themselves in the social sphere, creating friends and enemies. Once again, Wendt (1999: 21) contends that the "daily life of international politics is an on-going process of states taking identities in relation to others, casting them into corresponding counter-identities, and playing out the result." International and domestic structures generate the "rules of the game" within which states interact (Wendt, 1987: 360). One may argue that religious states and actors, after a time period during which communist states and allies were considered enemies of Western ideology, are now regarded as the "other."

Another important theme is the claim of the secular state on what had been religious. Although a "religious state" is seen as an anomaly by many, it is also an expected phenomenon. Mahmood (2006: 326) reminds us that the modern state itself is the transformation of pre-existing affiliations and in order to transform the religious domain "nation states have had to act as de facto theologians," creating new bonds without entirely giving up the religious premises that permeated pre-modern communities. Similarly, Carl Schmitt (2006: 36) argued that all significant concepts of modern state theory were transferred from theology; for example, the "omnipotent God" became the "omnipotent lawgiver." Religious ambitions, including politicized and securitized ones, do not disappear just because they have been declared irrelevant for the convenience of political rulers. Horowitz (2009: 192), in his study of the crusades and religious ideologies, maintains that "one conclusion of the Crusading case is the importance of new religious ideas in generating shifts in theological systems over time and the strong resistance of ingrained religious ideas to changes in material conditions – even very powerful conditions." Here, we can locate the argument that ideas generate material conditions, and religious ideas have indeed played a transformative role throughout political history.

Religious states are among the powerful reminders that religion is unlikely to be erased from the international public sphere, yet at the same time scholars of politics are increasingly aware that even in secular states' structures, there are religious elements that at times come to the fore. Whether they are remnants of the past social orders or harbingers of future ones – perhaps both – is a question that will occupy theoretical and empirical agendas for the foreseeable future.

Changing characters and role conceptions of the religious states

The fact that a state follows a particular religious ideology does not mean that the expectations from that state and its role conceptions will remain the same. A religious state may be perceived as peaceful or violent by other states; a secular state may become "religious" in time. The official state ideology also defines who can be part of that identity and who is excluded. These dynamics have inevitable international repercussions.

Hopf (1998: 176) states that "the social practices that constitute an identity cannot imply interests that are not consistent with the practices and structure that constitute that identity." How states conceive themselves (and how other states contribute to this self-conception) matters tremendously when it comes to their desires, interests, and attitudes in the international public sphere. Constructivist scholars have long recognized the importance of how states conceive of their identity including its religious aspect. A state does not even need to be qualified as a "religious state" in order to define itself through its religious credentials. For example, we may find that there is a predominant (Christian, democratic, white, civilized) identity being produced in the United States between state and society that accounts for broad swathes of identity relations between that state and the rest of the world (Hopf, 2010: 548). Wendt (1992a: 411) affirms that

> the level of resistance that these commitments induce will depend on the "salience" of particular role identities to the actor. The United States, for example, is more likely to resist threats to its identity as "leader of anticommunist crusades" than to its identity as "promoter of human rights".

Role conceptions, norms, and rules of interactions change over time and space. In his work on the peace process in the Middle East, Barnett (1999) explores how these changing norms function in temporal and spatial settings to make certain actions possible.

Identities and international interactions are fluid, since conditions and characterizations change quickly. However, in daily politics, this flexible nature of ideologies is easily forgotten. For example, although Islamic governments are sometimes seen as historically conditioned autocratic governments by scholars and practitioners, it is important to keep these political inferences in perspective. Donno and Russett (2004: 583) suggest that the effect of religion and culture on governance has changed dramatically over time. Before 1980, predominantly Catholic countries were "less likely than Islamic ones to have democratic governments, but this relationship subsequently turned strongly positive." They argue that rather than an effect of religion, it is cultural factors peculiar to the Arab region that may matter when determining the mode of governance. Constructivist scholarship is more sensitive to the overlaps between ethnicity and religion. Moreover, the critical strands of Constructivism in particular emphasize the importance of the colonial experience and how the dynamics of domination has had its repercussions on governance, especially in the Arab world.

Even secular states change characteristics in time, and these characteristics may involve religion. Civic nationalism has usually been represented as "neutral," especially with regard to the religious identities the state contains within itself. However, recent scholarship has revealed that the dominating aspects of civic nationalism have been "obscured by the myth of the ethnocultural neutrality of the state" (Kymlicka, 2001: 4). Almost every state has an establishment myth embedded in a particular religious tradition; the manifestations of that myth may become clear even under civic nationalism. Grigoriadis (2007) argues that in Turkey, the move from ethnic nationalism toward civic nationalism has strong similarities to the Ottoman civic identity. In this framework, the state embraces religious minorities with the condition that they will recognize the domination of a Sunni Muslim administration. Today, in many countries ranging from India and Egypt to Israel and the US, such tension between the "secular" and the "religious" is palpable. Secular states may become the religious states of tomorrow, and religious states may assume different features in time. These contestations of state identities and their contingency on numerous factors including public attitudes fall under the Constructivist agenda.

Transnational religious actors and Constructivism

Transnational religious actors, peaceful and violent, challenge the existing social order as they contest the secular ideologies that underlie its structure. We can analyze this challenge in multiple ways in the Constructivist tradition but here we focus on two of them. The first is through pondering the status and diffusion of "religious knowledge" in the social space, and the second is considering the political trajectory of religious agents.

Politics of knowledge and religious epistemic communities

Epistemic (or knowledge) communities, as an area of investigation, have already been discussed in the Constructivist literature. One may argue that religious actors constitute an epistemic community when it comes to issues like economic justice or conflict transformation. In the field of international relations, an epistemic community is defined as "a network of professionals with recognized expertise and competence in a particular domain and an authoritative claim to policy-relevant knowledge within that domain or issue-area" (Haas, 1992). These networks also contribute to the formation of rules and norms on an issue and the creation of new regimes on areas ranging from human rights to environment.

The theories which epistemic communities put forward need not be falsifiable. What matters is the formation of new norms and understandings which are informed by domestically developed theoretical expectations that were created by the experts of a specific field. Epistemic communities need to convince key players that the adoption of the proposed framework or ideas would be in the players' best interests. The key is not "inventing new concepts but raising them to new heights of public awareness" (Adler, 1992: 124). Accordingly, religious actors who possess a kind of systematic knowledge in an issue area may be considered an epistemic community. Employing this approach, Sandal (2011) argues that those religious actors throughout the world who changed the view that segregation is not "biblical," as was once claimed by the Dutch Reformed Church, constituted an epistemic community that helped topple the Apartheid system in South Africa. Thus, religious actors, relying on commonly held theological precepts, may pursue their own agenda independently of the states.

Values and knowledge go hand in hand. We see the discussions and tensions surrounding religious education, including the debate on creationism and Darwinism. Each religious tradition promotes a specific type of knowledge, and there can be multiple epistemic communities in one religion. We see the manifestations of these religious meanings in fields like finance, science, history, philosophy, peacebuilding, and war-making. Alkopher (2005:737) argues that in medieval society, the most important value was to defend the unity of Christendom: "this knowledge was formed by cognitive Christian structures and was manifested in the construction of particular interests and institutions such as the Crusade." Dismissing this knowledge creation and transformation capacity of the religious actors would be costly. Constructivists, taking mechanisms of knowledge seriously, would ask these questions on the nature of religious knowledge, its diffusion, and transformation.

Transnational religious actors, a world state, and other possible orders

How do transnational actors transform our social order? Are we moving toward religious civilizations forming units, or a tolerant world state that allows multiple faiths? Constructivists have already been asking the questions about the next "structures" and orders; integrating religion, therefore, into these discussions on world orders is straightforward.

Addressing the question of the ultimate order in political evolution, Wendt (2003: 528) argues that "a world state is inevitable because the teleological logic of anarchy, which channels struggles for recognition toward an end-state that transcends that logic." He also reminds us that some of the "worst historical excesses of human agency" have been committed with such a teleological faith. Historically, wars are partly the result of this clash of different understandings and discourses. Investigating recent history, Risse (2011: 592) describes the "cold war as primarily a competition about ideas about the better political and economic order." Current tensions between the religious and the secular are no different in this respect. All ideologies come with teleological understandings and the desire that the rest of the world join them. We are not in a position to agree or disagree with Wendt when it comes to the inevitability of a world state, but it is certain that some transnational religious actors, in all traditions, share this understanding and desire on their own terms.

Existing orders, with their gaps, failures, or successes, give way to alternative arrangements. Connolly (1999: 57) defines the politics of becoming as "new cultural identities formed out of unexpected energies and institutionally congealed injuries." Barbato and Kratochwil (2009) argue that Connolly's perspective is a fitting description of the "return of religion" after the fall of communism. The critique of secular ideologies facilitated the diffusion of religious norms, rules, and understandings. Studying institutionalism from a regional perspective, Katzenstein (2005: 167–172) draws attention to the structural gaps in the existent institutions and meanings when he says that "vaguely defined cultural Europeanization is amenable to reconstruction and transformation." This is true for almost all regions and institutions in the world. Transnational religious actors usually fill in these gaps and situate themselves in political arrangements, sometimes contesting their validity, sometimes not.

At the same time, transnational religious actors do not blindly succumb to a monolithic ideology. They form alliances and often blend into existing arrangements without questioning. Arguing that Islamist movements establish "imagined solidarities," Bayat (2005: 904) posits that religious groups converge, based on partial interests, through the "conscious use of religious or democratic symbols and resources for the cause of mobilization." He gives the Iranian Revolution as an example – although the leadership cadres included Islamic leaders (radical or liberal), the Revolution was conducted by diverse social groups including the secular middle class, workers, students, and minorities. These differences did not manifest until after the Revolution. Religious actors sometimes plan these temporary alliances, and sometimes they genuinely change in the process. Evaluating the Islamic political actors that come to power as a result of the so-called Arab Spring, Hamid (2011) claims that these actors have pragmatic tendencies and "they have proved willing to compromise their ideology and make difficult choices." El-Ghobashy (2005: 374) similarly argues that the Muslim Brotherhood has gone through a shift in its ideological plank "from politics as a sacred mission to politics as the public contest between rival interests." Discourses of opposition may differ from discourses of governance. The intersection of material benefits and religious ideologies, therefore, will lend itself to investigation for years to come.

Transnational religious issues and Constructivism

Unlike Neorealists or even Classical Realists, Constructivists engage all transnational issues in the field of international relations. This is arguably one of the implications of Constructivism's being a methodology and social approach. Conflict, peace, human rights, environmentalism, and development are among the primary fields of interest. In this section, we illustrate two main avenues in the intersection of transnational issues and Constructivism: the evolution of human rights and civil society as it relates to religion, and the role of religion in ethnic and national meanings.

Transformation of human rights and communities of interest

Human rights discourses occupy the agendas of many Constructivists. When combined with religion, how human rights discourses and actions transform in time and who falls under a protected category become major questions of interest. The actions of religious actors create new questions of human rights every day, and it is difficult to miss how liberal conceptions of human rights contest traditional societal values. How can one negotiate the social practice of the "caste system" of the Hindu culture with universal human rights norms? How did the pro-apartheid discourse of the Dutch Reformed Church evolve into an anti-apartheid one? Can one situate birth control within the framework of Catholic NGOs?

One question that arises from the tensions between the religious and the secular is the legitimacy and the future of religious humanitarianism. Lynch (2011) discusses how the context produced by the War on Terror shapes "the organizational component of contemporary religious humanitarianism" and "reify the identities of religious actors, equating an Islamic orientation with suspicious activities." Political and socioeconomic context replicates or challenges the identities of the agents. Constructivism also engages the question of which populations are of interest to policy-makers. Universal human rights, as a concept and argument that is increasingly recognized in the international arena, creates a challenge for the sovereignty principle. Due to changing norms and meanings, intervention in the name of human rights is more legitimate now than it was 50 years ago. Finnemore (1996: 183) argues that "a century ago, protecting nonwhite non-Christians was not an 'interest' of Western states, certainly not one that could prompt the deployment of troops." Religious narratives can also change the nature of the debate. Neta Crawford (2002) draws attention to the importance of religious arguments in abolishing slavery. Given that almost every major political move has been legitimized by religious arguments at some point, it is also important to point to different public theologies and the possibility of the same religious tradition evoked as support for and against a given case, as we have historically seen with colonization, apartheid, women rights, and slavery.

Human rights narratives can be as "ambivalent" as "the sacred" (see Appleby, 2000a). The same issue may be approached from two and sometimes more angles. One of the most contested subjects of the past decade has been the head-scarf debate. Freedman (2007) highlights how those who seek to ban head-scarves draw attention to the liberation of Muslim women from patriarchal oppression, whereas those who oppose the ban point to the basic rights of religious and cultural communities to express themselves. Similarly, issues like gay couples' right to adopt have caused rifts among Christian adoption agencies almost as much as the debates surrounding abortion. "Pro-choice" activists advocate that abortion is a woman's right over her body, whereas "pro-life" activists, not exclusively but usually influenced by their religious beliefs, claim that it is a violation of the baby's right to live. These issues brought those who are holding similar views together in the world, forming advocacy organizations or alliances that can influence political agendas.

Contestation of ethnic and national meanings

Religion is sometimes an intrinsic part of an ethnic or national identity, and hence has the power to reconstruct identity politics. Religious narratives may exacerbate an ethnic conflict or it can be part of the solution. Policy-makers and societies also situate religion in group belonging and citizenship, which may conflict with the liberal understanding of civic allegiances. Constructivists recognize the importance of these belongings. Highlighting the centrality of group attachment to world politics, Wendt states that "people do not easily shed group loyalties even if other groups are available as substitutes" (2003: 515).

The centrality of religion to the self-definition of groups has been challenged by multiculturalism which has transformed identities and practices. Kymlicka (2010:103) claims that many minority groups

> have their own histories of ethnic and racial prejudice, of anti-Semitism, of caste and gender exclusion, of religious triumphalism and of political authoritarianism, all of which are delegitimized by the norms of liberal-democratic multiculturalism and minority rights.

The extent of this delegitimization is open to question, yet multiculturalism and a liberal understanding of citizenship has challenged the preconceptions of groups. In addition, the religious identity and experience of citizens may transform the existing norms and borders of citizenship in a country. Knoll (2009) finds that in the US, those who more frequently attend religious services are more likely to support liberal immigration reform policies; members of minority religions (including Jews and Mormons) are also more likely to empathize with the undocumented immigrants. These attitudes will undoubtedly have an influence in the future demography of the US.

As we have touched upon in other chapters, it is also difficult to separate the religious dimension from national identities. Cederman and Daase (2003: 8) state that whereas nations' and ethnic groups' "corporate identities" define the membership criteria, their "social identities derive from scripts linked to their founding myths or to some other nation" and remind us that the Polish nation was mythologized as the Messiah. In Britain, however, Joppke (2008: 538) observes that being British is seen as a "set of values" (such as belief in democracy and tolerance) and not an "identity," which is a word reserved for different religious groups. Although the dynamics among religion, citizenship, and nationalism is always in flux, its power cannot be underestimated in politics. That is why Constructivism, with its emphasis on changing meanings, discourse, and narratives, is arguably the most equipped among all approaches to engage these intertwined belongings.

Religious identity and Constructivism

Identity, as a concept, is at the core of Constructivism, and everything we have covered in this chapter falls within the scope of this section. Therefore, we focus here on highlighting two dimensions that we believe we have not thus far adequately addressed. The first dimension is the interaction of religion with gender. The second is the reconstruction of religious beliefs and practices through imaginations, interactions, and changing social context.

Gender and religion

Before we examine the place of gender in religion and international relations, it is necessary to note that a number of Constructivist researchers pay close attention to their own position in creating knowledge and evaluating the outside world. Other strands of international relations theory are not as sensitive to this bias. Lynch (2008: 709) remarks that "a reflexive ethical stance by constructivists requires, in turn, an awareness of the existence of the hermeneutic circle, and an acknowledgement of our place as scholars within it." The research topics and emphases in scholarly works are defined by scholars themselves. Constructivists recognize this bias in the constitution of a "reality" by the dominant groups in society.

Hopf (1998: 180) argues that "constructivism conceives of the politics of identity as a continual contest for control over the power necessary to produce meaning in a social group"; this conception also means paying special attention to manifestations of social power and domination in discourses and practices. One of the major structural biases in both religion and international relations is the constitution of a history and social sphere without including female perspectives. Feminist scholars critique this approach, and deconstruct the concepts and orders that are the production of this one-dimensional thinking. Feminist scholarship has a significant intersection with Constructivism, but the movement itself goes far beyond the confines of the Constructivist strand of international relations. Tickner (2005: 19) underscores this notion by stating that "feminists share with other social constructivists an interest in constitutive questions; however, they are unique in asking questions about socially constructed gender hierarchies and the implications of these gender hierarchies for the behavior of states and the functioning of the global economy" (see also Tickner, 1992). Accordingly, Hutchings (2000: 130) notes that "any feminist international ethics will be focused primarily on pointing out how gendered relations of power are supported by existing norms, practices and institutions in international ethical life and on looking for ways of chipping away at those supports."

The feminist critique also has a significant bearing on how we understand religion and how history and tradition are created. Who is included in religious discourses and understandings? How do religious traditions portray women? Even the relatively more inclusive religious traditions have excluded women from their narratives. Bartkowski (2001: 20) emphasizes that "though Evangelicalism originated as a more socially egalitarian expression of Christian faith, evangelical values eventually converged with patriarchal Victorian ideals as evangelical Christianity entered the mainstream." Public theologies are influenced by local cultures and context, so it may be unrealistic to expect a gender-sensitive narrative of religion from a society that espouses patriarchal norms. To illustrate, the esteemed thirteenth-century theologian, Thomas Aquinas, was of the opinion that "Christ had to be incarnated as a male because only males possess full humanity" (Ruether, 2009: 94).

Inevitably, there are debates within feminism over whether the premises are biased in favor of the cultures from which it has emanated. To give an example, Halverson and Way (2011: 521) claim that "many Muslims, Islamist or otherwise, perceive Western feminism as a gender ideology predicated on secularization, the differentiation of secular and religious spheres, and Euro-American social norms." Brown (2005: 117) draws attention to race and gender issues embedded in religious traditions through the "domination and demonization of black bodies." Such conversations across cultures, races, geographies, and religious traditions may be conducted under the Constructivist framework, as the other theories of international relations we have covered do not problematize gender-based or racial dominations in international politics.

Transformation of religion

We have spelt out the approaches to defining religion in our introduction. The debates about defining the religious and secular, how they change in context and how religion itself is transformed in social spaces may be questioned under Constructivism. The transformation of identities and interests constitutes the dependent variable of Constructivism (Adler, 1997a: 344). Therefore, an understanding of religion and its transformation is vital to comprehend the manifestations associated with it. Defining oft-used concepts like religion, however, is not an easy task. Asad (1993: 29) acknowledges that "there cannot be universal definition of religion, not only because its constituent elements and relationships are histori-cally specific, but because that definition is itself the historical product of discur-sive processes." This emphasis on discursive processes necessitates an approach that is sensitive to intersubjectivity and meanings.

Beyond the challenge of defining religion, probing the political nature of the-ologies also poses a problem. Hewitt (2007: 455) states that "especially since the ideology critique of Karl Marx and its subsequent development in the critical social theory of the Frankfurt School, it is no longer possible to overlook the ideological and political dimensions of all theology." Religious meanings and practices are politically loaded and they may reflect or challenge the power rela-tions of the communities from which they emanated. In this light, how do reli-gious manifestations change? As we noted previously, some religious understandings are mutually constituted with national ideologies. In the Chris-tian Orthodox world, the Serbian religious elite "developed their theological concepts on the basis of the idea that Serbian orthodoxy forms the heart of the Serbian national identity and that from a historical perspective the Serbia nation is under constant threat" (Van Dartel, 1992: 281). Such securitization of a theo-logically constructed national identity places religion at the heart of international relations.

Religion, as an identity feature, also constitutes an alternative to other forms of identity that are prevalent in society but not able to fulfill citizens' demands. The leaders – both in democratic and authoritarian countries – need to cater to their citizens to be able to stay in power. In many Muslim-majority countries struggling with uneven modernization and corrupt bureaucracies, for example, citizens employ Islamist vehicles of political change to express their protest. These protests lead the rulers to revise their politics or to be replaced by actors who will implement a more egalitarian society on Islamic terms (Nasr, 2001). Islamic political theology is also transforming to answer the needs of Muslims. Abdulkarim Soroush (2002), among other influential progressive thinkers, emphasizes this inevitability of change and the freedom of Muslims to interpret the Qu'ran under contemporary challenges. Such transformations will have an impact on governance and different types of political challenges will lead to the reinterpretation of religious doctrines.

Similarly, Liberation Theology, a school of theology which emphasizes the emancipation of the poor and the oppressed, gained prominence in the Latin American countries. This occurred to the extent that it led the Catholic Church to reflect upon "the critiques of Latin American society and perhaps arrive at less radical, but still progressive conclusions" (Gill, 1998: 45). Liberation Theology is pursued by lay-led Christian communities (Ecclesial Base Communities) that aim to empower the masses by increasing political awareness. It has directly impacted the politics of Latin American countries by leading to the rise of prom-inent labor union and political leaders (Berryman, 1987; Roelofs, 1988). Due to its influence, national and transnational social issues were carried to the national interest level, changing the meaning of power and legitimacy. In Brazil, for the first time, a "working man," Luiz Ignacio Lula da Silva (the leader of the Workers' Party with its close links to liberation theology), was elected as President in 2002 (Flynn, 2005). In Venezuela, the conflict between the Catholic Church and President Chavez led to the birth of the Reform Catholic Church which is openly supportive of Chavez. Many claim that this Church is funded by the government, though Church officials deny this. They claim to share the humanistic and socialist goals to help the Venezuelan masses (Romero, 2008). The Catholic Church later condemned the Reform Catholic Venezuelan Church "for usurping its rites."[1]

In addition, some practices in religious traditions may lose their relevance in the face of rivaling norms that are more widely accepted. Zoya Hasan (2010) argues that the Indian state reformed religion in the interests of social justice and equality, abolishing practices such as untouchability and child marriage. Constructivism is the most suitable strand to approach such issues of transformation, replication, or elimination of social religious practices and contestation of existing political/religious norms and ideologies.

Religion and Constructivism: norms, meanings, and narratives

Unlike Classical Realism, Neorealism, Neoliberalism, and the English School, Constructivism is a general approach to understanding international relations rather than a specific theoretical strand. Many scholars in each of the strands we have covered have utilized Constructivist approaches in their research. There are still debates within the discipline as to what Constructivism is and whether it should be treated as a methodology, a social approach, or a theoretical strand. If one handled Constructivism as a theoretical strand, it would no doubt be the most conducive to accommodation of religious phenomena. Regardless of its epistemic status, Constructivism offers a rich terminology and a critique of discourses and interactions in our daily lives. It contains tools ranging from content analysis to participant observation, and constructivist scholars, especially critical Constructivists, question the possibility of conducting objective research. One may even claim that a significant portion of theology and religious studies as disciplines follow a Constructivist approach in the analysis discourses and meanings. Therefore, a religious studies scholar who wants to conduct research in the intersection of religion and international relations would most likely prefer Constructivism, since it is an approach that may be transferred to many other social science and humanities disciplines.

In this chapter we have covered a range of research possibilities and existing debates that shed light on the role of religion in international relations. We have argued that Constructivism provides (or has the potential to provide) us with insights into religious habits; religious narratives; gender and religion; religious epistemic communities; the role of religion in possible social orders; mutual constitution of religion and political structure; role conceptions and construction of imagined communities, among others. With its emphasis on subjectivity, agent–structure interaction, and context, Constructivism takes religious manifestations and discourses not only as an independent variable, but also as a dependent variable that changes in time. Especially for scholars who have an interest in religious identity, Constructivism is an attractive choice when it comes to international relations approaches.

8 Religion in international relations theory

Interactions and prospects

Religion has always been a part of local and international politics. Mainstream theories of international relations have not always paid sufficient attention to the religion dimension, yet this is not because these theories are unable to accommodate religion. Admittedly, each theoretical strand we examine has its own limits and strengths in accounting for religion's role in international relations. It is not realistic to expect a single theory to provide the optimal account. No theoretical framework can be all-encompassing. This result is not surprising, considering that each international relations theory – without regard to religion – is considered to explain some aspects of international relations better than others. This is especially true because the strengths and weaknesses of these theories in explaining religion closely parallel their generally recognized strengths and weaknesses.

That being said, we demonstrate in this volume that the multiple ways religion can influence international relations can be fruitfully explored using what most would consider to be mainstream theories, namely Classical Realism, Neorealism, Neoliberalism, the English School, and Constructivism. Again, as discussed in detail in Chapter 1, we make no claim that these are the only theories that can accommodate religion. Rather, these are the theories we chose to demonstrate that such an accommodation is possible. If religion is to be integrated into scholarly accounts of international relations, a novel theoretical framework is not a must. The existing theoretical tools have tremendous potential that still wait to be exploited. Some theoretical strands have already accommodated religion within themselves to an extent. In addition, by demonstrating that Neorealism can accommodate an understanding of religion, we show that such an understanding may be found even in those theoretical traditions that most would conclude are among the least compatible with religion.

In systematically analyzing the potential of these theories of international relations to accommodate religion, we have employed a general catalog that includes legitimacy, worldviews, non-state actors, states, transnational movements, transnational issues, and identity as they relate to religion. As expected, some strands of international relations theory prove to be more conducive than others to the incorporation of religion as it is manifested in a specific category. Below is a brief discussion of our survey of the possible interactions between these categories and bodies of international relations theory under investigation. This discussion is summarized in Table 8.1.

Table 8.1 Religion and theories of international relations

	Classical Realism	Structural Realism	Neoliberalism	English School	Constructivism
Religious worldviews	– Cognition is affected by religious worldviews – The "operational code" and preferences of policy-makers are influenced by religion – The religious beliefs of the constituency/audience might influence a policy-maker's options	– Religious worldviews complement the systemic accounts – Religious worldviews shape "threat perceptions" and the balance of threat – Religion is the "new nationalism," changing the balance of power	– Religious worldviews have an impact on regime formation – Religion influences the market, and vice versa – Religious worldviews influence the equilibrium and strategies in game theory	– Studies of ethics and worldviews are of interest to English School – Tensions among religious worldviews influence the international society	– Construction of religious habits and thoughts have an impact on political manifestations – Religious narratives and social practices shape worldviews and are continuously reconstructed in the public sphere
Religious legitimacy	– Religious legitimacy is a powerful tool of persuasion and religion is a form of social power	– Religious dimension might justify a state's existence – Religious pretexts can be sources of rallying and, hence, "hard power"	– Religion is a form of soft power – Religion (de) legitimizes regimes	– Diplomatic culture has religious roots – Religious legitimacy can create alternative orders – Religions can establish regional international societies	– Religious groups might constitute alternative communities of legitimacy – Religious legitimacy in public discourse creates borders and standards in politics

	Classical Realism	Structural Realism	Neoliberalism	English School	Constructivism
Non-state religious actors	– Security dilemma sheds light on the behavior of religious collectives – Religious institutions and minorities can challenge the state from inside and outside	– Balance of power and other realist terminology can be employed for the competition among religious groups – Lobbies and religious interest groups shape state agendas	– Supply-side of religion – Religious organizations compete in a market – Interfaith initiatives may be considered as "evolution of cooperation" – NRAs can reflect a collective public choice and be part of social capital	– Religious institutions might shape the norms of international society – Religious terrorist groups try to redefine international law	– Religious organizations socialize individuals into their roles in society – Religious actors and public attitudes mutually constitute each other
Religious States	– National interest is shaped by religious ideology in religious states	– Religious states strive for power like their secular counterparts – Religion changes policy preferences on a state level – Religious states define their goals in accordance with their religious identity	– Religious states employ faith-based diplomacy that might shape institutional frameworks	– Morality can be studied on a state level in ES – Religious states reproduce or challenge legal norms by reinterpretation of religious law – Religious states try to find ways of integration into international society	– Construction and situation of the (religious) state in international relations can be critically discussed within Constructivism – (Religious) states change characters and role conceptions in time, which affects other agents and the overall structure in international politics

Table 8.1 Continued

	Classical Realism	Structural Realism	Neoliberalism	English School	Constructivism
Transnational Religious Movements (TRMs)	– TRM challenges Realism in general in that it provide an alternative grouping/unit to the state, may facilitate formation of alliances based on religious ideology, or strive for a "state" that will be governed according to its religious perspective	– Classical Security Complex Theory recognizes the influence of TRM in interstate relations – TRM may be considered as a challenge or alternative to the state system	– Religious NGOs employ faith-based diplomacy and become involved in transnational politics – TRM is a critical part of civil society – Religious terrorist groups behave like corporations	– TRM may be regarded as a part of international society – Some TRMs may also be considered as a challenge to a Judeo-Christian international society	– Transnational religious actors might constitute religious epistemic communities, changing our understandings of transnational issues – Transnational religious actors contribute to the constitution of alternative world orders
Transnational issues	– Human rights, especially as construed by religious actors, may be a pretext for international political action – Sacred territories and holy places are considered as critical items on the security agenda	– Human rights, especially as construed by religious actors, may be a pretext for international political action – Possession of sacred territories changes the "balance of power"	– Economic development is tied to religion in certain settings – Ethics of scientific research is significantly influenced by religion – Missionary activities shape transnational dealings	– Human rights, albeit having different importance in solidarist and pluralist strands, are critical to ES and are shaped by religious actors – Modernity and development are central issues in ES and also for religious actors	– Religious actors create new questions of human rights – Ethnic and national meanings are contested through religion

	Classical Realism	Structural Realism	Neoliberalism	English School	Constructivism
Religious identity	– Religious identity defines who the actor and the "other" is – Access to political power might be shaped by the institutional structures of a faith tradition	– Religious identities are embedded in "structures"	– Religious identities define the partner – Religious identities define the issues and terms of cooperation	– There are universally shared moral premises that are embedded in all religions – Just War Traditions have been significantly influenced by religion	– There is a structural bias in religion and international relations literature when it comes to gender – Religious ideologies, identities, and practices are transformed in the face of new political and social rules and norms

Religious worldviews and international relations theory

Religious beliefs influence people's worldviews and identities. At an individual or group level, the convenient frameworks in this category are the Neoliberal, the English School and the Constructivist strands. Neoliberalism is compatible with the employment of religion as an explanatory factor in world politics. Religious actors can influence or even establish regimes. Religion can also be integrated into political economy investigations. One's religious beliefs have been shown to influence one's preferences in the market. As such, religion may be added to game-theoretical models as a factor that both defines one's goals and the paths taken to achieve those goals.

Although the English School may not be as conducive as Neoliberalism to the integration of religious worldviews into its accounts, it is still more flexible when compared to Classical Realism and Structural Realism. Despite the focus on state behavior, the English School regards the study of ethics and moral issues as a field of investigation in world politics. In addition, "international society," a central concept to the English School, arguably has its roots in a Judeo-Christian worldview. Tensions among different worldviews and attitudes toward international society may therefore be counted among the debates within the English School framework. Discussions on religion and political order have already been taking place in the English School framework, and the possibility of multiple international societies is explored. Both scholars of the English School and religious studies have challenged the Western-centricism of international society as it was once conceptualized, and different religious worldviews are taken into account. Constructivism is ideal for the investigation of the role of habits, religious narratives, and socio-religious practices.

Although it is not as flexible as the aforementioned three theoretical strands, Classical Realism starts its accounts at the individual level, and religion can be a powerful force in influencing policy-makers' beliefs. It may even be regarded as part of human nature in that it satisfies the basic human need for belonging. In addition to cognitive studies that take policy-makers as the unit, the investigations that study public opinion may also be studied under the Classical Realist framework. What the political audience believes may limit the policy options that are available to an even staunchly secular policy-maker. Although Classical Realism does not welcome normative moral arguments, it does not exclude religion as an explanatory variable in decision-making. That is, while Classical Realists consider using religion as a guide for policy-making to be a recipe for bad policy, there is ample room to accept that this nevertheless occurs.

Admittedly, Neorealism is not the ideal strand for individual- or societal-level explanations. However, this does not mean that religious worldviews cannot be integrated into any Neorealist accounts. To start with, even when it is interpreted very conservatively, Neorealist scholars recognize that system-level theories need to be accompanied by a unit-level theory. Although this unit-level theory may not be of primary interest, it is still crucial to complement the system-level accounts. There are other avenues in which religion is compatible with existing

Neorealist concepts and accounts; for example, "balance of threat," which means that the balance of power is not only dependent on material resources but also on threat perceptions. These threat perceptions may well be influenced by religious worldviews. In addition, the importance of nationalist ideologies in shaping the state system has already been recognized by Neorealists. Religious ideologies have the same power in today's world; they aim to establish either alternative groupings or religious states. These aspirations, influenced by religious world-views, can shape conflict and cooperation patterns on a system level.

Religious legitimacy and international relations theory

Religion is a powerful source of legitimacy, and it can function as such even in secular settings. Religious legitimacy could be covered under the "soft power" literature in Neoliberalism. In general, Neoliberalism is a convenient framework, since it recognizes multiple linkages and actors. Its definition of power and influence is not confined to military means. Soft power can be a useful tool when explaining how religious groups can influence not only their adherents, but also state politics. Since the emphasis is on the ideas and cultural identity as they relate to controlling others, a wide range of religious actors such as terrorist groups or churches qualify for the use of soft power within the context of religion. Religion may also be studied as a dimension of "regimes." These regimes range from human rights to environmental regimes. Norms, rules, and procedures that surround a particular issue may be legitimized with religious arguments.

With a flexible definition of power and the means to attain it in Classical Realism, religion may be seen as a form of social power that brings people together for a certain cause. This conception of religion as a form of power is similar to the concept of soft power in Neoliberalism but one that is somewhat less flexible and certainly more unorthodox. Neorealism proves to be more challenging with regard to religious legitimacy, since it is not as flexible as Neoliberalism in defining power, interest, and social control. In addition, Neorealist accounts usually black-box domestic politics, which makes it relatively difficult to trace (de)legitimizing acts. However, even in that limited context, religion may be studied as an integral part of the state's raison d'être. Since the state is the basic unit in Neorealism, any factor to which its existence is tied is critical. Religion can be one of these factors. Religious legitimacy is also a source of power in the anarchical system. If the states strive for power in a zero-sum fashion, religion can be an asset in this competition. Even staunch neorealists such as Walt and Mearsheimer now recognize how religion changes international politics.

Within the English School framework, religion may be understood and studied as part of the diplomatic culture that is accepted by the majority of states. This culture is the product of interactions among different faith traditions, the most dominant being the Judeo-Christian tradition. Inevitably, there are reactions to this culture and competing understandings of the world order. These reactions and tensions, along with the possibilities of multiple "regional" inter-national societies, can be covered under the English School. Constructivism also welcomes studies of religious legitimacy with its focus on discourse. The role of religious discourse in the construction of alternative political groupings and the transformation of public understandings are among the issues that might interest Constructivist researchers. Political theology literature which looks at the ideas which religious authorities and groups hold about political authorities is also rel-evant to the Constructivist agenda.

Non-state religious actors and international relations theory

We argue that non-state religious actors can be most fruitfully investigated under the Neoliberal and Constructivist frameworks, and to a lesser extent under the English School strand. Neoliberalism, with its focus on the market and issue linkages, is suitable for a variety of religion–international relations investigations in this context. First, non-state religious actors compete in the political market in an attempt to influence state policy. This competition may take place even within the same religion, among different denominations, or theologies. This concept of competition among religions, which is well developed in the sociology literature, can be translated to international relations to understand the role of religious organizations in the political market. Another concept, "evolution of coopera-tion," may be used in explaining inter-faith dialogue, which is a result of repeated interaction and reciprocity. The requirements for a sustainable dialogue and even conflict resolution in religious settings may be studied under the evolu-tion of cooperation framework. The public choice literature is another resource into which studies of religion and international relations can tap. Relevant queries include subjects that may be examined from a public choice perspective such as the cost–benefit calculus that religious communities evoke in individu-als, the types of public goods transnational religious movements present, and the kinds of social capital religious groups constitute or consolidate.

Similarly, Constructivism permits the study of non-state religious actors through multiple avenues, including organizational culture and socialization lit-eratures. Since the majority of Constructivist scholars do not prioritize state over non-state actors, this strand is a natural choice for those who would like to integ-rate this category into international relations theory. In addition, due to its atten-tion to change and mutual constitution of actors and structures, Constructivism accommodates studies that focus on the transformation of religious traditions, practices, and actors better than any other alternative.

The English School is another viable strand to study non-state religious actors. Its literature already recognizes the influence of non-state religious actors in international society, and how these actors can change the rules and norms. With their radically different vision of the world, terrorist organizations and their challenge to the legal norms may also be analyzed within the English School.

Inevitably, Realism is not the most ideal theoretical perspective for those who study religious institutions and religion at a societal level. However, this does not exclude any type of interaction between Realism and religion. The security dilemma concept of Classical Realism, for example, may be employed to investigate the threat perceptions of religious groups and how they compete for influence. In addition, religious groups can challenge the state's power by providing an alternative to existing governments, as was the case with the Catholic Church in Poland in the 1980s and the Dutch Reformed Church in South Africa before the demise of the Apartheid.

Similarly, Neorealist terminology (balancing, balance of threats, polarity) may be used to account for the politics of religion. In addition, Neorealists have started to draw attention to the influence of lobbies and religious interest groups in determining national security agendas. However, in accounting for non-state religious actors forming transnational networks to challenge state power, Neorealists may need to revise some of their assumptions and the definition of the "system."

Religious states and international relations theory

"Religious states" is probably the only category that can be conveniently analyzed in all five international relations traditions. In religious states, religion is intertwined with the national interest. A threat to religion in general may be interpreted as a threat to state. Religious states, therefore, are part of Classical Realist accounts. Similarly, Neorealism is conducive to the investigations of religious states at the system level. Religious states are similar to their counterparts: they compete with other states and they strive for power in an anarchical system. However, religious discourse resembles and arguably replaces the ideological discourses of the Cold War. In a desire to increase their power, religious states compete with other states and religious groupings, which adds another dimension to balancing behavior.

Neoliberalism and the English School are convenient to work with when investigating religious states in global politics. Faith-based diplomacy at the state level may be explored within the Neoliberal paradigm whereas the "rights and duties" of states that subscribe to a particular faith tradition would more likely to fall under the English School. The legal frameworks that are employed and also reinterpreted by the religious states would also be a dimension of interest within this strand. The focus on international society also raises the question of how religious states try to gain recognition without compromising their identity. In this sense, the English School can be an appropriate forum for the discussions on the compatibility or incompatibility of religious norms and laws with the implicit rules of international society.

Constructivist scholars adopt a more critical view of the assumptions of other strands; they do not take the definition of state and anarchy as given. States may be seen as temporal constructions. The role conceptions and characteristics of the states change over time. Religious states are no exceptions with their particular role conceptions and agendas.

Transnational religious movements and international relations theory

Inevitably, the strands that have taken the state as a "unit" do not fare as well as Neoliberalism or Constructivism (and to an extent the English School) when it comes to actors that are within or beyond state borders. Faith-based diplomacy and the activities of religious NGOs may be explored under the Neoliberal framework. In addition, the behavior of religious terrorist groups, transnational religious institutions (e.g., the Catholic Church) and religious civil society, all of which can behave like corporations or try to use soft (i.e., ideological) power, may be studied under this strand.

If one wants to treat religious actors as epistemic communities, then Constructivism would be an apt choice. Therefore, multiple works under religious studies can be integrated most easily to Constructivism. One may argue that similar to the affinity between economics and Neoliberalism (or legal studies and the English School), there is an overlap between religious studies and Constructivism. This is mostly due to the fact that religious studies scholars pay special attention to text and context. The possibility of a world state or alternative world orders may also be debated within this framework.

TRMs constitute a challenge to Realist thought, yet this challenge should not be interpreted as an obstacle. Classical Security Complex Theory, which takes states as the units yet recognizes their ties with transnational networks, is a step within Neorealism toward a more inclusive definition of the system level. Given the changing nature of threats to state survival, the meaning of balance of power is about to change. Neorealists acknowledge that TRMs (especially terrorist groups) can affect balancing and power distribution in the system; they can be part of the international structure and place constraints on state behavior. Both in Classical Realism and Neorealism, religion can be factored into alliance formation. Similarly, religion can lead to state formation. Members of the same faith tradition may come together and strive for a state, which is a topic of interest especially for Classical Realism.

The English School tradition can integrate TRMs into international society. This integration would not be too much of a theoretical stretch, since the English School scholars trace formation of international society and Rationalist thought to religious institutions. TRMs may either be framed as a part of the international society or as a challenge to it. The possibility of multiple international societies may also be explored through the English School.

Transnational religious issues and international relations theory

Transnational issues as they pertain to religion may be covered under all five theoretical frameworks. As is the case with non-state actors, Neorealism is the theoretical strand that is most resistant to accommodation religious transnational issues. However, when these transnational issues have the potential to change the "balance" in the system, it is possible to integrate them into the Neorealist framework. For example, human rights have been used as a pretext for intervention in another state's affairs. Controlling sacred territories has been seen as an element of power, and the attachment to a sacred territory is an important dimension of the statehood in states like Armenia, Ethiopia, Iran, and Israel. The same issues are also at the core of international relations theory and religion in Classical Realism. Any transnational issue that affects the power balance in the international system and the security agendas of states may be covered by Classical Realism and Neorealism, and religious issues are no exception.

The questions of human rights and states' responsibilities toward society have been at the center of the English School framework. The pluralist branch of the English School has traditionally viewed "order" (in other words, state sovereignty) as the core value that has to be respected, whereas the solidarist branch has advocated a universal conception of human rights that has to be heeded by the states. Different definitions of human rights within faith traditions have brought various issues ranging from abortion to religious dressing in public space to the international arena. With its focus on international law and society, the English School is arguably one of the most convenient theoretical frameworks when it comes to issues of human rights in the international sphere. Similarly, the transformation of the definition of human rights and the communities of interest to policy-makers are issues that spark the constructivists' interest. Among other transnational issues within the constructivist framework is the situation of religion in national and ethnic meanings and practices.

Neoliberalism is very much conducive to the integration of transnational religious issues into its accounts. In addition to human rights, issues at the intersection of economic development and religion have started to lend themselves to Neoliberal discussions. The ethics of scientific research as well as the relationships between scientific and religious communities may be studied using the Neoliberal framework. Missionary activities constitute another area of investigation which can benefit from the multiple linkages and soft power concepts that are embedded in Neoliberalism.

Religious identity and international relations theory

Religious identity is already part of the other categories that have been discussed thus far. However, it deserves special attention because there are identity-related discussions that cannot be accommodated in any other category. Within the context of Neorealism, identity may be defined as part of the "structure," especially given that the Westphalian state system was the product of the Western Christian tradition. Both in Neorealism and Classical Realism, religious identity contributes to the "threat perceptions" by defining who the actors are. As noted in the worldviews category, religious identity may influence decision-making and shape societies' or individuals' expectations. Religious traditions can act as structures, and constrain the range of actions and discourses available to a decision-maker. Depending on the issue, each faith tradition has its own rules and decision-making procedures. These rules, norms, and procedures can affect policies even in non-religious states. Religion can also be an alternative to the existing identity categories with which people are disillusioned, such as ethnicity and nationalism. Such an alternative political identity may end up in the revision of the existing units in the international system, balance of power and threat perceptions.

In Neoliberalism, religion may also be influential in defining the political partners. Religious actors may find it more convenient to associate with their counterparts in other religions rather than with secular actors in the political arena. Religion may also define the "rules of the game," be it economic partnership, political agreement, or cultural arrangements.

Within the English School framework, one possible avenue of linking religious identity and international society is through seeking the similarities among faith traditions, and how or whether these similarities can be manifested in one international society. In this vein, possibilities of inter-faith cooperation may be analyzed. The possibility of multiple "international societies" may also be explored through this framework, deriving from the studies of religion, modernity, and development. It may be argued that international society as we understand it, at its core, is a Judeo-Christian arrangement and there can be alternative arrangements that are in line with the Buddhist, Hindu, or Islamic principles. The English School, with its theological and legal roots, can constitute a convenient forum for the discussion of whether or not such multiple international societies would be compatible with one another. Along with these multiple understandings of international society, the different definitions and terms of war may be studied within the English School. The concept of "just war" has been at the center of contemporary political and legal debates. Given that the concept has theological origins, the English School is the most suitable theoretical framework to discuss *jus in bello* and *jus ad bellum* in contemporary conflict settings.

Identity issues may be investigated most conveniently by Constructivism. We mentioned only two possibilities that we believe have not been covered in other sections. First, the gender bias in religious studies and international relations has been gradually recognized. Inevitably, critical Constructivists continue to engage these debates and draw attention to the construction of exclusive categories. Second, religion is not a monolith and it does change in time. As noted previously, identity change can be captured through the Constructivist framework.

Some final thoughts

The purpose of this volume is to find ways to understand religion's multiple influences on international relations without losing the insights contained in mainstream international religion theory. Each of the five theories or approaches addressed here is able to integrate each of the influences discussed in Chapter 2, at least to some extent. That being said, many of these theories have relative blind spots. There are aspects of religion where our ability to understand religion through their lenses is at best strained and only partially successful. For example,

Classical Realism is adept at accounting for religious legitimacy as a form of power and religious worldviews as an inadvisable but nevertheless existent influence on policy. Yet it has difficulty dealing with non-state religious actors. However, these blind spots are similar to the blind spots that these theories are known to have in a more general sense. Realism does not deal with non-religious non-state actors any better than it deals with religious non-state actors.

Arguably, Constructivism has proven to be the most convenient approach to the study of religion within international relations. This is due to the relative ease of including identities, norms, and practices within this strand. The existence of positivist and critical camps within Constructivism also allows this perspective to be a hub for both mainstream researchers and scholars who question the assumptions of the positivist methodologies. This is also not surprising because Constructivism is generally considered to be the most flexible of mainstream international relations theories.

If one had to select a second-best theory that deals with religion's role in international relations, that theory would likely be Neoliberalism. This is because Neoliberalism is able to successfully integrate all aspects of religion's potential influence on international relations addressed here without any significant blind spots. To be clear, it is not necessarily successful in all aspects of religion's influences but there are no instances where its ability to integrate religion are strained or significantly limited. The English School likely runs a close third with few weak points, but is more often than not outperformed by Neoliberalism and Constructivism. Realism, not surprisingly, does not fare as well as other schools of thought. Yet Classical Realism, and to a lesser extent Neorealism, both prove to be compatible with accounts of religion.

However, as already noted, the purpose of this volume is not to select the best theory for understanding religion's multiple influences on international relations. Rather, it is to establish that we can understand religion without giving up the insights provided by existing international relations theories. As we point out in the introduction, we expect some debate over whether we have remained true to these theories in our efforts to integrate religion. In a narrow doctrinal sense it is certainly arguable that we have not, but from our perspective this is immaterial. We do not believe that the study of international relations – or any academic endeavor for that matter – is best served by a blind adherence to doctrine. Rather, it is best served by continuous efforts to modify and evolve theories to better suit the phenomena they seek to explain. As we learn more about these phenomena through experience and as new facets of politics are revealed through observation, theories must evolve to explain these new experiences and observations. Whether in our efforts to account for religion's influence we remain true to the core of existing theories or have in effect created new ones is to our eyes a subjective question. It is also one that in our minds proves insignificant next to the imperative of providing a better understanding of what we believe to be a vitally important aspect of international relations.

Whether religion has been a blind spot which had been ignored in international relations theory due to our preconceptions and biases or whether it is experiencing a resurgence, it is clear that religion is a significant phenomenon which influences international relations and is not accounted for adequately by existing international relations theories. Our efforts in this volume are intended to close this gap between theory and reality. We believe we have demonstrated that each of the five theories examined here can account for religion. We have also provided avenues that may be used in order to accomplish this, though we do not claim to have provided an exhaustive list of such avenues. That is, while we argue that the avenues we have provided for understanding religion's role in international relations are viable, we do not claim that they are the only viable avenues, and we expect that others will find different avenues that will be equally fruitful. This may include further insights into the five approaches we review here as well as efforts to understand religion's role in international relations through theories we have not addressed here. It is also our hope that others will use and further develop the avenues we suggest. In this spirit, we consider this volume the beginning of a discussion of religion in the context of mainstream international theories, rather than the final word on the topic.

Notes

1 Religions, paradigms, and international relations

1 For arguments regarding the dominance of secularization theory in the social sciences, see Appleby, 2000b: 3; Berger, 1999; Casanova, 1994: 17; Gill, 1998; Hadden, 1987b; Gorski and Altinordu, 2008; Philpott, 2009; Volf, 1996; Warner, 1993.
2 For a detailed discussion of how to define religion in the context of the social sciences, see Fox (2002: 11–30).
3 For a detailed discussion of different definitions of secularism and secularization in the social sciences, see Philpott (2009: 185–187).

2 Religion and its influence in the international arena

1 For a more complete review of the literature which argues that religion can act as a motivating force, see Fox (2002: 106–110).
2 For more on the intractability of religious conflict see Hassner (2009), Svensson and Harding (2011), and Wentz (1987).
3 For more information on the State Failure dataset see the project's website at http://global-policy.gmu.edu/pitf/. The analysis of the data used here is provided by the author.
4 Unpublished study by Jonathan Fox.
5 For a more detailed discussion of all these issues, see Fox and Sandler (2004: 77–79, 108–113).
6 For a full review of these critiques of Huntington's theories, see Fox (2004: 161–165).

3 Religion and Classical Realism: interactions within power politics

1 "Ram aur Roti" may be loosely translated as "God and Bread" within the framework of the Hindu culture.

4 Religion and Neorealism: interactions within the international system

1 Office of the Press Secretary, White House, "President Discusses Global War on Terror," Washington DC, September 5, 2006.

5 Religion and Neoliberalism: interactions within the market of ideas

1 "Secularism more threatening than Nazism – cardinal," *Irish Times*, May 5, 2000.
2 Full results are available at Pew Forum: Religion and Stem Cell Research (http://pew-forum.org/docs/?DocID=145).

3 Nicholas D. Kristoff, "Evangelicals a liberal can love," *New York Times*, February 3, 2008.

6   Religion and the English School: interactions within international society

1 Fred Barnes, "God and Man in the Oval Office," *The Weekly Standard* 8:26, March 17, 2003.

7   Religion and Constructivism: interactions, ideas, and identities

1 US Department of State, International Religious Freedom Report, 2008. Online: www.state.gov/g/drl/rls/irf/2008/108543.htm.

Bibliography

Abdul-Matin, Ibrahim "Muslim Market Power" *Huffington Post* October 31, 2011.

Abou El Fadl, Khalid "The Rules of Killing at War: An Inquiry into Classical Sources" *The Muslim World* 89(2), 1999, 144–157.

Abou Kazleh, Mohammad "Rethinking International Relations Theory in Islam: Toward a More Adequate Approach" *Alternatives: Turkish Journal of International Relations* 5(4), 2006, 41–56.

Abu Nimer, Mohammed "Conflict Resolution Training in the Middle East: Lessons To Be Learnt" *International Negotiation* 3(1), 1998, 99–116.

Abu Nimer, Mohammed "Conflict Resolution, Culture, Religion: Toward a Training Model of Interreligious Peacebuilding" *Journal of Peace Research* 38(6), 2001, 685–704.

Abu-Rabi, Ibrahim *Intellectual Origins of Islamic Resurgence in the Modern Arab World* Albany, NY: State University of New York Press, 1996.

Adler, Emanuel "The Emergence of Cooperation: National Epistemic Communities and the International Evolution of the Idea of Nuclear Arms Control" *International Organization* 46(1), 1992, 101–145.

Adler, Emanuel "Seizing the Middle Ground: Constructivism in World Politics" *European Journal of International Relations* 3(3), 1997a, 319–363.

Adler, Emanuel "Imagined (Security) Communities: Cognitive Regions in International Relations" *Millennium* 26(2), 1997b, 249–277.

Adler, Emanuel and Michael N. Barnett "Governing Anarchy: A Research Agenda for the Study of Security Communities" *Ethics and International Affairs* 10(1), 1996, 63–98.

Ahmed, Akbar "Ibn Khaldun's Understanding of Civilizations and the Dilemmas of Islam and the West Today" *Middle East Journal* 56(1), 2002, 20–45.

Akbaba, Yasemin "Who Discriminates More? Comparing Religious Discrimination in Western Democracies, Asia and the Middle East" *Civil Wars* 11(3), 2009, 321–358.

Akenson, Don *God's Peoples: Covenant and Land in South Africa, Israel and Ulster* Ithaca, NY: Cornell University Press, 1992.

Akiner, Shirin "Religion's Gap" *Harvard International Review* 22(1), 2000, 62–65.

Al Jazeera, "Switzerland Minaret Ban Condemned" December 1, 2009. Available at www.aljazeera.com/news/europe/2009/12/2009121142216681985.html (last accessed August 24, 2012).

Albright, Madeleine *The Mighty and The Almighty: Reflections on America, God, and World Affairs* New York: HarperCollins, 2006.

Alderman, Jon "Don't Stand So Close to Me: The War on Terror and U.S.–Saudi Relations" in Daniel Benjamin (ed.) *America and the World in the Age of Terror: A New Landscape in International Relations* Washington DC: CSIS, 2005, 151–173.

Ali, Muhamad "The Rise of the Liberal Islam Network (JIL) in Contemporary Indonesia" *American Journal of Islamic Social Sciences* 22(1), 2005, 1–29.

Alim, Samy H. "A New Research Agenda: Exploring the Transglobal Hip Hop Ummah" in Miriam Cooke and Bruce B. Lawrence (eds) *Muslim Networks from Hajj to Hip Hop* Chapel Hill: The University of North Carolina Press, 2005, 264–275.

Alkopher, Tal Dingott "The Social (and Religious) Meanings that Constitute War: The Crusades as Realpolitik vs. Socialpolitik" *International Studies Quarterly* 49(4), 2005, 715–738.

Almond, Gabriel, R. Scott Appleby, and Emmanuel Sivan *Strong Religion: The Rise of Fundamentalism around the World* Chicago, IL: University of Chicago Press, 2003.

Almond, Gabriel, Emmanuel Sivan, and R. Scott Appleby "Explaining Fundamentalisms" in Martin Marty and R. Scott Appleby (eds) *Fundamentalisms Comprehended* Chicago, IL: University of Chicago Press, 1995, 425–444.

Ammerman, Nancy T. "Operationalizing Evangelicalism: An Amendment" *Sociological Analysis* 43(2), 1982, 170–171.

Ammerman, Nancy T. "Accounting for Christian Fundamentalisms: Social Dynamics and Rhetorical Strategies" in Martin E. Marty and R. Scott Appleby (eds) *Accounting for Fundamentalisms: The Dynamic Character of Movements* Chicago, IL: University of Chicago Press, 1994, 149–170.

An-Na'im, Abdullahi Ahmed *Toward an Islamic Reformation: Civil Liberties, Human Rights and International Law* Syracuse, NY: Syracuse University Press, 1990.

An-Na'im, Abdullahi Ahmed "The Islamic Counter-Reformation" *New Perspectives Quarterly* 19(1), 2002, 29–35.

Anderson, Benedict *Imagined Communities: Reflections on the Origin and Spread of Nationalism* London: Verso, 1991.

Anderson, Liam and Gareth Stansfield *The Future of Iraq: Dictatorship, Democracy or Division* New York: Palgrave Macmillan, 2004.

Appiah, Kwame Anthony "Causes of Quarrel: What's Special about Religious Disputes?" in Thomas Banchoff (ed.) *Religious Pluralism, Globalization and World Politics* New York: Oxford University Press, 2008, 41–65.

Appleby, R. Scott *The Ambivalence of the Sacred: Religion, Violence, and Reconciliation* New York: Rowman and Littlefield, 2000a.

Appleby, R. Scott "Pope John Paul II" *Foreign Policy* 119(summer), 2000b, 12–25.

Appleby, R. Scott "Building Sustainable Peace: The Roles of Local and Transnational Religious Actors" in Thomas Banchoff (ed.) *Religious Pluralism, Globalization and World Politics* New York: Oxford University Press, 2008, 125–155.

Arrow, Kenneth J. *Social Choice and Individual Values* New Haven, CT: Yale University Press, 1970.

Art, Robert J. "A Defensible Defense: America's Grand Strategy after the Cold War" *International Security* 15(4), 1991, 5–53.

Asad, Talal *Genealogies of Religion: Discipline and Reasons of Power in Christianity and Islam* Baltimore, MD: The Johns Hopkins University Press, 1993.

Asad, Talal *Formations of the Secular: Christianity, Islam, Modernity* Stanford, CA: Stanford University Press, 2003.

Ashworth, Pat "South African Bishops Deplore Moral Decay" *Church Times*, February 19, 2010.

Asik, Mehmet Ozan "Contesting Religious Educational Discourses and Institutions in Contemporary Egypt" *Social Compass* 59(1), 2012, 84–101.

Axelrod, Robert *The Evolution of Cooperation* New York: Basic Books, 1984.

Axelrod, Robert and Robert Keohane "Achieving Cooperation under Anarchy: Strategies and Institutions" *World Politics* 38(1), 1985, 226–254.

Ayoob, Muhammed "Political Islam: Image and Reality" *World Policy Journal* 21(3), 2004, 1–14.

Bac, Meltem Muftuler "The Never-ending Story: Turkey and the European Union" *Middle Eastern Studies* 34(4), 1998, 240–258.

Bajoria, Jayshree and Greg Bruno *Al Qaeda: Backgrounder* New York: Council on Foreign Relations, 2009.

Banchoff, Thomas "Religious Pluralism and the Politics of Global Cloning Ban" in Thomas Banchoff (ed.) *Religious Pluralism, Globalization and World Politics* New York: Oxford University Press, 2008, 275–297.

Banchoff, Thomas *Embryo Politics: Ethics and Policy in Atlantic Democracies* Ithaca, NY: Cornell University Press, 2011.

Barbato, Mariano and Friedrich Kratochwil "Towards a Postsecular Order?" *European Political Science Review* 1(3), 2009, 317–340.

Barkawi, Tarak "Strategy as a Vocation: Weber, Morgenthau, and Modern Strategic Studies" *Review of International Studies* 24(2), 1998, 259–284.

Barkin, Samuel J. "Realist Constructivism" *International Studies Review* 5(3), 2003, 325–342.

Barnett, Michael "Culture, Strategy and Foreign Policy Change: Israel's Road to Oslo" *European Journal of International Relations* 5(1), 1999, 5–36.

Barnett, Michael *Eyewitness to Genocide: The United Nations and Rwanda* New York: Cornell University Press, 2002.

Barnett, Michael "Another Great Awakening?" in Jack Snyder (ed.) *Religion and International Relations Theory* New York: Columbia University Press, 2011, 91–115.

Barr, Michael D. "Confucianism, From Above and Below" in Jeffrey Haynes (ed.) *Routledge Handbook of Religion and Politics* New York: Routledge, 2009, 64–78.

Barro, Robert J. and Rachel M. McCleary "Religion and Economic Growth across Countries" *American Sociological Review* 68(5), 2003, 760–781.

Bartkowski, John P. *Remaking the Godly Marriage: Gender Negotiation in Evangelical Families* New Jersey: Rutgers University Press, 2001.

Baumgartner, Jody C., Peter L Fancia, and Jonathan S. Morris "A Clash of Civilizations? The Influence of Religion on Public Opinion of US Foreign Policy in the Middle East" *Political Research Quarterly* 61(2), 2008, 171–179.

Bayat, Asef "Islamism and Social Movement Theory" *Third World Quarterly* 26(6), 2005, 891–908.

BBC News "Vatican and Muslims Condemn Swiss Minaret Ban Vote" November 30, 2009. Available at http://news.bbc.co.uk/2/hi/europe/8385893.stm (last accessed August 24, 2012).

Bebbington, David *Evangelicalism in Modern Britain; A History from the 1730s to the 1980s* London: Unwin Hyman, 1989.

Bellah, Robert N. "Christianity and Symbolic Realism" *Journal for the Scientific Study of Religion* 9(2), 1970, 89–96.

Bellin, Eva "Faith in Politics: New Trends in the Study of Religion and Politics" *World Politics* 60(1), 2008, 315–347.

Benhabib, Seyla "The Return of Political Theology: The Scarf Affair in Comparative Constitutional Perspective in France, Germany and Turkey" *Philosophy and Social Criticism* 36(3), 2010, 451–471.

Benthall, Jonathan *Returning to Religion: Why a Secular Age Is Haunted by Faith* London: I.B. Tauris, 2008.

Berger, Peter *The Desecularization of the World: Resurgent Religion and World Politics* Washington DC: Ethics and Public Policy Center and Wm. B. Eerdmans Publishing, 1999.

Berggren, D. Jason and Nicol C. Rae "Jimmy Carter and George W. Bush: Faith, Foreign Policy and an Evangelical Presidential Style" *Presidential Studies Quarterly* 36(4), 2006, 606–632.

Berman, Eli and David Laitin "Religion, Terrorism and Public Goods: Testing the Club Model" *Journal of Public Economics* 92(10), 2008, 1942–1967.

Berryman, Phillip *Liberation Theology* Philadelphia, PA: Temple University Press, 1987.

Betances, Emelio *The Catholic Church and Power Politics in Latin America* Lanham, MD: Rowman and Littlefield, 2007.

Beyerlein, Kraig and Mark Chaves "The Political Activities of Religious Congregations in the US" *Journal for the Scientific Study of Religion* 42(2), 2003, 229–246.

Biersteker, Thomas J. and Sue E. Eckert (eds) *Countering the Financing of Terrorism* New York: Routledge, 2007.

Biersteker, Thomas J. and Cynthia Weber *State Sovereignty as Social Construct* Cambridge: Cambridge University Press, 1996.

Bilewicz, Michal and Ireneusz Krzeminski "Anti-Semitism in Poland and Ukraine: The Belief in Jewish Control as a Mechanism of Scapegoating" *International Journal of Conflict and Violence* 4(2), 2010, 234–243.

Black, Amy E., Douglas L. Koopman, and David K. Ryden *Of Little Faith: The Politics of George W. Bush's Faith-based Initiatives* Washington DC: Georgetown University Press, 2004.

Blaney, David and Naeem Inayatullah "The Westphalian Deferral" *International Studies Review* 2(2), 2000, 28–64.

Blau, Peter "Critical Remarks on Weber's Theory of Authority" *American Political Science Review* 57(2), 1963, 305–316.

Boisard, Marcel A. "The Probable Influence of Islam on Western Public and International Law" *International Journal of Middle East Studies* 11(4), 1980, 429–450.

Boyle, Kevin and Juliet Sheen (eds) *Freedom of Religion and Belief: A World Report* London: Routledge, 1997.

Brettschneider, Corey "A Transformative Theory of Religious Freedom: Promoting the Reasons for Rights" *Political Theory* 38(2), 2010, 187–213.

Brooks, Stephen G. "Dueling Realisms" *International Organization* 51(3), 1997, 445–477.

Brouwer, Steve, Paul Gifford, and Susan Rose (eds) *Exporting the American Gospel: Global Christian Fundamentalism* New York: Routledge, 1996.

Brown, Keith and Dimitrios Theodossopoulos "The Performance of Anxiety: Greek Narratives of War in Kosovo" *Anthropology Today* 16(1), 2002, 3–8.

Brown, Carl *Religion and State: The Muslim Approach to Politics* New York: Columbia University Press, 2000a.

Brown, Chris "The English School: International Theory and International Society" in Mathias Albert, Lothar Brock, and Klaus Dieter Wolf (eds) *Civilizing World Politics: Society and Community Beyond the State* Boston, MA: Rowman and Littlefield, 2000b, 91–102.

Brown, Seyom *New Forces, Old Forces, and the Future of World Politics* (post-Cold War edition) New York: HarperCollins, 1995.

Brown, Seyom *New Forces, Old Forces, and the Future of World Politics* New York: HarperCollins, 2005.

Brubaker, Rogers "Religion and Nationalism: Four Approaches" *Nations and Nationalism* 18(1), 2012, 2–20.

Bruce, Steve *Politics and Religion* Cambridge: Polity Press, 2003.

Buchanan, James and Gordon Tullock *The Calculus of Consent* Ann Arbor, MI: University of Michigan Press, 1962.

Bull, Hedley "Grotian Conception of International Society" in Herbert Butterfield and Martin Wight (eds) *Diplomatic Investigations: Essays in the Theory of International Politics* London: Allen and Unwin, 1966, 51–73.

Bull, Hedley *The Anarchical Society: A Study of Order in World Politics* London: Macmillan, 1977.

Bull, Hedley "Natural Law and International Relations" *British Journal of International Studies* 5(2), 1979, 171–181.

Butterfield, Herbert *Christianity and History* London: Fontana, 1950.

Buzan, Barry "Rethinking System and Structure" in Barry Buzan, Charles Jones, and Richard Little (eds) *The Logic of Anarchy: Neorealism to Structural Realism* New York: Columbia University Press, 1993a, 19–80.

Buzan, Barry "From International System to International Society: Structural Realism and Regime Theory Meet the English School" *International Organization* 47(3), 1993b, 327–352.

Buzan, Barry, Charles Jones, and Richard Little *The Logic of Anarchy* NY: Columbia University Press, 1993.

Buzan, Barry, Ole Waever, and Jaap de Wilde *Security: A New Framework for Analysis* Boulder, CO: Lynne Rienner, 1997.

Carment, David and Patrick James (eds) *Wars in the Midst of Peace* Pittsburgh: University of Pittsburgh Press, 1997.

Carr, Edward H. *The Twenty Years Crisis 1919–1939* (2nd edn) London: Macmillan, 1946.

Casanova, Jose *Public Religions in the Modern World* Chicago, IL: University of Chicago Press, 1994.

Casanova, Jose "Cosmopolitanism, The Clash of Civilizations and Multiple Modernities" *Current Sociology* 59(2), 2011, 252–267.

Cederman, Lars-Erik and Christopher Daase "Endogenizing Corporate Identities: The Next Step in Constructivist IR Theory" *European Journal of International Relations* 9(1), 2003, 5–35.

Chase, Anthony "Mutual Renewal: On the Relationship of Human Rights to the Muslim World" in Patrick James (ed.) *Religion, Identity and Global Governance: Ideas, Evidence and Practice* Toronto: Toronto University Press, 2011, 57–81.

Checkel, Jeffrey T. "International Institutions and Socialization in Europe: Introduction and Framework" *International Organization* 59(4), 2005, 801–826.

Chernus, Ira "The War in Iraq and the Academic Study of Religion" *Journal of the American Academy of Religion* 76(4), 2008, 844–873.

Cho, Il Hyun and Peter Katzenstein "In the Service of State and Nation: Religion in East Asia" in Jack Snyder (ed.) *Religion and International Relations Theory* New York: Columbia University Press, 2011, 168–199.

Christensen, Thomas J. *Useful Adversaries: Grand Strategy, Domestic Mobilization and Sino–American Conflict 1947–1958* Princeton, NJ: Princeton University Press, 1996.

Clark, Ian *Legitimacy in International Society* New York: Oxford University Press, 2005.

Clark, John *Worlds Apart: Civil Society and the Battle for Ethical Globalization* London: Earthscan, 2003.

Cleary, Edward *The Struggle for Human Rights in Latin America* Westport, CT: Praeger, 1997.

Cohen, Stuart A. "The Changing Jewish Discourse on Armed Conflict: Themes and Implications" *Terrorism and Political Violence* 17(3), 2005, 353–370.

Cole, Juan (quoted in Ethan Bronner) "Just How Far Did They Go, Those Words Against Israel?" *New York Times* June 11, 2006. Available at www.nytimes.com/2006/06/11/weekinreview/11bronner.html?_r=2 (last accessed July 20, 2012).

Connolly, William *Why I Am Not a Secularist* Minneapolis: University of Minnesota Press, 1999.

Corstange, Daniel "Religion, Pluralism and Iconography in the Public Sphere: Theory and Evidence from Lebanon" *World Politics* 64(1), 2012, 116–160.

Cortell, Andrew P. and James W. Davis "Understanding the Impact of International Norms: A Research Agenda" *International Studies Review* 1(2), 2000, 65–87.

Council on Foreign Relations, Backgrounder, "Kach and Kahane Chai" 2008. Available at www.cfr.org/publication/9178/kach_kahane_chai_israel_extremists.html?breadcrumb=%2Fabout%2Fnewsletters%2Feditorial_detail%3Fid%3D1332 (last accessed June 7, 2012).

Cox, Brian and Daniel Philpott "Faith-based Diplomacy: An Ancient Idea Newly Emergent" *Bradywine Review of Faith and International Affairs* 1(2), 2003, 31–40.

Crawford, Neta C. *Argument and Change in World Politics: Ethics, Decolonization, and Humanitarian Intervention* Cambridge: Cambridge University Press, 2002.

Crawford, Neta C. "Just War Theory and the U.S. Counterterror War" *Perspectives on Politics* 1(1), 2003, 5–25.

Crossette, Barbara "Vatican Holds up Abortion Debate at Talks in Cairo" *New York Times* September 8, 1994.

Cumming-Bruce, Nick and Steven Erlanger "Swiss Ban Minarets on Mosques" *New York Times* November 20, 2009.

Currie, Chuck "The Ahmadiyya Community Rejects Revenge and Embraces Peace" *Huffington Post* October 28, 2011.

Dalacoura, Katarina "Unexceptional Politics? The Impact of Islam on International Relations" *Millennium* 29(3), 2000, 879–887.

Dallmayr, Fred "Beyond Monologue: For a Comparative Political Theory" *Perspectives on Politics* 2(2), 2004, 249–257.

Daniels, Timothy "Liberals, Moderates and Jihadists: Protesting Danish Cartoons in Indonesia" *Contemporary Islam* 1(3), 2007, 231–246.

Davie, Grace *The Sociology of Religion* London: Sage, 2007.

Davis, David R., Keith Jaggers, and Will H. Moore "Ethnicity, Minorities, and International Conflict" in David Carment and Patrick James (eds) *Wars In the Midst of Peace* Pittsburgh: University of Pittsburgh Press, 1997, 148–164.

de Gruchy, John W. and Charles Villa-Vicencio (eds) *Apartheid is a Heresy* Cape Town: David Philip, 1983.

Dean, Cornelia "Believing Scripture but Playing by Science's Rules" *New York Times* February 12, 2007. Available at www.nytimes.com/2007/02/12/science/12geologist.html?pagewanted=all (last accessed August 24, 2012).

Den Dulk, Kevin R. "Evangelical 'Internationalists' and U.S. Foreign Policy during the Bush Administration" in Mark J. Rozell and Gleaves Whitney (eds) *Religion and The Bush Presidency* New York: Palgrave Macmillan, 2007, 213–235.

Denoeux, Guilain "The Forgotten Swamp: Navigating Political Islam" *Middle East Policy* 9(2), 2002, 56–81.

Dessler, David "Constructivism within a Positivist Social Science" *Review of International Studies* 25(1), 1999, 123–137.

Deutsch, Karl, Sidney Burrell, Robert Kahn, Maurice Leem Jr., Martin Lichterman, Raymond Lindgren, Francis Lowenheim, and Richard van Wagenen *Political Community and the North Atlantic Area: International Organization in Light of Historical Experience* Princeton, NJ: Princeton University Press, 1957.

DeVotta, Neil "Sinhalese Buddhist Nationalist Ideology: Implications for Politics and Conflict Resolution in Sri Lanka" *East-West Center Policy Studies* 40, Washington DC: East-West Center, 2007.

Djupe, Paul A. and Christopher P. Gilbert "Politics and Church: By-product or Central Mission?" *Journal for the Scientific Study of Religion* 47(1), 2008, 45–62.

Donnelly, Jack *International Human Rights* (2nd edn) Boulder, CO: Westview Press, 1998.

Donno, Daniela and Bruce Russett "Islam, Authoritarianism, and Female Empowerment: What are the Linkages?" *World Politics* 56(4), 2004, 582–607.

Douglas, Kelly Brown *What's Faith Got to Do with It? Black Bodies/Christian Souls* New York: Orbis Books, 2005.

Douglas, William "Religious Leaders, Lawmakers Wrangle over Ethics of Immigration Reform" *Miami Herald* July 14, 2010.

Dunne, Tim "Society and Hierarchy in International Relations" *International Relations* 17(3), 2003, 303–320.

Eberts, Mirella W. "The Roman Catholic Church and Democracy in Poland" *Europe-Asia Studies* 50(5), 1998, 817–842.

Economist "The New Wars of Religion: An Old Menace has Returned but in Very Different Forms" November 3, 2007.

Edkins, Jenny *Trauma and the Memory of Politics* New York: Cambridge University Press, 2003.

Edwards, Michael and David Hulme *Non-governmental Organizations: Performance and Accountability* London: Earthscan, 1995.

Eisenstadt, Shmuel E. "The Reconstruction of Religious Arenas in the Framework of 'Multiple Modernities'" *Millennium* 29(3), 2000a, 591–611.

Eisenstadt, Shmuel E. "Multiple Modernities" *Daedalus* 129(1), 2000b, 1–29.

Eisenstein, Marie A. *Religion and the Politics of Tolerance: How Christianity Builds Democracy* Waco, TX: Baylor University Press, 2008.

Elie, Paul "A Man for All Reasons" *Atlantic Monthly* 300(4), 2007. Available at www.theatlantic.com/magazine/archive/2007/11/a-man-for-all-reasons/306337/ (last accessed August 19, 2012)

Emmett, Chad F. "The Capital Cities of Jerusalem" *Geographical Review* 86(2), 1996, 233–258.

Enders, Walter and Todd Sandler *The Political Economy of Terrorism* New York: Cambridge University Press, 2005.

Esposito, John *Unholy War* Oxford: Oxford University Press, 2003.

Esposito, John L. and James P. Piscatori "Democratization and Islam" *Middle East Journal* 45(3), 1991, 427–440.

Esposito, John L. and John O. Voll "Islam and the West: Muslim Voices of Dialogue" *Millennium* 29(3), 2000, 613–639.

Esterhuyse, Willie P. *Apartheid Must Die* Cape Town: Tafelberg Publishers, 1981.

Etzioni, Amitai *Political Unification: A Comparative Study of Leaders and Forces* New York: Holt, Rinehart and Winston, 1965.

Farr, Thomas F. *World of Faith and Freedom: Why International Religious Liberty is Vital to American National Security* New York: Oxford University Press, 2008.

Farrell, Theo "Constructivist Security Studies: Portrait of a Research Program" *International Studies Review* 4(1), 2002, 49–72.

Fars News Agency "President Urges Iran's Proactive Role on International Scene", March 3, 2010. Available at http://english.farsnews.com/newstext.php?nn=8812221256 (last accessed August 23, 2012).

Ferrari, Lisa L. "The Vatican as a Transnational Actor" in Paul Christopher Manuel, Lawrence C. Reardon, and Clyde Wilcox (eds) *The Catholic Church and the Nation State: Comparative Perspectives* Washington DC: Georgetown University Press, 2006, 33–53.

Fierke, Karin M. "Whereof We Can Speak, Thereof We Must Not Be Silent: Trauma, Political Solipsism and War" *Review of International Studies* 30(4), 2004, 471–491.

Finke, Roger and Rodney Stark *The Churching of America, 1776–1990: Winners and Losers in Our Religious Economy* New Brunswick, NJ: Rutgers University Press, 1992.

Finnemore, Martha "Constructing Norms of Humanitarian Intervention" in Peter Katzenstein (ed.) *The Culture of National Security: Norms and Identity of World Politics* New York: Columbia University Press, 1996, 153–175.

Firestone, Reuven "Holy War in Modern Judaism? 'Mitzvah War' and the Problem of the 'Three Vows'" *Journal of the American Academy of Religion* 74(4), 2006, 954–982.

Fisch, M. Steven "Islam and Authoritarianism" *World Politics* 55(1), 2002, 4–37.

Fischer, Michael M.J. "Islam: The Odd Civilization Out?" *New Perspectives Quarterly* 19(1), 2002, 62–71.

Fiske, Susan T. and Shelley E. Taylor *Social Cognition* New York: Random House, 1991.

Fleet, Michael and Brian H. Smith *The Catholic Church and Democracy in Chile and Peru* Notre Dame, IN: University of Notre Dame Press, 1997.

Fletcher, Holly *Egyptian Islamic Jihad: Backgrounder* New York: Council on Foreign Relations, 2008.

Flynn, Peter "Brazil and Lula, 2005: Crisis, Corruption and Change in Political Perspective" *Third World Quarterly* 26(8), 2005, 1221–1267.

Fox, Jonathan "Do Religious Institutions Support Violence or the Status Quo?" *Studies in Conflict and Terrorism* 22(2), 1999a, 119–139.

Fox, Jonathan "The Influence of Religious Legitimacy on Grievance Formation by Ethnoreligious Minorities" *Journal of Peace Research* 36(3), 1999b, 289–307.

Fox, Jonathan *Ethnoreligious Conflict in the Late 20th Century: A General Theory* Lanham, MD: Lexington Books, 2002.

Fox, Jonathan *Religion, Civilization and Civil War: 1945 Through the New Millennium* Lanham, MD: Lexington Books, 2004.

Fox, Jonathan "World Separation of Religion and State into the 21st Century" *Comparative Political Studies* 39(5), 2006, 537–569.

Fox, Jonathan *A World Survey of Religion and the State* New York: Cambridge University Press, 2008.

Fox, Jonathan "The Religious Wave: Religion and Domestic Conflict from 1960 to 2009" *Civil Wars* 14(2), 2012, 141–158.

Fox, Jonathan *An Introduction to Religion and Politics: Theory and Practice* London: Routledge, 2013.

Fox, Jonathan and Shmuel Sandler *Bringing Religion into International Relations* New York: Palgrave Macmillan, 2004.

Freedman, Jane "Women, Islam and Rights in Europe: Beyond a Universalist/Culturalist Dichotomy" *Review of International Studies* 33(1), 2007, 29–44.

Freston, Paul "Popular Protestants in Brazilian Politics" *Social Compass* 41(4), 1994, 537–570.

Freston, Paul "Moved by the Spirit: Pentecostal Power and Politics after 100 years" The Pew Forum on Religion and Public Life, April 24, 2006, Event Transcript. Available at http://pewforum.org/Politics-and-Elections/Moved-by-the-Spirit-Pentecostal-Power-and-Politics-after-100-Years(2).aspx (last accessed November 5, 2011).

Freyberg-Inan, Annette, Ewan Harrison, and Patrick James (eds) *Rethinking Realism in International Relations* Baltimore, MD: The Johns Hopkins University Press, 2009.

Friedlander, Nuri "From Tahrir to Wall Street: The Role of Religion in Protest Movements" *Huffington Post* October 17, 2011.

Froese, Paul and F. Carson Mencken "A U.S. Holy War? The Effects of Religion on Iraq War Policy Attitudes" *Social Science Quarterly* 90(1), 2009, 103–116.

Fukuyama, Francis "Social Capital, Civil Society, and Development" *Third World Quarterly* 22(1), 2001, 7–20.

Fuller, Graham E. and Ian O. Lesser *A Sense of Siege: The Geopolitics of Islam and the West* Boulder: Westview Press, 1995.

Fuller, Graham E. "The Future of Political Islam" *Foreign Affairs* 81(2), 2002, 48–60.

Fuller, Graham E. "The Hizballah–Iran Connection: Model For Sunni Resistance" *The Washington Quarterly* winter 2006, 139–150.

Fuller, Graham E. and Ian O. Lesser *A Sense of Siege: The Geopolitics of Islam and the West* Boulder, CO: Westview Press, 1995.

Gallagher, Nancy *Quakers in the Israeli–Palestinian Conflict: The Dilemmas of NGO Humanitarian Activism* Cairo: American University of Cairo Press, 2007.

Ganiel, Gladys *Evangelicalism and Conflict in Northern Ireland* New York: Palgrave Macmillan, 2008.

Geertz, Clifford "Centers, Kings and Charisma: Reflections on the Symbolics of Power" in J. Ben-David and C. Nichols Clark (eds) *Culture and its Creators* Chicago, IL: Chicago University Press, 1977.

Gellner, Ernest *Postmodernism, Reason and Religion* London: Routledge, 1992.

George, Alexander "The Operational Code: A Neglected Approach to the Study of Political Leaders and Decision-making" *International Studies Quarterly* 13(2), 1969, 190–222.

El-Ghobashy, Mona "The Metamorphosis of the Egyptian Muslim Brothers" *International Journal of the Middle East Studies* 37(3), 2005, 373–395.

Ghose, Ghovav and Patrick James "Third Party Intervention in Ethno-religious Conflict: Role Theory, Pakistan and War in Kashmir, 1965" *Terrorism and Political Violence* 17(3), 2005, 427–445.

Ghumman, Sonia and Linda Jackson "The Downside of Religious Attire: The Muslim Headscarf and Expectations of Obtaining Employment" *Journal of Organizational Behavior* 31(1), 2010, 4–23.

Gifford, Paul *African Christianity: Its Public Role* London: Hurst and Company, 1998.

Gill, Anthony *Rendering unto Caesar: The Catholic Church and the State in Latin America* Chicago, IL: University of Chicago Press, 1998.

Gill, Anthony *The Political Origins of Religious Liberty* New York: Cambridge University Press, 2008.

Gilpin, Robert *War and Change in International Politics* New York: Cambridge University Press, 1981.

Goddard, Stacie E. and Daniel H. Nexon "Paradigms Lost? Reassessing Theory of International Politics" *European Journal of International Relations* 11(9), 2005, 9–61.

Goff, Patricia M. "World Religions and Local Identities: The Case of Islamic Arbitration in Ontario, Canada" in Patrick James (ed.) *Religion, Identity and Global Governance: Ideas, Evidence and Practice* Toronto: Toronto University Press, 2011, 187–203.

Gold, Dore *Hatred's Kingdom: How Saudi Arabia Supports the New Global Terrorism* Washington DC: Regnery Publishing, 2003.

Goldewijk, Berma K. (ed.) *Religion, International Relations, and Cooperation Development* Wageningen, Netherlands: Wageningen Academic, 2007.

Gopin, Marc *Between Eden and Armageddon: The Future of World Religions, Violence, and Peacemaking* Oxford: Oxford University Press, 2000.

Gorski, Phillip S. and Ates Altinordu "After Secularization" *Annual Review of Sociology* 34(1), 2008, 55–85.

Gottlieb, Roger S. *A Greener Faith: Religious Environmentalism and Our Planet's Future* Oxford: Oxford University Press, 2006.

Greif, Avner "Culture Beliefs and the Organization of Society: A Historical and Theoretical Reflection on Collectivist and Individualist Societies" *Journal of Political Economy* 102(5), 1994, 912–950.

Grieco, Joseph M. "Anarchy and the Limits of Cooperation: A Realist Critique of the Newest Liberal Institutionalism" *International Organization* 42(3), 1988, 485–507.

Grigoriadis, Ioannis N. "Turk or Turkiyeli? The Reform of Turkey's Minority Legislation and the Rediscovery of Ottomanism" *Middle Eastern Studies* 43(3), 2007, 423–438.

Guillermo, Trejo "Religious Competition and Ethnic Mobilization in Latin America: Why the Catholic Church Promotes indigenous Movements" *American Political Science Review* 103(3), 2009, 323–342.

Guner, Serdar S. "Religion and Preferences: A Decision-theoretic Explanation of Turkey's New Foreign Policy" *Foreign Policy Analysis* 8(3), 2012, 217–230.

Gurr, Ted R. *Minorities At Risk* Washington DC: United States Institute of Peace, 1993.

Gurr, Ted R. "Peoples against the State: Ethnopolitical Conflict and the Changing World System" *International Studies Quarterly* 38(3), 1994, 347–377.

Guth, James L. "Religion and Public Opinion: Foreign Policy Issues" in Corwin E. Smidt, Lyman A. Kellstedt, and James L. Guth (eds) *The Oxford Handbook of Religion and American Politics* New York: Oxford University Press, 2009, 243–265.

Haas, Ernst *The Uniting of Europe: Political, Economic and Social Forces 1950–1957* Stanford, CA: Stanford University Press, 1958.

Haas, Peter M. "Introduction: Epistemic Communities and International Policy Coordination" *International Organization* 46(1), 1992, 1–35.

Habermas, Jurgen "On the Relations between the Secular Liberal State and Religion" in Hent De Vries and Lawrence E. Sullivan (eds) *Political Theologies: Public Religions in a Post-secular World* New York: Fordham University Press, 2006, 251–261.

Hadden, Jeffrey K. "Religious Broadcasting and the Mobilization of the New Christian Right" *Journal for the Scientific Study of Religion* 26(1), 1987a, 1–24.

Hadden, Jeffrey K."Toward Desacralizing Secularization Theory" *Social Forces* 65(3), 1987b, 587–611.

Haggard, Stephen and Beth A. Simmons "Theories of International Regimes" *International Organization* 41(3), 1987, 491–517.

Hall, Rodney Bruce and Thomas J. Biersteker "The Emergence of Private Authority in the International System" in Rodney Bruce Hall and Thomas J. Biersteker (eds) *The Emergence of Private Authority in Global Governance* New York: Cambridge University Press, 2002, 3–23.

Halliward, Maia Carter "Situation the 'Secular': Negotiating the Boundary between Religion and Politics" *International Political Sociology* 2(1), 2008, 1–16.

Halverson, Jeffry R. and Amy K. Way "Islamist Feminism: Constructing Gender Identities in Postcolonial Muslim Societies" *Politics and Religion* 4(3), 2011, 503–525.

Hamid, Shadi "The Rise of the Islamists: How Islamists will Change Politics, and Vice Versa" *Foreign Affairs* 90(3), May/June 2011, 40–47.

Hamilton, Fiona "Sharia Courts Hearing More Cases for Non-Muslims" *The Times* June 21, 2009.

Hamilton, Malcolm *Sociology of Religion* New York: Routledge, 1995.

Hardgrave, Jr., Robert L. "Hindu Nationalism and the BJP: Transforming Religion and Politics in India" in Rafiq Dossani and Henry S. Rowan (eds) *Prospects for Peace in South Asia* Palo Alto, CA: Stanford University Press, 2005, 185–215.

Harris, Fredrick C. "Something Within: Religion as a Mobilizer of African-American Political Activism" *Journal of Politics* 56(1), 1994, 42–68.

Harris, Ian "Order and Justice in 'the Anarchical Society'" *International Affairs* 69(4), 1993, 793–841.

Hasan, Zoya "Not Quite Secular Political Practice" in Linell E. Cady and Elizabeth Shakman Hurd (eds) *Comparative Secularisms in a Global Age* New York: Palgrave Macmillan, 2010, 197–217.

Hasenclever, Andreas and Volker Rittberger "Does Religion Make a Difference? Theoretical Approaches to the Impact of Faith on Political Conflict" *Millennium* 29(3), 2000, 641–674.

Hashmi, Sohail H. "International Society and Its Islamic Malcontents" *Fletcher Forum of World Affairs* 20, 1996, 13–31.

Hashmi, Sohail H. "Saving and Taking Life in War: Three Modern Views" *The Muslim World* 89(2), 1999, 158–180.

Hassan, Amro "Mubarak Names New Al Azhar Top Cleric" *Los Angeles Times*, March 19, 2010. Available at http://latimesblogs.latimes.com/babylonbeyond/2010/03/egypt-mubarak-names-new-azhar-cleric.html (last accessed August 24, 2012).

Hassner, Ron E. "Understanding and Resolving Disputes Over Sacred Space" *Stanford Center on Conflict and Negotiation Papers* No. 62, 2002.

Hassner, Ron E. "'To Halve and to Hold': Conflict over Sacred space and the Problem of Indivisibility" *Security Studies* 12(4), 2003, 1–33.

Hassner, Ron E. *War on Sacred Grounds* London: Cornell University Press, 2009.

Hassner, Ron E. "Religion and International Affairs: The State of the Art" *Religion, Identity and Global Governance: Ideas, Evidence and Practice*, Toronto: Toronto University Press, 2011, 37–56.

Hayes, Bernadette C. "The Impact of Religious Identification on Political Attitudes: An International Comparison" *Sociology of Religion* 56(2), 1995, 177–194.

Haynes, Jeffrey *Religion in Third World Politics* Boulder, CO: Lynne Rienner, 1994.

Haynes, Jeffrey *Religion in Global Politics* New York: Longman, 1998.

Haynes, Jeffrey "Religion and the Foreign Policy Making in the USA, India and Iran: Towards A Research Agenda" *Third World Quarterly* 29(1), 2008, 143–165.

Haynes, Jeffrey "Religion and Foreign Policy" in Jeffrey Haynes (ed.) *Routledge Handbook of Religion and Politics* New York: Routledge, 2009a, 293–307.

Haynes, Jeffrey "Transnational Religious Actors and International Order" *Perspectives* 17(2), 2009b, 43–70.

Hearn, Julie "The 'Invisible' NGO: US Evangelical Missions in Kenya" *Journal of Religion in Africa* 32(1), 2002, 32–60.

Hefner, Robert W. *Civil Islam: Muslims and Democratization in Indonesia* Princeton, NJ: Princeton University Press, 2000.

Heft, James L. "John Paul II and the 'Just War' Doctrine: Make Peace through Justice and Forgiveness, Not War" in Patrick James (ed.) *Religion, Identity and Global Governance: Ideas, Evidence and Practice* Toronto: Toronto University Press, 2011, 203–219.

Hehir, J. Bryan. "Religious Freedom and U.S. Foreign Policy" in Elliott Abrams (ed.) *The Influence of Faith: Religious Groups and U.S. Foreign Policy* Lanham MD: Rowman and Littlefield, 2001, 33–52.

Herbert, David *Religion and Civil Society: Rethinking Public Religion in the Contemporary World* Aldershot, Surrey: Ashgate Publishing, 2003.

Hermann, Margaret and Charles Hermann "Who Makes Foreign Policy Decisions and How" *International Studies Quarterly* 33(4), 1989, 361–388.

Hertzke, Allen D. *Freeing God's Children: The Unlikely Alliance for Global Human Rights* Lanham, MD: Rowman and Littlefield, 2004.

Hertzke, Allen D. "The Catholic Church and Catholicism in Global Politics" in Jeffrey Haynes (ed.) *Routledge Handbook of Religion and Politics*, New York: Routledge, 2009, 48–63.

Herz, John H. "Idealist Internationalism and the Security Dilemma" *World Politics* 2(2), 1950, 157–180.

Herz, John H. "The Security Dilemma in International Relations: Background and Present Problems" *International Relations* 17(4), 2003, 411–416.

Hewitt, Marsha Aileen "Critical Theory" in Peter Scott and William T. Cavanaugh (eds) *The Blackwell Companion to Political Theology* Oxford: Blackwell Publishing, 2007, 455–471.

Hillman, Arye "Economic Security Consequences of Supreme Values" *Public Choice* 131(3), 2007, 259–280.

Hobbes, Thomas *The Leviathan* New York: Penguin, [1651] 1985.

Hobden, Steven *Historical Sociology: Back to the Future in International Relations* Cambridge: Cambridge University Press, 2001.

Hoffman, Bruce " 'Holy Terror': The Implications of Terrorism Motivated by a Religious Imperative" *Studies in Conflict and Terrorism* 18(4), 1995, 271–284.

Hoffman, Bruce *Inside Terrorism* New York: Columbia University Press, 1998.

Hoffman, Bruce "The Changing Face of Al Qaeda and The Global War on Terrorism" *Studies in Conflict and Terrorism* 27(6), 2004, 549–560.

Hopf, Ted "The Promise of Constructivism in International Relations Theory" *International Security* 23(1), 1998, 171–200.

Hopf, Ted "The Logic of Habit in IR" *European Journal of International Relations* 16(4), 2010, 539–561.

Horowitz, Donald *Ethnic Groups in Conflict* Berkeley: University of California Press, 1985.

Horowitz, Michael C. "Long Time Going: Religion and the Duration of Crusading" *International Security* 34(2), 2009, 162–193.

Human Rights Watch *China: End Crackdown on Tibetan Monasteries* October 12, 2011. Available at www.hrw.org/news/2011/10/12/china-end-crackdown-tibetan-monasteries (last accessed August 23, 2012).

Huntington, Samuel P. *The Third Wave: Democratization in the Late Twentieth Century* Oklahoma: University of Oklahoma Press, 1991.

Huntington, Samuel P. "The Clash of Civilizations?" *Foreign Affairs* 72(3), 1993, 22–49.

Huntington, Samuel P. *The Clash of Civilizations and the Remaking of the World Order* New York: Simon and Schuster, 1996.

Hurd, Elizabeth S. "The Political Authority of Secularism in International Relations" *European Journal of International Relations* 10(2), 2004a, 235–262.

Hurd, Elizabeth S. "The International Politics of Secularism: US Foreign Policy and the Islamic Republic of Iran" *Alternatives* 29(2), 2004b, 115–138.

Hurd, Elizabeth S. "Negotiating Europe: The Politics of Religion and the Prospects for Turkish Accession" *Review of International Studies* 32, 2006, 401–418.

Hurd, Elizabeth "Theorizing Religious Resurgence" *International Politics* 44, 2007, 647–665.

Hurd, Elizabeth *The Politics of Secularism in International Relations* Princeton, NJ: Princeton University Press, 2008.

Hurd, Ian "Legitimacy and Authority in International Politics" *International Organizations* 53(2), 1999, 379–408.

Hurrell, Andrew "One World? Many Worlds? The Place of Regions in the Study of International Society" *International Affairs* 83(1), 2007, 127–146.

Hurriyet Daily News "Opposition BDP Decries 'Police-State' Practices in Turkey" October 17, 2011. Available at www.hurriyetdailynews.com/opposition-bdp-decries-police-state-practices-in-turkey.aspx?pageID=438&n=opposition-bdp-decries-8216police-state-practices8217-in-turkey-2011–10–17 (last accessed August 24, 2012).

Hutchings, Kimberly "Towards a Feminist International Ethics" *Review of International Studies* 26(5), 2000, 111–130.

Iannaccone, Laurence "Sacrifice and Stigma: Reducing Free-riding in Cults, Communes, and Other Collectives" *Journal of Political Economy* 100(2), 1992, 271–291.

Iannaccone, Laurence "'Voodoo Economics?': Reviewing the Rational Choice Approach to Religion" *Journal for the Scientific Study of Religion* 34(1), 1995, 76–89.

Ibrahim, Azeem "Muslims and Government: Contrasting America and Britain" *Huffington Post* October 28, 2011.

Iftikhar, Arsalan *Islamic Pacifism: Global Muslims in the Post-Osama Era* Dulles, VA: Potomac Books, 2011.

Inboden, William Charles *Religion and American Foreign Policy, 1945–1960* Cambridge: Cambridge University Press, 2008.

Irish Times "Secularism More Threatening than Nazism – Cardinal" May 5, 2000.

Jackson, Lynne M. and Victoria M. Esses "Of Scripture and Ascription: The Relation between Religious Fundamentalism and Intergroup Helping" *Personality and Social Psychology Bulletin* 23(8), 1997, 893–906.

Jackson, Patrick Thaddeus and Daniel H. Nexon (eds) "Bridging the Gap: Toward a Realist–Constructivist Dialogue" *International Studies Review* 6(2), 2004, 337–352.

Jackson, Robert H. "The Political Theory of International Society" in Ken Booth and Steve Smith (eds) *International Relations Theory Today* University Park, PA: Penn State University Press, 1995, 110–129.

Jackson, Robert H. "Is There a Classical International Theory?" in Steve Smith, Ken Booth, and Marysia Zalewski (eds) *International Theory: Positivism and Beyond* Cambridge: Cambridge University Press, 1996, 203–221.

Jackson, Robert H. *The Global Covenant: Human Conduct in a World of States* Oxford: Oxford University Press, 2000.

Jaggers, Keith and Ted R. Gurr "Tracking Democracy's Third Wave with the Polity III Data" *Journal of Peace Research* 32(4), 1995, 469–482.

James, Carolyn and Ozgur Ozdamar "Religion as a Factor in Ethnic Conflict: Kashmir and Indian Foreign Policy" *Terrorism and Political Violence* 17(3), 2005, 447–467.

James, Patrick "Neorealism as a Scientific Research Enterprise: Toward Elaborated Structural Realism" *International Political Science Review* 14(2), 1993, 123–248.

James, Patrick *International Relations and Scientific Progress: Structural Realism Reconsidered* Columbus: Ohio State University Press, 2002.

James, Patrick (ed.) *Religion, Identity and Global Governance: Ideas, Evidence and Practice* Toronto: University of Toronto Press, 2010.

Jansen, Thomas "Europe and Religions: The Dialogue between the European Commission and Churches or Religious Communities" *Social Compass* 47(1), 2000, 103–112.

Jelen, Ted G. "Notes for a Theory of Clergy as Political Leaders" in Sue E.S. Crawford and Laura R. Olson (eds) *Christian Clergy in American Politics* Baltimore, MD: The Johns Hopkins University Press, 2001, 15–30.

Jervis, Robert *Perception and Misperception in International Politics* Princeton, NJ: Princeton University Press, 1976.

Jervis, Robert "Realism in the Study of World Politics" *International Organization* 52(4), 1998, 971–991.

Johnston, Douglas "The Churches and Apartheid in South Africa" in Douglas Johnston and Cynthia Sampson (eds) *Religion, The Missing Dimension of Statecraft* New York: Oxford University Press, 1994, 177–208.

Johnston, Douglas (ed.) *Faith-based Diplomacy: Trumping Realpolitik* New York: Oxford University Press, 2003.

Johnston, Hank and Jozef Figa "The Church and Political Opposition: Comparative Perspectives on Mobilization against Authoritarian Regimes" *Journal for the Scientific Study of Religion* 27(1), 1988, 32–47.

Jones, Eric *Cultures Merging: A Historical and Economic Critique of Culture* Princeton, NJ: Princeton University Press, 2006.

Jones, Roy E. "The English School of International Relations: A Case for Closure" *Review of International Studies* 7(1), 1981, 1–13.

Joppke, Christian "Immigration and the Identity of Citizenship: The Paradox of Universalism" *Citizenship Studies* 12(6), 2008, 533–546.

Jordan, Borimir "Religion in Thucydides" *Transactions of the American Philological Association* 116, 1986, 119–147.

Juergensmeyer, Mark *The New Cold War?* Berkeley: University of California Press, 1993.

Juergensmeyer, Mark "Terror Mandated by God" *Terrorism and Political Violence* 9(2), 1997, 16–23.

Juergensmeyer, Mark *Global Rebellion: Religious Challenges to the Secular State, from Christian Militias to Al Qaeda* Berkeley: University of California Press, 2008.

Juergensmeyer, Mark "The Global Rise of Religious Nationalism" *Australian Journal of International Affairs* 64(3), 2010, 262–273.

Jung, Dietrich "The Political Sociology of World Society" *European Journal of International Relations* 7(4), 2001, 443–474.

Kalyvas, Stathis "Commitment Problems in Emerging Democracies: The Case of Religious Parties" *Comparative Politics* 32(4), 2000, 379–398.

Kamil, Omar "Rabbi Ovadia Yosef and his 'Culture War' in Israel" *Middle East Review of International Affairs* 4(4), 2000, 22–29.

Kaplan, Eben "Tracking Down Terrorist Financing" *Council on Foreign Relations Back-grounder* April 4, 2006.

Karyotis, Georgios and Stratos Patrikios "Religion, Securitization and Anti-immigration Attitudes: The Case of Greece" *Journal of Peace Research* 47(1), 2010, 43–57.

Katzenstein, Peter J. *A World of Regions: Asia and Europe in the American Imperium* Ithaca, NY: Cornell University Press, 2005.

Katzenstein, Peter J. and Timothy A. Byrnes "Transnational Religion in an Expanded Europe" *Perspectives on Politics* 4(4), 2006, 679–694.

Kaufman, Stuart J. "Spiraling to Ethnic War: Elites, Masses and Moscow in Moldova's Civil War" *International Security* 12(2), 1996, 108–138.

Keck, Margaret and Katherine Sikkink *Activists beyond Borders: Advocacy Networks in International Politics* Ithaca, NY: Cornell University Press, 1998.

Kedourie, Elie *Nationalism in Asia and Africa* London: Weidenfeld and Nicolson, 1971.

Kedourie, Elie *Democracy and Arab Political Culture* Washington DC: Washington Institute for Near East Studies, 1992.

Kelley, Colleen "With God on His Side: Deconstructing the Post-9/11 Discourse of George W. Bush" Paper presented at the Annual Meeting of the Australian and New Zealand Communication Association, Christchurch, New Zealand, July 4–7.

Kemp, Geoffrey *Iran and Iraq: The Shia Connection, Soft Power, and the Nuclear Connection* Washington DC: United States Institute of Peace, 2005.

Kengor, Paul *God and George W. Bush: A Spiritual Life* New York: HarperCollins, 2004.

Kennan, George F. *Memoirs 1925–1950* Boston, MA: Little, Brown, 1967.

Kennedy, Robert "Is One Person's Terrorist Another's Freedom Fighter? Western and Islamic Approaches to 'Just War' Compared" *Terrorism and Political Violence* 11(1), 1999, 1–21.

Keohane, Robert O. *After Hegemony: Cooperation and Discord in World Political Economy* Princeton: Princeton University Press, 1984.

Keohane, Robert O. (ed.) *Neorealism and Its Critics* New York: Columbia University Press, 1986.

Keohane, Robert O. "International Institutions: Two Approaches" *International Studies Quarterly* 32(4), 1988, 379–396.

Keohane, Robert O. *International Institutions and State Power* Boulder, CO: Westview Press, 1989.

Keohane, Robert O. and Lisa L. Martin "The Promise of Institutionalist Theory" *International Security* 20(1), 1995, 39–51.

Keohane, Robert O. and Helen V. Milner (eds) *Internationalization and Domestic Politics* New York: Cambridge University Press, 1996.

Keohane, Robert O. and Joseph Nye *Power and Interdependence* Boston, MA: Little Brown, 1977.

Keohane, Robert O. and Joseph Nye "Power and Interdependence Revisited" *International Organization* 41(4), 1987, 725–753.

Keohane, Robert O. and Joseph Nye "Power and Interdependence in the Information Age" *Foreign Affairs* 77(5), 1998, 81–94.

Kessler, Markus "Religio-Secular Metamorphoses: The Remaking of Turkish Alevism" *Journal of the American Academy of Religion* 76(2), 2008, 280–311.

Khosla, Deepa "Third World States as Intervenors in Ethnic Conflicts: Implications for Regional and International Security" *Third World Quarterly* 20(6), 1999, 1143–1156.

Kimball, Charles *When Religion Becomes Evil* San Francisco, CA: HarperCollins, 2002.

Kim-Prieto, Chu and Ed Diener "Religion as a Source of Variation in the Experience of

Positive and Negative Emotions" *The Journal of Positive Psychology* 4(6), 2009, 447–460.

Kinghorn, Johann "On the Theology of Church and Society in the DRC" *Journal of Theology for Southern Africa* 70, 1990, 21–36.

Kirkpatrick, Lee A. "Fundamentalism, Christian Orthodoxy, and Intrinsic Religious Orientation as Predictors of Discriminatory Attitudes" *Journal for the Scientific Study of Religion* 32(3), 1993, 256–268.

Kissinger, Henry "Domestic Structure and Foreign Policy" *Daedalus* 95(2), 1966, 503–529.

Kitiarsa, Pattana "In Defense of the Thai Style Democracy" National University of Singapore: Asia Research Institute, 2006. Paper available at www.ari.nus.edu.sg/showfile. asp?eventfileid=188 (last accessed August 22, 2012).

Klausen, Jytte *The Islamic Challenge: Politics and Religion in Western Europe* Oxford: Oxford University Press, 2005.

Klotz, Audie and Cecelia Lynch *Strategies for Research in Constructivist International Relations* New York: M.E. Sharpe, 2007.

Knoll, Benjamin R. " 'And Who Is My Neighbor?' Religion and Immigration Policy Attitudes" *Journal for the Scientific Study of Religion* 48(2), 2009, 313–331.

Kokoslakis, Nikos "Legitimation, Power and Religion in Modern Society" *Sociological Analysis* 46(4), 1985, 367–376.

Kolas, Ashild "Tibetan Nationalism: The Politics of Religion" *Journal of Peace Research* 33(1), 1996, 51–66.

Krasner, Stephen D. *International Regimes* Ithaca, NY: Cornell University Press, 1983.

Kratochwil, Friedrich "Religion and (Inter-)National Politics: On the Heuristics of Identities, Structures, and Agents" *Alternatives* 30(2), 2005, 113–140.

Kraus, Rachel "Thou Shall Not Take the Name of Thy God in Vain: Washington Offices' Use of Religious Language to Shape Public and Political Agendas" *Journal of Media and Religion* 8(2), 2009, 115–137.

Krebs, Ronald R. and Patrick Thaddeus Jackson "Twisting Tongues and Twisting Arms: The Power of Political Rhetoric" *European Journal of International Relations* 13(1), 2007, 35–66.

Kroessin, Mohammed and Abdulfatah Mohamed "Saudi Arabian NGOs in Somalia: 'Wahhabi' Da'wah or Humanitarian Aid?" in Gerard Clarke and Michael Jennings (eds) *Development, Civil Society and Faith-based Organizations: Bridging the Sacred and the Secular* Basingstoke: Palgrave Macmillan, 2008, 187–214.

Kubalkova, Vendulka "Towards an International Political Theology" *Millennium* 29, 2000, 675–704.

Küng, Hans *The Catholic Church* trans. J. Bowden London: Weidenfeld and Nicolson, 2001.

Kuran, Timur "Why the Middle East is Economically Underdeveloped: Historical Mechanisms of Institutional Stagnation" *Journal of Economic Perspectives* 18(3), 2004, 71–90.

Kuru, Ahmet T. "Passive and Assertive Secularism: Historical Conditions, Ideological Struggles, and State Policies toward Religion" *World Politics* 59(4), 2006, 568–594.

Kymlicka, Will *Politics in the Vernacular: Nationalism, Multiculturalism and Citizenship* New York: Oxford University Press, 2001.

Kymlicka, Will "The Rise and Fall of Multiculturalism: New Debates on Inclusion and Accommodation in Diverse Societies" *International Social Science Journal* 61(199), 2010, 97–112.

Kymlicka, Will "Multicultural Citizenship within Multination States" *Ethnicities* 11(3), 2011, 281–302.

Laaman, Peter *Getting on Message: Challenging the Christian Right from the Heart of the Gospel* Boston, MA: Beacon Press, 2006.

Lamy, Steven "The Role of Religious NGOs in Shaping Foreign Policy: Western Middle Powers and Reform Internationalism" in Patrick James (ed.) *Religion, Identity and Global Governance: Ideas, Evidence and Practice* Toronto: Toronto University Press, 2011, 244–271.

Lapid, Yosef "Culture's Ship: Returns and Departures in International Relations Theory" in Yosef Lapid and Friedrich Kratochwil (eds) *The Return of Culture and Identity in International Relations Theory* Boulder, CO: Lynne Rienner, 1996, 3–20.

Laudy, Mark "The Vatican Mediation of the Beagle Channel Dispute: Crisis Intervention and Forum Building" in Melanie Barton, John H. McGuinness, and Margaret E. Greenberg (eds) *Words Over War: Mediation and Arbitration to Prevent Deadly Conflict* New York: Rowman and Littlefield, 2000, 293–321.

Laustsen, Carsten B. and Ole Waever "In Defense of Religion: Sacred Referent Objects for Securitization" *Millennium* 29(3), 2000, 705–739.

Lawler, Peter "Janus-faced Solidarity: Danish Internationalism Reconsidered" *Cooperation and Conflict* 42(1), 2007, 101–126.

Layne, Christopher "The Unipolar Illusion: Why New Great Powers will Rise" *International Security* 7(4), 1993, 5–51.

Laythe, Brian, Deborah Finkel, and Lee A. Kirkpatrick "Predicting Prejudice from Religious Fundamentalism and Right Wing Authoritarianism: A Multiple Regression Approach" *Journal for the Scientific Study of Religion* 40(1), 2002, 1–10.

Lebow, Richard N. "Classical Realism" in Tim Dunne, Milja Kurki, and Steve Smith (eds) *International Relations Theories: Discipline and Diversity* Oxford: Oxford University Press, 2007, 52–70.

Lederach, John Paul *Preparing for Peace: Conflict Transformation Across Cultures* New York: Syracuse University Press, 1995.

Leenders, Reinoud "Regional Conflict Formations? Is the Middle East Next?" *Third World Quarterly* 28(5), 2007, 959–982.

Legro, Jeffrey and Andrew Moravcsik "Is Anybody Still a Realist?" *International Security* 24(2), 1999, 5–55.

Leigh, Karen "The Saudi–Iran Cold War: Will the Assassination Plot Heat it Up?" *TIME* October 13, 2011. Available at www.time.com/time/world/article/0,8599,2096764,00.html.

Leites, Nathan *The Operational Code of the Politburo* New York: McGraw-Hill, 1951.

Leites, Nathan *A Study of Bolshevism* New York: Free Press, 1953.

Levitt, Matthew *Hamas: Politics, Charity and Terrorism in the Service of Jihad* New Haven, CT: Yale University Press, 2006.

Levitt, Peggy "Religion as a Path to Civic Engagement" *Ethnic and Racial Studies* 31(4), 2008, 766–791.

Levy, Yagil "The Israeli Military: Imprisoned by the Religious Community" *Middle East Policy* 18(2), 2011, 67–83.

Lewis, Bernard *The Middle East and the West* New York: Harper & Row, 1964.

Lewis, Bernard *Islam and the West* Oxford: Oxford University Press, 1993.

Lewis, Bernard "License to Kill: Usama bin Ladin's Declaration of Jihad" *Foreign Affairs* 77(6), 1998, 14–19.

Lim, Chaeyoon and Robert D. Putnam "Religion, Social Networks, and Life Satisfaction" *American Sociological Review* 75(6), 2010, 914–933.

Lincoln, Bruce (ed.) *Religion, Rebellion and Revolution* London: Macmillan, 1985.

Lincoln, Bruce *Holy Terrors: Thinking About Religion After 9/11* Chicago, IL, and London: University of Chicago Press, 2003.

Linklater, Andrew *The Transformation of Political Community: Ethical Foundations of the Post-Westphalian Era* Cambridge: Polity Press, 1998.

Lippman, Walter *US Foreign Policy: Shield of the Republic* Boston, MA: Little, Brown, 1943.

Lipson, Charles "International Cooperation in Economic and Security Affairs" *World Politics* 37(1), 1984, 1–23.

Lloyd, Robert B. "Christian Mediation in International Conflicts" in Patrick James (ed.) *Religion, Identity and Global Governance: Ideas, Evidence and Practice* Toronto: Toronto University Press, 2011, 220–243.

Longman, Timothy *Christianity and Genocide in Rwanda* Cambridge: Cambridge University Press, 2010.

Loriaux, Michael "The Realists and St. Augustine: Skepticism, Psychology and Moral Action in International Relations" *International Studies Quarterly* 36(4), 1992, 401–420.

Luoma-aho, Mika "Political Theology, Anthropomorphism and Person-hood of the State: The Religion of IR" *International Political Sociology* 3, 2009, 293–309.

Luttwak, Edward "The Missing Dimension" in Douglas Johnston and Cynthia Sampson (eds) *Religion: The Missing Dimension in Statecraft* Oxford: Oxford University Press, 1994, 8–19.

Lynch, Cecelia "Acting on Belief: Christian Perspectives on Suffering and Violence" *Ethics and International Affairs* 14(1), 2000, 83–97.

Lynch, Cecelia "Reflexivity in Research on Civil Society: Constructivist Perspectives" *International Studies Review* 10(4), 2008, 708–721.

Lynch, Cecelia "A Neo-Weberian Approach to Religion in International Politics" *International Theory* 1(3), 2009, 381–408.

Lynch, Cecelia "Religion, Identity and the 'War on Terror': Insights from Religious Humanitarianism" in Patrick James (ed.) *Religion, Identity and Global Governance: Ideas, Evidence and Practice* Toronto: Toronto University Press, 2011, 108–128.

Machiavelli, Niccolo *The Discourses* ed. Bernard Crick trans. Leslie J. Walker New York: Penguin, [1513] 1984.

Madan, T.N. "Indian Secularism: A Religio-Secular Ideal" in Linell E. Cady and Elizabeth Shakman Hurd (eds) *Comparative Secularisms in a Global Age* New York: Palgrave Macmillan, 2010, 181–197.

Madeley, John T.S. "European Liberal Democracy and the Principle of State Religious Neutrality" *West European Politics* 26(1), 2003, 1–22.

Madsen, Richard *Democracy's Dharma: Religious Renaissance and Political Development in Taiwan* Berkeley: University of California Press, 2007.

Mahmood, Saba "Secularism, Hermeneutics, and the Empire: The Politics of Islamic Reformation" *Public Culture* 18(2), 2006, 323–347.

Mainwaring, Scott *The Catholic Church and the Politics in Brazil* Stanford, CA: Stanford University Press, 1986.

Malici, Akan and Allison L. Buckner "Empathizing with Rogue Leaders: Mahmoud Ahmadinejad and Bashar al-Asad" *Journal of Peace Research* 45(6), 2008, 783–800.

Manji, Firoze and Carl O'Coill "The Missionary Position: NGOs and Development in Africa" *International Affairs* 78(3), 2002, 567–583.

Manor, James "Organizational Weakness and the Rise of Sinhalese Buddhist Extremism" in Martin E. Marty and R. Scott Appleby (eds) *Accounting for Fundamentalisms: The Dynamic Character of Movements*, Chicago, IL: University of Chicago Press, 1994, 770–784.

Marsden, Lee "Religion, Identity and American Power in the Age of Obama" *International Politics* 48, 2011, 326–343.

Marshall, Katherine and Lucy Keough *Mind, Heart and Soul in the Fight Against Poverty* Washington DC: World Bank, 2004.

Marshall, Katherine and Marisa Van Saanen *Development and Faith: Where Mind, Heart and Soul Work Together* Washington DC: The World Bank Press, 2007.

Marty, Martin E. and R. Scott Appleby (eds) *Fundamentalisms and the State: Remaking Politics, Economies and Militance*, Chicago, IL: University of Chicago Press, 1991.

Marty, Martin E. and R. Scott Appleby (eds) *Fundamentalisms and Society: Reclaiming the Sciences, Family and Education* Chicago, IL: University of Chicago Press, 1993.

Massaro, Thomas *Living Justice: Catholic Social Teaching in Action* Lanham, MD: Rowman and Littlefield, 2008.

Massimo, Introvigne "Religious Minorities and Anti-cult Opposition: The Italian Situation in Comparative Perspective" Paper presented on June 9, 2001 at an International Conference at the University of Heidelberg.

Mayall, James "National Identity and the Revival of Regionalism" in Louise Fawcett and Andrew Hurrell (eds) *Regionalism in World Politics: Regional Organization and International Order* Oxford: Oxford University Press, 1995, 169–201.

Mayer, Elizabeth Ann *Islam and Human Rights: Tradition and Politics* Boulder, CO: Westview Press, 2006.

Mazrui, Ali *Cultural Forces in World Politics* London: James Currey, 1990.

McCarthy John D. and Mayer N. Zald "Resource Mobilization and Social Movements: A Partial Theory" *American Journal of Sociology* 82(6), 1976, 1217–1218.

McCleary, Rachel M. and Robert J. Barro "Religion and Economy" *Journal of Economic Perspectives* 20(2), 2006, 49–72.

McCloskey, Deirdre *The Bourgeois Virtues: Ethics for an Age of Commerce* Chicago, IL: University of Chicago Press, 2006.

McDermott, Monica L. "Voting for Catholic Candidates: The Evolution of a Stereotype" *Social Science Quarterly* 88(4), 2007, 953–969.

McDuie-Ra, Duncan and John A. Rees "Religious Actors, Civil Society and the Development Agenda: The Dynamics of Inclusion and Exclusion" *Journal of International Development* 22(1), 2010, 20–36.

McIntosh, Mary and Dan Abele *Tolerance for a Multi-ethnic Bosnia Hercegovina: Testing Alternative Theories* Scotland: University of Strathclyde, Centre for the Study of Public Policy, 1996.

Mead, Walter Russell "God's Country?" *Foreign Affairs* 85(5), 2006, 24–43.

Mearsheimer, John J. "Back to the Future: Instability in Europe after the Cold War" *International Security* 15(1), 1990, 5–56.

Mearsheimer, John J. *The Tragedy of Great Power Politics* New York: W.W. Norton, 2001.

Mearsheimer, John J. *Hans Morgenthau and the Iraq War: Realism versus Neoconservatism* London: Open Democracy, 2005.

Mearsheimer, John and Stephen Walt "An Unnecessary War" *Foreign Policy* 134, 2003, 50–59.

Mearsheimer, John and Stephen Walt "The Israel Lobby" *London Review of Books* 28(6), 2006, 3–12.

Mendelsohn, Barak "Sovereignty under Attack: The International Society Meets the Al Qaeda Network" *Review of International Studies* 31(1), 2005, 45–68.

Mendelsohn, Barak "English School, American Style: Testing the Preservation-seeking Quality of the International Society" *European Journal of International Relations* 15(2), 2009, 291–318.

Mentak, Said "Islam and Modernity: Islamist Movements and Politics of Position" *Contemporary Islam* 3(2), 2009, 113–119.

Metz, Johan Baptist and Jurgen Moltmann *Faith and the Future: Essays on Theology, Solidarity and Modernity* Maryknoll, NY: Orbis, 1995.

Meyer, Josh "Al Qaeda Said to Focus again on WMD" *Los Angeles Times* February 3, 2008.

X   Midlarsky, Manus I. "Democracy and Islam: Implications for Civilizational Conflict and the Democratic Peace" *International Studies Quarterly* 42(3), 1998, 458–511.

Miles, Jack "Religion and American Foreign Policy" *Survival* 46(1), 2004, 23–37.

Miller, Alan S. "The Influence of Religious Affiliation on the Clustering of Social Attitudes" *Review of Religious Research* 37(3), 1996, 123–136.

Miller, David *Citizenship and National Identity* Cambridge: Polity Press, 2000.

Miller, Marjorie "Israeli Opens Fire in Hebron Market: 7 Arabs Wounded" *Los Angeles Times*, January 2, 1997.

Mintz, Alex "How Do Leaders Make Decisions? A Poliheuristic Perspective" *Journal of Conflict Resolution* 48(1), 2004, 3–13.

Mitzen, Jennifer "Ontological Security in World Politics" *European Journal of International Relations* 12(3), 2006, 341–370.

Mojzes, Paul *Yugoslavian Inferno: Ethno-religious Warfare in the Balkans* New York: Continuum, 1995.

Mollov, Benjamin M. *Power and Transcendence: Hans J. Morgenthau and the Jewish Experience* Lanham, MD: Lexington Books, 2002.

Moore, James "The Creationist Cosmos of Protestant Fundamentalism" in Martin E. Marty and R. Scott Appleby (eds) *Fundamentalisms and Society: Reclaiming the Sciences, Family and Education* Chicago, IL: University of Chicago Press, 1993, 42–73.

Moreau, Scott (cited in Peter Waldman) "Evangelicals Give U.S. Foreign Policy an Activist Tinge" *The Wall Street Journal* May 26, 2004.

Morgenthau, Hans J. "The Evil of Politics and the Ethics of Evil" *Ethics* 56(1), 1945, 1–18.

Morgenthau, Hans J. *Politics among Nations* New York: Knopf, 1948.

Morgenthau, Hans J. "Book Review: Modern Nationalism and Religion by Salo Wittmayer Baron" *Ethics* 59(2), 1949, 147–148.

Morgenthau, Hans J. "What Is the National Interest of the United States?" *Annals of the American Academy of Political and Social Science* 282(1), 1952, 1–7.

Morgenthau, Hans J. *Politics among Nations* (2nd edn) New York: Knopf, 1956.

Morgenthau, Hans J. *Politics among Nations* (4th edn) New York: Knopf, 1967.

Morgenthau, Hans J. *Science: Servant or Master?* New York: W.W. Norton, 1972.

Mostafa, Mohamed M. and Mohamed T. Al-Hamdi "Political Islam, Clash of Civilizations, U.S. Dominance and Arab Support of Attacks on America: A Test of a Hierarchical Model" *Studies in Conflict and Terrorism* 30(8), 2007, 723–736.

Mouffe, Chantal "Religion, Liberal Democracy, and Citizenship" in Hent De Vries and Lawrence E. Sullivan (eds) *Political Theologies: Public Religions in a Post-secular World* New York: Fordham University Press, 2006, 318–327.

Murray, Douglass " 'To What Extent is Sharia Law Already Operating in Britain?' The

2009 Charles Douglas-Home Memorial Trust Award Essay" *The Times*, December 30, 2009.

Muslim Public Affairs Council Statement "Examining the Root Causes of Abu Ghraib" May 7, 2004. Available at www.mpac.org/issues/islamophobia/examining-the-root-causes-of-abu-ghraib.php (last accessed August 23, 2012).

Nahshoni, Kobi "Segregated Facebook for Haredim" ynetnews.com July 7, 2011. Availableatwww.ynetnews.com/Ext/Comp/ArticleLayout/CdaArticlePrintPreview/1,2506,L-4098443,00.html (last accessed 8 November 2011).

Narayan, Deepa, Robert Chambers, Meera Shah, and Patti Petesch *Voices of the Poor: Crying Out for Change* Washington DC: World Bank, and New York: Oxford University Press, 2000.

Nardin, Terry "Legal Positivism as a Theory of International Society" in David Mapel and Terry Nardin (eds) *International Society: Diverse Ethical Perspectives* Princeton, NJ: Princeton University Press, 1999, 17–35.

Nasr, Vali Reza *Islamic Leviathan: Islam and the Making of State Power* Oxford: Oxford University Press, 2001.

Nexon, Daniel "Religion and International Relations: No Leap of Faith Required" in Jack Snyder (ed.) *Religion and International Relations Theory* New York: Columbia University Press, 2011.

Niebuhr, Reinhold *Moral Man and Immoral Society: A Study of Ethics and Politics* New York: Charles Scribner's Sons, 1932.

Niebuhr, Reinhold "Repeal the Neutrality Act!" *Christianity and Crisis* 1, 1941.

Niebuhr, Reinhold *Christian Realism and Political Problems* London: Faber and Faber, 1954.

Niebuhr, Reinhold *Nature and Destiny of Man II* Westminster: John Knox Press, 1996.

Noland, M. "Religion, Islam et Croissance Economique" *Revue Francaise de Gestion* 2007, 171, 97–118.

Norman, Wayne *Negotiating Nationalism Nation-building, Federalism, and Secession in the Multinational State* Oxford: Oxford University Press, 2006.

Norris, Pippa and Ronald Inglehart *Sacred and Secular: Religion and Politics Worldwide* New York: Cambridge University Press, 2004.

Nussbaum, Martha C. *Upheavals of Thought: The Intelligence of Emotion* Cambridge: Cambridge University Press, 2001.

Nye, Joseph "Neorealism and Neoliberalism" *World Politics* 40, 1988, 235–251.

Nye, Joseph *Soft Power* New York: Perseus Books, 2004.

Nye, Joseph "Public Diplomacy and Soft Power" *Annals of the American Academy of Political and Social Science* 616(1), 2008, 94–109.

Nye, Joseph and Robert Keohane "Transnational Relations and World Politics: An Introduction" *International Organization* 25(3), 1971, 326–350.

O'Dwyer, Shaun "The Yasukuni Shrine and the Competing Patriotic Pasts of East Asia" *History and Memory* 22(2), 2010, 142–177.

Olson, Mancur *The Logic of Collective Action* Cambridge, MA: Harvard University Press, 1965.

Omer, Atalia "Can a Critic be a Caretaker Too? Religion, Conflict and Conflict Transformation" *Journal of the American Academy of Religion* 79(2), 2011, 459–496.

Onuf, Nicholas *World of Our Making: Rules and Rule in Social Theory and International Relations* Columbia, SC: University of South Carolina Press, 1989.

Oren, Ido "The Subjectivity of the 'Democratic' Peace: Changing US Perceptions of Imperial Germany" *International Security* 20(2), 1995, 147–184.

Pach, Chester "The Reagan Doctrine: Principle, Pragmatism and Policy" *Presidential Studies Quarterly* 36(1), 2006, 75–88.

Pan, Esther and Jayshree Bajoria "The U.S.–India Nuclear Deal" *Council on Foreign Relations Backgrounders* October 2, 2008.

Pape, Robert "The Strategic Logic of Suicide Terrorism" *American Political Science Review* 97(3), 2003, 343–361.

Pape, Robert "Soft-balancing Against the United States" *International Security* 30(1), 2005, 7–45.

Patterson, Eric *Just War Thinking: Morality and Pragmatism in the Struggle Against Contemporary Threats* Lanham, MD: Lexington Books, 2007.

Patterson, Eric *Christianity and Power Politics Today: Christian Realism and Contemporary Political Dilemmas* New York: Palgrave Macmillan, 2008.

Pattison, James "Just War Theory and the Privatization of the Military Force" *Ethics and International Affairs* 22(2), 2008, 143–162.

Perica, Vjekoslav *Balkan Idols: Religion and Nationalism in Yugoslav States* New York: Oxford University Press, 2004.

Peterson, Scott "Iran Flexes its 'Soft Power' in Iraq" *Christian Science Monitor* May 20, 2005. Available at www.csmonitor.com/2005/0520/p06s02-woiq.html (last accessed February 7, 2012).

Philpott, Daniel "The Religious Roots of International Relations" *World Politics* 52, 2000, 206–245.

Philpott, Daniel *Revolutions in Sovereignty: How Ideas Shaped Modern International Relations* Princeton, NJ: Princeton University Press, 2001.

Philpott, Daniel "The Challenge of September 11 to Secularism in International Relations" *World Politics* 55(1), 2002, 66–95.

Philpott, Daniel "Christianity and Democracy: The Catholic Wave" *Journal of Democracy* 15(2), 2004, 32–46.

Philpott, Daniel "Explaining the Political Ambivalence of Religion" *American Political Science Review* 101, 2007, 505–525.

Philpott, Daniel "Has the Study of Global Politics Found Religion?" *Annual Review of Political Science* 12, 2009, 183–202.

Philpott, Daniel *Just and Unjust Peace: An Ethic of Reconciliation* New York: Oxford University Press, 2012.

Philpott, Daniel and Timothy Samuel Shah "The Fall and Rise of Religion in International Relations: History and Theory" in Jack Snyder (ed.) *Religion and International Relations Theory* New York: Columbia University Press, 2012, 24–60.

Phongpaichit, Pasuk and Chris Baker *A History of Thailand* New York: Cambridge University Press, 2005.

Pichler, Hans-Karl "'The Godfather of 'Truth': Max Weber and Carl Schmitt in Morgenthau's Theory of Power Politics" *Review of International Studies* 24(2), 1998, 259–294.

Pickering, W.S.F. *Durkheim's Sociology of Religion: Themes and Theories* London: Routledge and Kegan Paul, 1984.

Pierson, Paul and Theda Skocpol "Historical Institutionalism in Contemporary Political Science" in Ira Katznelson and Helen Milner (eds) *Political Science: The State of the Discipline* New York: Norton, 2002, 693–721.

Pieris, Aloysius "Political Theologies in Asia" in Peter Scott and William T. Cavanaugh (eds) *The Blackwell Companion to Political Theology* Oxford: Blackwell, 2007, 256–271.

Piscatori, James *Islam in a World of Nation-States* Cambridge: Cambridge University Press, 1986.

Polkinghorn, Brian and Sean Byrne "Between War and Peace: an Examination of Conflict Management Styles in Four Conflict Zones" *International Journal of Conflict Management* 12(1), 2001, 23–46.

Posen, Barry "The Security Dilemma and Ethnic Conflict" *Survival* 35(1), 1993, 27–47.

Powell, Emilia Justyna and Stephanie J. Rickard "International Trade and Domestic Legal Systems: Examining the Impact of Islamic Law" *International Interaction* 36(4), 2010, 335–362.

Preus, Samuel "Machiavelli's Functional Analysis of Religion: Context and Object" *Journal of the History of Ideas* 40(2), 1979, 171–190.

Price, Richard M. and Christian Reus-Smit "Dangerous Liaisons? Critical International Theory and Constructivism" *European Journal of International Relations* 4(3), 1998, 259–261.

Prodromou, Elizabeth "The Ambivalent Orthodox" *Journal of Democracy* 15(2), 2004, 62–75.

Prokop, Michaela "Saudi Arabia: The Politics of Education" *International Affairs* 79(1), 2003, 77–89.

Putnam, Robert "Diplomacy and Domestic Politics: The Logic of Two-level Games" *International Organization* 42(3), 1988, 427–460.

Putnam, Robert "Bowling Alone: America's Declining Social Capital" *Journal of Democracy* 6(1), 1995, 65–78.

Putnam, Robert *Bowling Alone: The Collapse and Revival of American Community* New York: Simon and Schuster, 2000.

Ralph, Jason "International Society, the International Criminal Court and American Foreign Policy" *Review of International Studies* 31(1), 2005, 27–44.

Ramachandran, Sudha "Who's Behind the LTTE Split?" *Asia Times* March 26, 2004.

Ramazani, Rouhoullah K. "Reflections on Iran's Foreign Policy: Defining the National Interests" in John L. Esposito and Rouhoullah K. Ramazani (eds) *Iran at the Crossroads* New York: Palgrave, 2001, 211–239.

Rapoport, David C. "Fear and Trembling: Terrorism in Three Religious Traditions" *American Political Science Review* 78(3), 1984, 658–677.

Rapoport, David C. "Messianic Sanctions for Terror" *Comparative Politics* 20(2), 1988, 195–213.

Reed, Charles and David Ryall (eds) *The Price of Peace: Just War in the Twenty First Century* Cambridge: Cambridge University Press, 2007.

Reese, Thomas *Inside the Vatican: The Politics and Organization of the Catholic Church* Cambridge, MA: Harvard University Press, 1998.

Rengger, Nicholas "On the Just War Tradition in Twenty-first Century" *International Affairs* 78(2), 2002, 353–363.

Reporters Without Borders "Sayed Pervez Kambaksh is Freed and Goes Abroad" September 7, 2009.

Richardson, James T. "Religion, Law and Human Rights" in Peter Beyer and Lori Beaman (eds) *Religion, Globalization and Culture* Leiden: Martinus Nijhoff, 2007, 407–431.

Risse, Thomas "Constructivism and International Institutions: Toward Conversations across Paradigms" in Ira Katznelson and Helen Milner (eds) *Political Science: The State of the Discipline* New York: Norton, 2002.

Risse, Thomas "Ideas, Discourse, Power and the End of the Cold War: 20 Years On" *International Politics* 48(4), 2011, 591–606.

Roelofs, H. Mark "Liberation Theology: The Recovery of Biblical Radicalism" *American Political Science Review* 88(2), 1988, 549–566.

Romero, Simon "Sympathetic to Chavez, A New Church Draws Fire" *New York Times* August 1, 2008.

Roof, Wade Clark *Spiritual Market Place: Baby Boomers and the Remaking of American Religion* Princeton, NJ: Princeton University Press, 2001.

Rose, Gideon "Neoclassical Realism and Theories of Foreign Policy" *World Politics* 51(1), 1998, 144–172.

Rose, Susan *Keeping Them Out of the Hands of Satan: Evangelical Schooling in America* New York: Routledge, 1988.

Rosenak, Michael "Jewish Fundamentalism in Israeli Education" in Martin E. Marty and R. Scott Appleby (eds) *Fundamentalisms and Society: Reclaiming the Sciences, Family and Education* Chicago, IL: University of Chicago Press, 1993, 374–415.

Ross, Andrew A.G. "Coming in from the Cold: Constructivism and Emotions" *European Journal of International Relations* 12(2), 2006, 197–222.

Rubin, Barry "Religion and International Affairs" in Douglas Johnston and Cynthia Sampson (eds) *Religion, the Missing Dimension of Statecraft* Oxford: Oxford University Press, 1994, 20–34.

Rudolph, Susanne H. "Religion, States and Transnational Civil Society" in Susanne H. Rudolp and James Piscatori (eds) *Transnational Religion and Fading States* Boulder, CO: Westview Press, 1997, 1–27.

Ruether, Rosemary Radford *Christianity and Social Systems: Historical Constructions and Ethical Challenges* New York: Rowman and Littlefield, 2009.

Ruggie, John G. *The Antinomies of Interdependence* New York: Columbia University Press, 1983.

Ruggie, John G. *Constructing the World Polity* New York: Routledge, 1998.

Rummel, Rudolph J. "Is Collective Violence Correlated with Social Pluralism?" *Journal of Peace Research* 34(2), 1997, 163–175.

Saat, Norshahril "Islamising Malayness: Ulama Discourse and Contemporary Authority in Malaysia" *Contemporary Islam* 6(2), 2012, 135–153.

Sachedina, Abdulaziz *The Islamic Roots of Democratic Pluralism* New York: Oxford University Press, 2001.

Sala-i-Martin, X., Doppelhofer, G., and Miller, R.I. "Determinants of Long-term Growth: A Bayesian Averaging of Classical Estimates (BACE) Approach" *American Economic Review* 94(4), 2004, 813–835.

Salim, Arskal *Challenging the Secular State: The Islamization of Law in Modern Indonesia* Honolulu: University of Hawaii Press, 2008.

Salvatore, Armando and Mark LeVine (eds) *Religion, Social Practice, and Contested Hegemonies* New York: Palgrave Macmillan, 2005.

Salvatore, Armando and Mark LeVine "Reconstructing the Public Sphere in Muslim Majority Societies" in Armando Salvator and Mark LeVine (eds) *Religion, Social Practice and Contested Hegemonies* New York: Palgrave Macmillan, 2005, 1–27.

Samuelsson, Kurt *Religion and Economic Action: The Protestant Ethic, the Rise of Capitalism, and the Abuses of Scholarship* Toronto: University of Toronto Press, 1993.

Sandal, Nukhet "Religious Actors as Epistemic Communities in Conflict Transformation: The Cases of Northern Ireland and South Africa" *Review of International Studies* 37(3), 2011, 929–949.

Sandal, Nukhet "Clash of Public Theologies? Rethinking the Concept of Religion in Politics" *Alternatives* 37(1), 2012, 66–83.

Sandal, Nukhet "Public Theologies of Human Rights and Citizenship: The Case of Turkey's Christians" *Human Rights Quarterly* forthcoming (August 2013).

Sandal, Nukhet and Patrick James "Religion and International Relations Theory: Towards a Mutual Understanding" *European Journal of International Relations* 17(1), 2011, 3–25.

Sandal, Nukhet, Enyu Zhang, Patrick James, and Carolyn James "Poliheuristic Theory and Crisis Decision-making: A Comparative Analysis of Turkey with China" *Canadian Journal of Political Science* 44(1), 2011, 27–57.

Saniotis, Arthur "Muslims and Ecology: Fostering Islamic Environmental Ethics" *Contemporary Islam* 2011 (online).

Saroglou, Vassilis, Vanessa Delpierre, and Rebecca Dernelle "Values and Religiosity: A Meta-analysis of Studies using Schwartz's Model" *Personality and Individual Differences* 37(4), 2004, 721–734.

Scheve, Kenneth and David Stasavage "Religion and Preferences for Social Insurance" *Quarterly Journal of Political Science* 1(3), 2006, 255–286.

Schmitt, Carl *Political Theology: Four Chapters on the Concept of Sovereignty* trans. George Schwab Cambridge, MA: MIT University Press, 2006.

Schweller, Randall *Deadly Imbalances: Tripolarity and Hitler's Strategy of World Conquest* New York: Columbia University Press, 1988.

Schweller, Randall "Unanswered Threats: A Neoclassical Realist Theory of Underbalancing" *International Security* 29(2), 2004, 159–201.

Seul, Jefferey R. "'Ours is the Way of God': Religion, Identity and Intergroup Conflict" *Journal of Peace Research* 36(3), 1999, 553–569.

Shadid, Anthony *Legacy of the Prophet: Despots, Democrats, and the New Politics of Islam* Boulder, CO: Westview Press, 2002.

Shadid, Anthony and David Kirkpatrick, "Activists in the Arab World Vie to Define Islamic State" *New York Times*, September 29, 2011. Available at www.nytimes.com/2011/09/30/world/middleeast/arab-debate-pits-islamists-against-themselves.html?pagewanted=all&_r=0 (last accessed February 7, 2013).

Shah, Timothy Samuel and Daniel Philpott, "The Fall and Rise of Religion in International Relations" in Jack Snyder (ed.) *Religion and International Relations Theory* New York: Columbia University Press, 2011, 24–60.

Shahin, Emad Eldin *Political Ascent: Contemporary Islamic Movements in North Africa* Boulder, CO: Westview Press, 1998.

Shahin, Emad Eldin "Political Islam in Egypt" in Michael Emerson and Richard Yougs (eds) *Political Islam and European Foreign Policy* Brussels: Center for European Studies, 2007, 65–86.

Shahin, Emad Eldin "Toleration in a Modern Islamic Polity: Contemporary Islamist Views" in Ingrid Creppell, Russell Hardin, and Stephen Macedo (eds) *Toleration on Trial* Boulder, CO: Lexington Books, 2008, 169–191.

Shani, Giorgio "Toward a Post-Western IR: The Umma, Khalsa Panth, and Critical International Relations Theory" *International Studies Review* 10(4), 2008, 722–734.

Sharp, Paul "Mullah Zaeef and Taliban Diplomacy: An English School Approach" *Review of International Studies* 29(4), 2003, 481–498.

Shavit, Uria and Frederic Wiesenbach "Muslim Strategies to Convert Christians" *The Middle East Quarterly* 16(2), 2009, 3–14.

Shimko, Keith L. "Realism, Neorealism, and American Liberalism" *The Review of Politics* 54(2), 1992, 281–301.

Shupe, Anson "The Stubborn Persistence of Religion in the Global Arena" in Emile

Sahliyeh (ed.) *Religious Resurgence and Politics in the Contemporary World* New York: SUNY Press, 1990, 17–26.

Sidahmed, Abdal Salam "Islamism, Nationalism and Sectarianism" in Markus E. Bouillon, David M. Malone and Ben Rowswell (eds) *Iraq: Preventing a New Generation of Conflict* Boulder, CO: Riener, 2007, 71–87.

Sigmund, Paul E. "The Catholic Tradition and Modern Democracy" *The Review of Politics* 49(4), 1987, 530–548.

Silverman, Adam L. "Just War, Jihad and Terrorism: A Comparison of Western and Islamic Norms for the Use of Political Violence" *Journal of Church and State* 44(1), 2002, 73–92.

Singh, Bhrigupati "Reinhabiting Civil Disobedience" in Hent De Vries and Lawrence E. Sullivan (eds) *Political Theologies: Public Religions in a Post-secular World* New York: Fordham University Press, 2006, 365–382.

Skocpol, Theda and Morris Fiorina *Civic Engagement in American Democracy* Washington DC: Brooking Institution, 1999.

Slack, James D. "Barack Obama and the Public Administration of Faith" *International Journal of Public Administration* 32(9), 2009, 786–791.

Smith, Adam *The Theory of Moral Sentiments* Edinburgh: Kincaid and Bell, 1759.

Smith, Adam *An Inquiry into Nature and Causes of The Wealth of Nations* New York: Modern Library, [1776] 1965.

Smith, Anthony D. "Ethnic Election and National Destiny: Some Religious Origins of Nationalist Ideals" *Nations and Nationalism* 5(3), 1999, 331–355.

Smith, Anthony "The Sacred Dimension of Nationalism" *Millennium* 29(3), 2000, 791–814.

Smith, Anthony *Chosen Peoples: Sacred Sources of National Identity* New York: Oxford University Press, 2004.

Smith, Rogers "Religious Rhetoric and the Ethics of Public Discourse: The Case of George W. Bush" *Political Theory* 36(2), 2008, 272–300.

Snidal, Duncan "The Game Theory of International Politics" *World Politics* 38(1), 1985, 25–57.

Snyder, Glenn H. and Paul Diesing *Conflict among Nations: Bargaining, Decision Making and System Structure in International Crises* Princeton, NJ: Princeton University Press, 1977.

Snyder, Jack "Introduction" in Jack Snyder (ed.) *Religion and International Relations Theory* New York: Columbia University Press, 2011.

Sofer, Roni "Peres Calls for Moral Sanctions on Iran" *Israel News* June 10, 2010.

Soroush, Abdulkarim *Reason, Freedom and Democracy in Islam: Essential Writings of Abdulkarim Soroush* trans. and ed. Mahmoud Sadri and Ahmad Sadri New York: Oxford University Press, 2002.

South African Democracy Education Trust *The Road to Democracy in South Africa: 1960–1970*, 2004.

Stahnke, Tad "Obama's Indonesian Opportunity" *Washington Post* March 17, 2010.

Stark, Rodney and William S. Bainbridge *The Future of Religion* Berkeley: University of California Press, 1985.

Stark, Rodney and Roger Finke *Acts of Faith: Explaining the Human Side of Religion* Berkeley: University of California Press, 2000.

Stein, Arthur "Coordination and Collaboration: Regimes in an Anarchic World" *International Organization* 36(2), 1982, 299–324.

Stepan, Alfred "Religion, Democracy, and the 'Twin Tolerations'" *Journal of Democracy* 11(4), 2000, 37–56.

Stepan, Alfred and Graeme B. Robinson "An 'Arab' More than 'Muslim' Electoral Gap" *Journal of Democracy* 14(3), 2003, 30–44.

Stern, Jessica *Terror in the Name of God: Why Religious Militants Kill* New York: HarperCollins, 2003.

Stern, Jessica and Amit Moti "Producing Terror: Organizational Dynamics of Survival" in Thomas J. Biersteker and Sue E. Eckert (eds) *Countering the Financing of Terrorism* New York: Routledge, 2007, 19–47.

Svensson, Isak "Fighting with Faith: Religion and Conflict Resolution in Civil Wars" *Journal of Conflict Resolution* 51(6), 2007, 930–949.

Svensson, Isak and Emily Harding "How Holy Wars End: Exploring The Termination Patters of Conflicts with Religious Dimensions in Asia" *Terrorism and Political Violence* 23(2), 2011, 133–149.

Sylvest, Casper "John H. Herz and the Resurrection of Classical Realism" *International Relations* 22(4), 2008, 441–455.

Takim, Liyakat "Holy Peace or Holy War: Tolerance and Co-existence in the Islamic Juridical Tradition" *Islam and Muslim Societies: A Social Science Journal* 3(2), 2007, 159–171.

Taliaferro, Jeffrey W., Steven E. Lobell, and Norrin M. Ripsman (eds) *Neoclassical Realism, the State and Foreign Policy* Cambridge: Cambridge University Press, 2009.

Tarrow, Sidney *Democracy and Disorder: Protest and Politics in Italy 1965–1975* Oxford: Clarendon Press, 1989.

Tarzi, Shah M. "Neorealism, Neoliberalism and the International System" *International Studies* 41(1), 2004, 115–128.

Taspinar, Omer "Europe's Muslim Street" *Foreign Policy* 135, 2003, 76–77.

Tawney, Richard H. *Religion and the Rise of Capitalism* New York: Harper & Row, 1926.

Taydas, Zeynep and Ozgur Ozdamar "A Divided Government, an Ideological Parliament and an Insecure Leader: Turkey's Indecision about Joining the Iraq War" *Social Science Quarterly* 2012 (online). DOI: 10.1111/j.1540–6237.2012.00871.x.

Taylor, Charles *A Secular Age* Cambridge, MA: Harvard University Press, 2007.

Taylor, Mark C. "Reconfiguring Religion" *Journal of the American Academy of Religion* 77(1), 2009, 105–119.

Tehran Times "West Hypocritically Using Human Rights Issue to Criticize other Nations" October 19, 2009. Available at http://old.tehrantimes.com/Index_view.asp?code=205838 (last accessed August 23, 2012).

Telhami, Shibley "Kenneth Waltz, Neorealism, and Foreign Policy" *Security Studies* 11(3), 2002, 158–170.

Tepe, Sultan "Moderation of Religious Parties: Electoral Constraints, Ideological Commitments, and the Democratic Capacities of Religious Parties in Israel and Turkey" *Political Research Quarterly* 65(3), 2012, 467–485.

Tetlock, Philip "Social Psychology and World Politics" in Daniel Gilbert, Susan Fiske, and Gardner Lindzey (eds) *The Handbook of Social Psychology* New York: McGraw Hill, 1998, 868–912.

Thomas, Scott "Religion and International Society" in Jeffrey Haynes (ed.) *Religion, Globalization and Political Culture in the Third World* New York: Palgrave Macmillan, 1999.

Thomas, Scott M. "Religion and International Conflict" in Ken R. Dark *Religion and International Relations* New York: Palgrave Macmillan, 2000, 1–23.

Thomas, Scott "Faith, History and Martin Wight: The Role of Religion in the Historical

Sociology of the English School of International Relations" *International Affairs* 77(4), 2001, 905–929.

Thomas, Scott M. "Taking Religious and Cultural Pluralism Seriously: The Global Resurgence of Religion and the Transformation of International Society" in Fabio Petito and Pavlos Hatzopoulos (eds) *Religion in International Relations: The Return from Exile* New York: Palgrave Macmillan, 2003, 21–55.

Thomas, Scott M. *The Global Resurgence of Religion and the Transformation of International Relations: The Struggle for the Soul of the Twenty-first Century* New York: Palgrave Macmillan, 2005.

Thucydides *The Peloponnesian War* trans. Rex Warner Baltimore, MD: Penguin Books, [400 BCE] 1972.

Tibi, Bassam "Islamic Law/Shari'a, Human Rights, Universal Morality and International Relations" *Human Rights Quarterly* 16(2), 1994, 277–299.

Tibi, Bassam "Post-bipolar Order in Crisis: The Challenge of Politicized Islam" *Millennium* 29(3), 2000, 843–859.

Tickner, Ann J. *Gender in International Relations: Feminist Perspectives on Achieving Global Security* New York: Columbia University Press, 1992.

Tickner, Ann "What is your Research Program? Some Feminist Answers to International Relations Methodological Questions" *International Studies Quarterly* 49(1), 2005, 1–21.

Todd, Jennifer "Symbolic Complexity and Political Division: The Changing Role of Religion in Northern Ireland" *Ethnopolitics* 9(1), 2010, 85–102.

Toft, Monica D. "Getting Religion? The Puzzling Case of Islam and Civil War" *International Security* 31(4), 2007, 97–131.

Toft, Monica D. "Religion, Rationality and Violence" in Jack Snyder (ed.) *Religion and International Relations Theory* New York: Columbia University Press, 2011, 115–141.

Toft, Monica D., Daniel Philpott, and Timothy S. Shah *God's Century: Resurgent Religion and Global Politics* New York: W.W. Norton, 2011.

Toly, Noah "Changing the Climate of Religious Internationalism: Evangelical Responses to Global Warming and Human Suffering" in Jeffrey Haynes (ed.) *Routledge Handbook of Religion and Politics* London: Routledge, 2009, 403–419.

Triandis, Harry C. *The Analysis of Subjective Culture* New York: Wiley Interscience, 1972.

Turam, Berna *Between Islam and the State: The Politics of Engagement* Palo Alto, CA: Stanford University Press, 2006.

Turner, Brian S. "Managing Religions: State Responses to Religious Diversity" *Contemporary Islam* 1(2), 2007, 123–137.

Turner, Brian S. *Religion and Social Theory* (2nd edn) London: Sage, 1991.

Vallier, Ivan "The Roman Catholic Church: A Transnational Actor" *International Organization* 25(3), 1971, 479–502.

Van Dartel, Geert "The Nations and the Churches in Yugoslavia" *Religion, State and Society* 20(3), 1992, 275–288.

Van Evera, Stephen "Hypotheses on Nationalism and War" *International Security* 15(1), 1994, 5–39.

Van Staveren, Irene *The Values of Economics: An Aristotelian Perspective* London: Routledge, 2001.

Varshney, Ashutosh "Contested Meanings: India's National Identity, Hindu Nationalism, and the Politics of Anxiety" *Daedalus* 122(3), 1993, 227–261.

Vassort-Rousset, Brigitte "Religion, Identity and International Politics" *Ares* 23(1), 2006, 11–24.

Verba, Sidney, Kay L. Scholzman, Henry Brady, and Norman H. Nie "Race, Ethnicity, and Political Resources: Participation in the United States" *British Journal of Political Science* 23(4), 1993, 453–497.

Vincent, R. *Human Rights and International Relations* Cambridge: Cambridge University Press, 1986.

Vincent, R. John and Paul Watson "Beyond Non-intervention" in Ian Forbes and Mark J. Hoffman (eds) *Political Theory, International Relations and the Ethics of Intervention* London: Macmillan, 1993.

Vinjamuri, Leslie and Aaron P. Boesenecker "Religious Actors and Transitional Justice" in Thomas Banchoff (ed.) *Religious Pluralism, Globalization and World Politics* New York: Oxford University Press, 2008, 155–195.

Viroli, Maurizio *Machiavelli's God* Princeton, NJ: Princeton University Press, 2010.

Volf, Miroslav *Exclusion and Embrace: A Theological Exploration of Identity, Otherness and Reconciliation* Nashville, TN: Abingdon Press, 1996.

Vriens, Lauren *Armed Islamic Group: Backgrounder* New York: Council on Foreign Relations, 2009.

Vries, Lloyd de "General Faulted for Satan Speeches" CBS News. Available at www.cbsnews.com/stories/2003/10/16/attack/main578471.shtml (last accessed April 13, 2010).

Wald, Kenneth, Lyman Kellstedt, and David Leege "Church Involvement and Political Behavior" in David Leege and Lyman Kellstedt (eds) *Rediscovering the Religious Factor in American Politics* New York: M.E. Sharpe, 1993.

Walker, Stephen G., Mark Schafer, and Michael D. Young "Presidential Operational Codes and Foreign Policy Conflicts in the Post-Cold War World" *Journal of Conflict Resolution* 43(5), 1999, 610–625.

Wallis, Jim *God's Politics: Why the American Right gets it Wrong and the Left Doesn't get it* San Francisco, CA: Harper, 2005.

Walt, Stephen M. "Alliance Formation and the Balance of World Power" *International Security* 9(4), 1985, 3–43.

Walt, Stephen M. *The Origins of Alliances* Ithaca, NY: Cornell University Press, 1987.

Walt, Stephen M. "Building up New Bogeymen" *Foreign Policy* 106, 1997, 177–189.

Walt, Stephen M. "International Relations: One World, Many Theories" *Foreign Policy* 110, 1998, 29–46.

Walt, Stephen M. "Taming American Power" *Foreign Affairs* 84(5), 2005, 105–120.

Walt, Stephen M. and John Mearsheimer *The Israel Lobby and the U.S. Policy* New York: Farrar, Strauss, and Giroux, 2007.

Walters, LeRoy "Human Embryonic Stem Cell Research: An Intercultural Perspective" *Kennedy Institute of Ethics Journal* 14(1), 2004, 3–38.

Waltz, Kenneth *Man, the State, and War* New York: Columbia University Press, 1959.

Waltz, Kenneth *Theory of International Politics* Cambridge, MA: Addison-Wesley, 1979.

Waltz, Kenneth "Anarchic Orders and Balances of Power" in Robert O. Keohane (ed.) *Neorealism and Its Critics* New York: Columbia University Press, 1986, 98–131.

Waltz, Kenneth "The Origins of War in Neorealist Theory" *Journal of Interdisciplinary History* 18(4), 1988, 615–628.

Waltz, Kenneth "Evaluating Theories" *American Political Science Review* 91(4), 1997, 913–917.

Waltz, Kenneth "Globalization and Governance" *PS: Political Science and Politics* 32(4), 1999, 693–700.

Walzer, Michael *Just and Unjust Wars: A Moral Argument with Historical Illustrations* (3rd edn) New York: Basic Books, 2000.

Wander, Andrew "2009: A Year in Human Rights" *Al Jazeera* December 17, 2009.

Warner, R. Stephen (1993) "Work in Progress toward a New Paradigm for the Sociological Study of Religion in the United States" *American Journal of Sociology* 98(5), 1993, 1044–1093.

Warr, Kevin "The Normative Promise of Religious Organizations in Global Civil Society" *Journal of Church and State* 41(3), 1999, 499–523.

Watson, Adam "Hedley Bull, States Systems and International Societies" *Review of International Studies* 13(2), 1987, 147–153.

Watson, Adam *The Evolution of International Society: A Comparative Historical Analysis* New York: Routledge, 1992.

Weber, Max [1905] *The Protestant Ethic and The Spirit of Capitalism* New York: Dover Publications, 1958.

Weber, Max [1922] *Sociology of Religion* Boston, MA: Beacon Press, 1963.

Weber, Max [1922] *The Sociology of Religion* Boston, MA: Beacon Press, 1991.

Weigel, George *The Final Revolution: The Resistance Church and the Collapse of Communism* Oxford: Oxford University Press, 1992.

Weigel, George "Roman Catholicism in the Age of John Paul" in Peter L. Berger (ed.) *The Desecularization of the World: Resurgent Religion and World Politics* Washington DC: Ethics and Public Policy Center, and Grand Rapids, MI: William B. Eerdmans, 1999, 19–37.

Weinberg, Leonard B. and William L. Eubank "Terrorism and Democracy: What Recent Events Disclose" *Terrorism and Political Violence* 10(1), 1998, 108–118.

Weinberg, Leonard, William Eubank, and Ami Pedahzur "Characteristics of Terrorist Organizations 1910–2000" Presented at the 25th Annual Meeting of the International Society of Political Psychology in Berlin, Germany, July 2002.

Weisman, Steven R. "India Airlifts Aid to Tamil Rebels" *New York Times*, June 5, 1987.

Wendt, Alexander "The Agent–Structure Problem in International Relations Theory" *International Organization* 41(3), 1987, 335–370.

Wendt, Alexander "Anarchy is What States Make of it: The Social Construction of Power Politics" *International Organization* 46(2), 1992a, 391–425.

Wendt, Alexander "Levels of Analysis vs. Agents and Structures: Part III" *Review of International Studies* 18(2), 1992b, 181–185.

Wendt, Alexander "Constructing International Politics" *International Security* 20(1), 1995, 71–81.

Wendt, Alexander *Social Theory of International Politics* Cambridge: Cambridge University Press, 1999.

Wendt, Alexander "Why a World State is Inevitable" *European Journal of International Relations* 9, 2003, 491–542.

Wentz, Richard *Why People Do Bad Things in the Name of Religion* Macon, GA: Mercer, 1987.

Westbrook, David A. "Islamic International Law and Public International Law: Separate Expressions of World Order" *Virginia Journal of International Law* 33, 1993, 819–899.

Wheeler, Nicholas J. *Saving Strangers: Humanitarian Intervention in International Society* New York: Oxford University Press, 2001.

Wight, Martin "Christian Pacifism" *Theology* 33, July 1936.

Wight, Martin "Western Values in International Relations" in Herbert Butterfield and Martin Wight (eds) *Diplomatic Investigations* London: Allen and Unwin, 1966, 89–131.

Wight, Martin "International Legitimacy" *International Relations* 4, 1972, 1–28.

Wight, Martin *Systems of States* Leicester: Leicester University Press, 1977.

Wight, Martin *International Theory: The Three Traditions* New York: Holmes and Meier, 1992.

Williams, Robert E. Jr. and Dan Caldwell "Jus Post Bellum: Just War Theory and the Principles of Just Peace" *International Studies Perspectives* 7(4), 2006, 309–320.

Williams, Michael J. "Why Ideas Matter in International Relations? Hans Morgenthau, Classical Realism, and the Moral Construction of Power Politics" *International Organization* 58(4), 2005, 633–665.

Wilmer, Franke *The Indigenous Voice in World Politics* Newbury Park: Sage, 1993.

Wilson, Bryan R. *Religion in Sociological Perspective* Oxford: Oxford University Press, 1982.

Wilson, Erin "Beyond Dualism: Expanded Understandings of Religion and Global Justice" *International Studies Quarterly* 54(3), 2010, 733–754.

Wiseman, Geoffrey "Pax Americana: Bumping into Diplomatic Culture" *International Studies Perspectives* 6, 2005, 409–430.

Wolfers, Arnold "Statesmanship and Moral Choice" *World Politics* 1(2), 1949, 175–195.

Wolfers, Arnold " 'National Security' as an Ambiguous Symbol" *Political Science Quarterly* 67(4), 1952, 481–502.

Wolfers, Arnold *Discord and Collaboration* Baltimore, MD: Johns Hopkins University Press, 1962.

Woodberry, Robert D. "The Missionary Roots of Liberal Democracy" *American Political Science Review* 106(2), 2012, 244–274.

Woodward, Bob *Bush at War* New York: Simon and Schuster, 2002.

World Council of Churches "A Spiritual Declaration on Climate Change" April 4, 2005. Available at www.oikoumene.org/en/resources/documents/wcc-commissions/international-affairs/climate-change/a-spiritual-declaration-on-climate-change.html (last accessed February 7, 2012).

Wuthnow, Robert *Christianity and Civil Society: The Contemporary Debate* Harrisburg, PA: Trinity Press International, 1996.

Yadav, Stacey Philbrick "Understanding 'What Islamists Want': Public Debates and Contestation in Lebanon and Yemen" *Middle East Journal* 64(2), 2010, 199–213.

Yavuz, Hakan "The Gulen Movement" in Hakan Yavuz and John Esposito (eds) *Turkish Islam and The Secular State* New York: Syracuse University Press, 2003.

Young, Oran R. "Regime Dynamics: The Rise and Fall of International Regimes" *International Organization* 36(2), 1982, 277–297.

Zakaria, Fareed *From Wealth to Power: The Unusual Origins of America's World Role* Princeton, NJ: Princeton University Press, 1999.

Zakaria, Fareed "Islam, Democracy and Constitutional Liberalism" *Political Science Quarterly* 119(1), 2004, 1–20.

Zehfuss, Maja "Constructivism and Identity: A Dangerous Liaison" *European Journal of International Relations* 7(3), 2001, 315–348.

Zhang, Yongjin "The 'English School' in China: A Travelogue of Ideas and their Diffusion" *European Journal of International Relations* 9(1), 2003, 87–114.

Index

Page numbers in *italics* denote tables.